Preppers: History and the Cultural Phenomenon

by

Lynda King

Dystopian Fiction & Survival Nonfiction

www.PrepperPress.com

Preppers: History and the Cultural Phenomenon

ISBN 978-0692225509

Printed in the United States of America.

Prepper Press Trade Paperback Edition: July 2014

Prepper Press is a division of Kennebec Publishing, LLC

- This book is dedicated to my dear family, who all roll their eyes at each new adventure I embark on, but who, I know, love me just the same.

About the Author:

Lynda King is a freelance writer who lives with her husband in a 19th-century farmhouse on a one-acre "mini-farm" in Central Massachusetts, where they maintain a large organic garden and a small flock of chickens. As a Girl Scout, Lynda learned "Always be prepared!" ... and took that early lesson to heart. Today her grandchildren frequently quote her oft-repeated adage: "I'd rather have it and not need it, than need it and not have it."

Lynda is president and cofounder of a group in her town dedicated to creating a self-reliant community. The group has worked closely with the town's emergency management personnel on organizing a CERT team and has hosted educational programs on emergency preparedness. The group also organizes sustainable living workshops that have included skills such as bread- and cheese-making, home canning, beekeeping, and understanding alternative energy.

Born and raised in New England, and a proud Yankee through and through, Lynda values self-reliance, and has as one of her favorite quotes a line from the children's story "The Little Red Hen":

"Then I will do it myself," said the Little Red Hen. And she did.

Table of Contents

APPENDIX

Part One:

The History of Preparedness

"Prepare for the unknown

by studying how others in the past

have coped with the unforeseeable and the unpredictable."

— Gen. George S. Patton

"During bad circumstances, which is the human inheritance, you must decide not to be reduced. You have your humanity, and you must not allow anything to reduce that."

— Maya Angelou, American author and poet

Introduction

Anyone who has been a member of the Boy Scouts or Girl Scouts has had the motto "be prepared" drummed into their heads at countless meetings, ceremonies, and outings. Since 1910 these two organizations have been teaching youths of our country responsibility, citizenship, character, courage, personal fitness, environmental stewardship—and preparedness.

Once thought of primarily as a collection of skills for camping and wilderness survival, today's preparedness is far more encompassing, and is accepted by many as an important aspect of living in a modern, complex world. The U.S. Federal Emergency Management Agency (FEMA), emphasizes emergency preparedness for individuals and businesses as a way to reduce or prevent loss of property or loss of life in the face of disaster.

On its website, www.Ready.gov, FEMA maintains a list of possible disasters—from a host of natural disasters to dozens attributable to man, through accidents or terrorism. The site offers instructions for people on how to assess their risks for experiencing some of them, how to develop emergency plans, and how to put together a kit of disaster supplies.

FEMA also offers resources to help communities start Citizens Emergency Response Teams (CERT teams) to assist first responders in the wake of disaster. Trainees learn about natural, technological, and other disasters and their potential impact on a community's infrastructure and stability.

Beyond the emergency readiness advocated by the government, preparedness has emerged as a cultural phenomenon of which many people have only recently become aware. The term "prepper" was thrust into the public spotlight in February 2012, when the National Geographic Channel launched its reality series, "Doomsday Preppers." The show looks at the lives of people who are focused on emergency preparedness in ways that most people are not, people anticipating a number of different events that could bring an end to "the world as we know it."

The preppers making up this new cultural phenomenon prepare for emergencies beyond short-term power outages and damaging weather,

3

focusing on events with wide-ranging, long-term impact, such as a worldwide pandemic, destruction of the country's power grid, global warming, and economic collapse. They organize their lives to provide for their basic needs should the worst happen, and refer to the things they do and the things they buy for this purpose as their "preps"; and their preps can include everything from food storage and water purification to building underground bunkers and stockpiling weapons.

The public's curiosity has been aroused. According to Nielsen Media, more than 2 million viewers tuned in to the Season 2 premiere of Doomsday Preppers. [1]

The *Washington Post*, in a report on its website in November 2012 about the popularity of Doomsday Preppers, claimed that the show attracts viewers with an "apocalyptic mentality," and went on to say that the show had become a hit "in part because of the paranoia and survivalist instincts it conjures."

In December 2012, the term "prepper" came into full public view by way of the country's major news outlets, in the aftermath of the horrific massacre of 20 schoolchildren and seven adults in Newtown, Connecticut. The shooter, Adam Lanza, killed his mother, Nancy Lanza, at her home, before using several of her guns to carry out the school shooting that ended the lives of 20 young students and six school administrators. Marsha Lanza, Nancy's sister-in-law, described her as a "prepper" who was concerned about economic collapse. Marsha told reporters her sister-in-law had a collection of guns for self-defense and said she liked to shoot them. Subsequent news accounts reported that Nancy often took her son to the shooting range for target practice.

The tragic and horrifying incident sparked an outcry for more gun control, but it also raised questions for the uninitiated about who and what preppers are. The association of the term "prepper" with this event caused many people to equate preppers with radical extremists seen to be on the fringes of normal society, evoking images of people like reclusive survivalist Ted Kaczynski, the so-called "Unabomber," who engaged in a nationwide reign of home-grown terror from 1978 to 1995.[2]

In an article about the Newtown incident, posted on the website www.foreignpolicy.com, writer JM Berger said, "While there's not much solid research to be had, anecdotal observations certainly give the impression that there's a higher incidence of mental illness among hardcore preppers than in the general population, and the nature of their beliefs and social networks may create obstacles to diagnosis and treatment."

Questioned by this author about a source for these observations, Berger said, "When I say anecodotal, it means there isn't data, but when you go look at prepper media and writings, you can obviously see a certain amount of crazy on display to an extent that should be acknowledged even if it can't be measured."

Preppers in Popular Culture

Lacking any hard data, people newly exposed to the idea of prepping are left to form their own opinions about who preppers are, based on their own experience, their own worldview, and whatever they find in the media, in popular culture, or on the Web.

Since the debut of Doomsday Preppers, many media outlets have picked up on the prepping story, which has been featured on television, online, and in print. In addition, there has been a recent explosion of books written about possible catastrophic events, from both the fictional and nonfictional perspective, all offering inspiration for would-be preppers.

Books

Apocalyptic fiction looks at the struggles of people surviving some calamitous event—people who are prepared, and people who are not. However, despite the recent spate of disaster-themed books filling store shelves and booklists at Amazon.com, apocalyptic story-telling is not new. As far back as 1826, Mary Shelley wrote *The Last Man*, a futuristic novel about a world devastated by disease. George R. Stewart repeated this theme in his 1949 novel, *Earth Abides*.

It seems that society has long been fascinated by doomsday stories; and although some of them are fantastic enough that we can just sit back and enjoy the story—like *The Day of the Triffids* (John Wyndham, 1951), about aggressive plants taking over the world—recent literature has brought us face-to-face with things some believe really could happen, because we've seen elements of them in real life.

Pat Frank's 1959 classic, *Alas, Babylon,* is one of several post-World War II novels dealing with nuclear war. Frank's book looks at the effects of such a war on the United States, specifically a small town in Central Florida. We know of the horror and ruin unleashed by the U.S.'s nuclear attack on Japan in 1945, but the idea of such an event happening in our country seems unthinkable. *Alas, Babylon* and its ilk are scarier than *The Day of the Triffids,* because readers can visualize in real terms the nuclear devastation that *could* happen—it has happened before; the potential is there. Increasingly, themes of modern apocalyptic literature deal with threats that were unimagined in Mary Shelley's time.

In James Wesley Rawles' book, *Patriots* (1998, 2009), the disintegration of society is brought about by an economic collapse, for which only small groups of people are prepared. In David Dalglish's *A Land of Ash* (2010), the Yellowstone caldera, identified by scientists in the 1960s-1970s,[3] is what lays waste to the world. In Willam R. Forstchen's 2011 book release, *One Second After,* an electromagnetic pulse, or EMP, ends civilization as we know it, knocking out everything powered by electricity—including modern transportation.

It is important to note that much of today's apocalyptic fiction focuses on some disastrous event that brings about The End Of The World As We Know It—"TEOTWAWKI" (pronounced "tee-ought-wah-key") in prepper parlance—not the end of the planet.

Nonfiction books on the subject offer an abundance of information about threats that could truly doom society, such as those enumerated in Lawrence E. Joseph's 2008 entry, *Apocalypse 2012: An Investigation into Civilization's End.* The book, written ahead of the much-heralded 2012 "Mayan doomsday" allegedly foretold by the ancient Mayans' long-count calendar, discusses a long list of possibilities that include catastrophic earthquakes, deadly solar flares, and the alignment of the Solar System's orbit with a "gravitationally dense" region of the Milky

Way that could set off a storm of asteroids raining down upon the Earth.

But beyond offering events to fear, the growing body of disaster-related nonfiction also offers practical advice on steps people can take to survive any number of disasters. Dr. Arthur T Bradley's *Handbook to Practical Disaster Preparedness for the Family* (2010), presents 440 pages of information on putting together an emergency preparedness plan, covering everything from first aid to food storage, water purification, financial preparations, and more. Bernie Carr's *Prepper's Pocket Guide: 101 Easy Things You Can Do to Ready Your Home for a Disaster* (2011), gives suggestions about the basics — creating a 72-hour survival kit, an emergency contact list, and a master list of passwords — as well as the not-so-routine: calculating your family's requirements for water and food, investing in precious metals, and using sunlight to disinfect water, to name a few.

Television and Movies

Books are not the only means by which reasons to prepare have infiltrated the public psyche. Television and movies have served up their own share of apocalyptic stories, and have for many years. (In movies, Godzilla was wreaking havoc on Japan as far back as 1954.) But while some of these productions have focused on the end of the world, or parts of it, others have focused on actually surviving cataclysms, making them more appealing to the prepper community — offering not only entertainment, but also practical information.

In 2006 CBS launched the TV series *Jericho*, which ran through September 2008. The show centered around the residents of a small, fictional town in Kansas that was spared the direct wrath of 23 nuclear attacks in the U.S., but, along with other communities that were similarly fortunate, was left isolated from the outside world, with no power, no transportation, and no food, beyond the two days' worth of groceries on the shelf in the local store. The residents found themselves woefully unprepared, and throughout the course of the series, struggled to survive. *TV Guide*, in 2007, ranked the program #11 on its list of top "cult" shows.[4]

NBC launched its doomsday-themed TV series, *Revolution,* in the fall of 2012. The series follows a cast of characters and their exploits several years after some unknown event triggers a worldwide blackout on the scale of an EMP, affecting both the lights and motor-powered transportation. It is in the background of the story that we see the primitive culture with which they have survived, where the manicured lawns of today's familiar "McMansions" have been transformed into vegetable gardens that abut crude wattle fences helping to contain goats and chickens. According to a report in *USA Today* on January 6, 2013, the show was "fall's most popular new series among younger viewers."[5]

In the world of movies, *The Divide* (2011) explores how survivors of a nuclear attack continue on after the end of contemporary society, and a 2012 offering, *Remnants,* looks at how a community pulls together after a disaster from the heavens causes a worldwide blackout and illustrates what can happen in a community when some people are prepared for disaster and others are not.

A Renewal of Prepping

A look at history shows that there have always been survivalists of one kind or another. There is often renewed interest in preparedness following some kind of catastrophe. In a presentation for a "National Severe Weather Workshop" in 2008, the National Emergency Management Association (NEMA) confirmed, "Emergency management almost has no natural constituency base until an emergency or disaster occurs."[6]

By some accounts, renewed interest in preparedness started after the September 11, 2001, attacks on the U.S. Others say it is more recent. According to author James Wesley Rawles, interest in the preparedness movement has doubled annually since Hurricane Katrina struck the Gulf Coast in 2005.

The Survival Podcast website (www.TheSurvivalPodcast.com), launched in 2008, says its members number around 45,000. Tom Martin, one of the cofounders of the American Preppers Network (http://americanpreppersnetwork.com), says that 32,000 people have joined the network since the debut of the website in 2008, and that number, he says, is constantly going up.[7]

It's unclear how to measure the number of people who are preppers. By some estimates that number is 3 to 4 million in the U.S. alone. Martin says he thinks the number is impossible to track, since many people might not classify themselves that way. "Anyone who prepares is a prepper," he says. "But many of them never heard of the word 'prepper' before." If you take into account members of the Church of Jesus Christ of Latter-Day Saints, who live by the precept of "providing for every needful thing," storing at least a year's supply of food, the number of preppers in the U.S. alone is more than 5 million people.

With millions of people out there purported to be prepping for disaster, it begs the questions: Who are preppers, really? Are they radical, fringe extremists? Or are they rational people responding to real, potential threats? And if so, what are they preparing for exactly — how, and why? This book will attempt to answer these questions by first looking at events in our country's distant and not-so-distant past that have helped the prepper movement evolve into what it is today.

Part One:

The History of Preparedness

Chapter One: Pre-1950s

Early Warnings

It has been said that people have been preparing for the end of time since the beginning of time. Indeed, many of the predictions about the end or the world have their origins in cultural and religious traditions, legends, and myths about how the world came to be.

Scores of end-times predictions are rooted in the theology of the Abrahamic faiths— Christianity, Judaism, and Islam. In the Qur'ran, *Surah 54:1* talks about signs in the heavens that will signal the end of the world—the splitting of the moon and the falling of stars. The Old Testament book *Numbers* foretells that the appearance of a Messiah will herald the end of days, and the New Testament is filled with symbolic prophecies about the end of the world. Although a preponderance of doomsayers point to the book of *Revelation*, with its hellfire-and-brimstone imagery, as the source for beliefs about the end of time, there is another Biblical prophecy in *2 Peter, 3:10* that succinctly and vividly describes the end:

> *"But the Day of the Lord will come like a thief. On that Day the heavens will disappear with a shrill noise, the heavenly bodies will burn up and be destroyed, and the earth with everything in it will vanish."*[8]

But it is not just the traditions of the Judeo-Christian-Islamic faiths that hold a belief about end times. As far back as the 22nd century B.C., the Assyrians were predicting the end of the world. Writer Mark Strauss, in a 2009 article for Smithsonian.com, noted this inscription on an Assyrian clay tablet dating from 2800 B.C.:

> *"Our Earth is degenerate in these later days; there are signs that the world is speedily coming to an end; bribery and corruption are*

common; children no longer obey their parents; every man wants to write a book and the end of the world is evidently approaching."[9]

Some of the world's great non-Abrahamic religions characterize the end of the world as part of a repeating cycle of birth, growth, downfall, recovery, and rebirth—a cycle that usually ends with the Earth's destruction. Hinduism foretells the arrival of the final incarnation of Vishnu on a white horse ushering in the end of the world after eradicating evil and freeing the worthy from this cycle. Buddhism tradition describes an enlightened being named Maitreya bringing about the end of the world as we know it by rescuing humanity and promoting a universal brotherhood on Earth.

One of the most famous predictions about the world's end originated with the 1996 translation of hieroglyphs on a portion of an ancient Mayan monument discovered in Tabasco, Mexico in the 1960s.[10] After the stone, dubbed "Monument 6," was unearthed during the construction of a concrete factory in Tabasco, the location in which it was found was preserved as an archaeological site known as El Tortuguero. The translated excerpt that caused such a stir is known as the Tortuguero passage.

Scholars believe that the ancient Mayan civilization was one of those that held beliefs about cycles of birth, death, and renewal, and that those cycles were represented by dates noted on the so-called Mayan long-count calendar. Many scholars believed that the Tortuguero passage pointed to a date at the end of the long-count calendar that was interpreted to be December 21, 2012. According to authors Matthew Restall and Amara Solari, in their book, *2012 and the End of the World,* one translation of the passage in question is: "The thirteenth calendrical cycle will end on the day 4 Ahua, the third of Uniiw, when there will occur blackness (or a spectacle) and the God of the Nine will come down to the red (or be displayed in a great investiture)." The conclusion reached by many was that the passage predicted the end of creation on December 21, 2012.

However, in their book, Restall and Solari go on to make the argument that this monument was not prophetic in nature, but was, rather, celebratory, possibly part of a building dedication, akin to a cornerstone that might say, "Built in 1900, this building will stand until 2012."[11] Their theory might have been right—December 21, 2012, has come and gone, but creation has not.

History is filled with predictions about the end of the world, but in most of these predictions, mankind does not survive, and no one expects much forewarning about the cataclysm that will bring about the end. Many of the end-times prophecies come with an admonition for people to prepare for the end by mending their evil ways, that they might be spared the wrath of the gods and selected for eternal life in a post-cataclysm paradise. Some early cultures — the Mayans among them — adopted the practice of sacrificing animals, or even humans, as a way of appeasing the gods. History has few accounts of ancient preppers expecting to survive, through their own efforts, the foretold destruction of the world.

However, one exception can be found in the Old Testament book *Genesis* — believed by some to have been written sometime around the 6th or 5th centuries B.C. — which tells the story of Noah. Noah may well have been history's first-known prepper. According to the story, God forewarns Noah of a catastrophic flood, and gives him detailed instructions on building an ark for the purpose of saving a select number of humans and animals from the deluge. Clearly, Noah expected to survive, and according to the story, he did. The flood arrived as foretold, and Noah not only survived, but lived until the ripe old age of 950.[12]

Most end-times predictions are not as hopeful as Noah's story: Noah and his family *survived*, along with representative animals from every species, according to the Biblical account. In most ancient stories about the end of the world, it's really the end — no one survives.

Some end-of-the-world predications are based on the approach of dates that are seen to be significant; others are based on astronomy, astrology, or disasters that people have experienced. Many early religious leaders, including Pope Sylvester II, a French pope born around 940 AD, predicted that the apocalypse would take place at the end of the Christian Milliennium, in January 1000 CE.[13] In the 14th century, the appearance of the Black Death sparked speculation that the end-times were imminent.[14]

Spanish adventurer Christopher Columbus wrote in his 16th-century manuscripts, which were published as the *Book of Prophecies* in the late 19th century[15], that the world would come to an end in 1658, 7,000 years after what he believed to be its beginning, in 5343 BCE. Famed Colonial

American preacher and witch hunter Cotton Mather predicted three times that the world would end: 1697, 1716, and 1736.

The celebrated 16th-century French prophet Nostradamus made many predictions in his work, *The Prophecies*, published in 1555. Some of his predictions are said to have accurately predicted several modern-day events, among them World War II and the rise of Hitler, the detonation of an atomic bomb at Hiroshima, and even the terrorist attacks in the U.S. on September 11, 2001. Some who study his writings say that his predictions for the 21st century include periods of war, famine, disease, extreme weather events, and an upheaval of religious and social orders. Although he made no specific predictions calling out the end of the world, he did write that his prophecies went only as far as 3797, leaving some to infer that we have until then to worry about the end.

End-of-the-world predictions notwithstanding, early traditions also offer warnings about the need to assess the risks of misfortune and prepare accordingly. The Biblical book of *Proverbs* (6: 6-11), thought to have been written around 900 BC, offers this caution:

> *"Lazy people should learn a lesson from the way ants live. They have no leader, chief, or ruler, but they store up their food during the summer, getting ready for winter. How long is the lazy man going to lie around? When is he ever going to get up? 'I'll just take a short nap,' he says; 'I'll fold my hands and rest awhile.' But while he sleeps, poverty will attack him like an armed robber."*

The book repeats this commendation of ants in chapter 30:25, calling them out as one of four animals in the world "that are small, but very, very clever":

> *"Ants ... are weak, but they store up their food in the summer."*

These warnings in *Proverbs* likely influenced the well-known tale of the ant and the grasshopper credited to storyteller Aesop (of *Aesop's Fables*), who is thought to have lived between 620 and 564 BC. The story is about a grasshopper that spends the summer months singing and playing, and invites the ant to join in. The ant replies:

> *"I am helping to lay up food for the winter, and recommend you to do the same."*

14

The grasshopper responds:

"Why bother about winter? We have got plenty of food at present."

When winter comes, the grasshopper, dying of hunger, crawls to the ant, begging for food. The ant scolds the grasshopper, saying that since it spent the summer singing, it could spend the winter dancing. The lesson for the grasshopper?

"It is best to prepare for the days of necessity."

Traditions of the Church of Jesus Christ of Latter-Day Saints also offer counsel in preparing for hard times. Its beliefs about preparedness are rooted in the 19th century, when the church's prophet, Joseph Smith, was said to have received a number of revelations recorded for posterity in its Doctrines and Covenants. Among them, in *D&C 109:8,* are these words of warning:

"Organize yourselves; prepare every needful thing ..."

Smith's disciples have, since that time, taken care to follow these words, and the church today advises followers in ways to prepare. Expounding upon Smith's original pronouncement, the church offers these words:

"Our Heavenly Father created this beautiful earth, with all its abundance, for our benefit and use. His purpose is to provide for our needs as we walk in faith and obedience. He has lovingly commanded us to 'prepare every needful thing' (see D&C 109:8) so that, should adversity come, we may care for ourselves and our neighbors and support bishops as they care for others."

Preparing for seasons of want was a theme that resonated with the ancients. Our ancestors were well acquainted with the hardships of early life—drought and famine among them—and from the earliest times took steps to protect themselves from those privations by engaging in some sort of food preservation. According to Brian A. Nummer, Ph.D., in a 2002 paper for the National Center for Home Food Preservation, some of the food-preservation processes we are rediscovering today date back thousands of years. He says, "Evidence shows that Middle East and oriental cultures actively dried foods as early as 12,000 B.C. in the hot sun."[16]

15

While food preservation was an essential part of daily life in early times, Nummer says that today's interests in it have changed from "preserve because we have to," to "preserve because we like to." It has become more of a hobby, particularly here in the U.S. But some people have returned to the belief that preserving food is an indispensable part of life. Some consider it a vital part of emergency preparedness planning, regardless of the nature or scope of any potential disaster. This may have its roots in some of America's more recent history, when misfortune in all its forms taught hard lessons about what can befall those who greet it unprepared.

Weather, War, and Woe

Hurricanes Catch Our Attention

Much of the information about the destruction wrought by early hurricanes along U. S. coasts has been preserved only in the oral traditions passed from generation to generation by people who live in areas where the threats of these tempests are well known and their potential for destruction well respected. But in the late 1800s the government recognized the value in trying to predict and prepare for any extreme weather events Nature might conjure up and formed the National Weather Service.

President Ulysses S. Grant signed a joint resolution of Congress on February 9, 1870, establishing the service, for the purpose of "*taking meteorological observations at the military stations in the interior of the continent and at other points in the States and Territories...and for giving notice on the northern (Great) Lakes and on the seacoast by magnetic telegraph and marine signals, of the approach and force of storms.*"[17]

Tracking by the agency shows that the deadliest hurricane to strike the U.S. since its record-keeping began was the one that struck Galveston, Texas, in September 1900, killing an estimated 8,000 people.[18]

Lacking today's weather-tracking technologies, forecasters made educated guesses about the path of the storm based on observations made at key tracking stations. The Galveston Weather Bureau started getting warnings from the National Service four days before the storm hit, saying that a tropical storm was heading north, over Cuba. U.S. and Cuban forecasters disagreed about the likely track of the storm, and

16

although those in Washington predicted that it would make landfall in Florida and then head out to sea in the Atlantic, a Cuban forecaster saw a track that brought it into Texas.[19]

Looking to the skies as the storm made its unsuspected approach, Galveston residents saw few clouds and no need to worry, so paid little attention to the warning about a possible landfall in Texas. Only a small number of people evacuated to the mainland. Few made preparations of any kind.

Blizzards to Remember

While hurricanes are nightmares mainly for mariners and those who live along the coast, blizzards are the furies of nature most feared by people living in the northern part of the country, and they strike terror into the hearts of those living in the South with their occasional anomalous appearances there.

As with hurricanes, the lack of advance warning available to those in the paths of blizzards in the early 20th century left most people little, if any, time to prepare. Every generation has in its collective memory tales of "the blizzard of the century," and each subsequent ferocious blizzard tends to fade the memory about "the worst." We in the 21st century think we have seen the most extreme weather winter has to offer. But, according to the National Weather Service, the worst winter storm in U.S. history occurred in March 1888.

Earning the monikers "The Great Blizzard of 1888" and "The Great White Hurricane," the storm battered the Eastern seaboard from Chesapeake Bay to Maine for three days.[20] People in the path of the unexpected blizzard were caught off-guard after enjoying a period of unseasonably mild weather that cued the appearance of crocuses and cherry blossoms and prompted farmers to start readying their fields for planting.[21] But what started as a gentle rain in some areas on the evening of March 11, 1888, and as light snow in others, turned into heavy snow overnight, and by noon on March 12 had brought life in the Northeast to a standstill. Temperatures plummeted into the single digits, and snow piled up in unprecedented amounts. Hardest hit were Connecticut, Rhode Island, Massachusetts, New York, and New Jersey. Connecticut, Rhode Island, and Massachusetts were buried under 50 inches of snow, while 40 inches blanketed New Jersey and New York. Driven by winds that gusted to as much as 80 miles per hour, the snow massed in drifts 40 to 50 *feet* high.

Telegraph, telephone, and power lines and poles were down, isolating people from the outside world and throwing those who had electricity into darkness. Buried under the snow, trains were – for close to a week – unable to move supplies of food and coal, the fuel with which most homes were heated at the time. Thousands of passengers were stranded in rail cars without food, heat, or water, and thousands more were trapped in their homes with stores of those necessities running low.

People in the cities suffered more than those who lived in rural communities, where farmers, self-sufficient and naturally leading lives of preparedness, were in the habit of stocking their own food and fuel.[22] More than 400 people lost their lives, 200 of them in New York City. One hundred seamen died in the storm when more than 200 ships were either lost at sea or run aground.[23]

In New York, property losses from flooding and fires were staggering. With communications down and fire stations crippled, the losses from fire alone totaled nearly $25 million. Chronicling for the *New York Times* the events of the storm he witnessed, a reporter wrote in its aftermath, "...the most amazing thing to the residents of this great city must be the ease with which the elements were able to overcome [the] boasted triumph of civilization...."[24]

The impact of "The Great Blizzard of 1888" left its mark. The blizzard convinced city officials in Boston and New York to work on plans to prepare against the impact of any such future storms by putting transportation and utilities underground. Those preparations gave rise to the subway systems in both cities.

Tornadoes for the Record Books

In the late 19th century, the government started to make a concerted effort at predicting severe weather in order to provide enough advance warning for people to prepare for coming storms. The Army Signal Corps launched an effort in the mid-1880s to understand one of nature's most-feared weather events: the tornado.

Few who have lived through them would disagree that tornadoes are the worst of weather's rages. Their elusive and unpredictable nature makes them almost impossible to prepare for specifically, even with advance notice. The dark, menacing funnel clouds that inspire terror in the hearts of all who see them often appear out of nowhere and touch down randomly, sometimes leaving houses on one side of a street in total ruin and those on the opposite side fully intact. They are powerful enough to lift anything into the air and fling it down like so much trash. Who can forget the image of Dorothy Gale's house being tossed about like a cardboard box in the classic movie, *The Wizard of Oz*?

As part of the Army Signal Corps' initiative to learn more about tornadoes, Sgt. John P. Finley organized a team to document the weather patterns that seemed to breed them, and began using the data to issue tornado alerts. However, fearing that the word "tornado" would cause a panic among the public, the Weather Bureau decided to forbid the use of the term in weather forecasts, a ban that lasted until the mid-20th century. It wasn't until after two Air Force weather officers accurately predicted a tornado at the Tinker Air Force Base in Oklahoma City five days before it happened that the government focused serious attention on predicting tornadoes. In 1951 the Air Force established the Severe Weather Warning Center, with a unit responsible for predicting tornadoes threatening all Air Force bases on the U.S. mainland.[25]

The United States experiences more tornadoes than any other country in the world.[26] They usually strike east of the Rockies, and happen often enough in the middle of the country for that region to have earned the nickname "Tornado Alley." But they have occurred at one time or another in every state in the union—including Alaska and Hawaii. From our frozen north to our tropical paradises, there is no place in the country that is immune to severe weather.

According to the U.S. National Oceanic and Atmospheric Administration, the ten deadliest tornadoes in U.S. history occurred between 1840 and 1953, before Americans received tornado warnings of any kind. The worst was the Tri-State Tornado of 1925. The massive twister, believed to have been part of a deadly tornado outbreak that hit at least seven states, roared across Missouri, Illinois, and Indiana in a matter of three-and-a-half hours, leaving in its wake a 219-mile path of destruction that is the longest ever recorded in the world. Nearly 700 deaths and more than 2,000 injuries were attributed to the Tri-State

Tornado alone. More than twenty towns were completely destroyed. Scientists who have studied it believe the tornado was an "F5" class as measured on the Fujita scale, which ranks tornadoes based on the amount and type of damage they leave behind. The Fujita scale describes an F5 as an "incredible tornado," ranking second only to an F6, which is described as an "inconceivable tornado." An estimated $16.5 million in damages were attributed to the Tri-State Tornado.[27]

Without early warning systems for tornadoes, the first notice people got about a tornado's approach, if they were lucky enough, was when they saw the funnel cloud. People took shelter in root cellars or basements, if they could, but were susceptible to being trapped or injured by falling rubble from their collapsing homes.

In the 1930s, people in Tornado Alley began building storm shelters as specific preparations against the threat of tornadoes. These shelters took the form of small cement bunkers built into an embankment or underground, close enough to the house to provide a quick escape from a storm, but not so close that the occupants could be trapped by debris from the house if it were destroyed. The use of these shelters gave rise to a whole industry devoted to perfecting and selling them throughout the country, an industry that is thriving today.

The Earth Moves

In the early 20th century people learned that weather disasters were not the only calamities the natural world had to offer. On April 18, 1906, the most significant earthquake in history struck the western part of the country, from southern California to southern Oregon, and as far inland as central Nevada.[28] The rupture ran along 296 miles of the San Andreas Fault, first identified in 1895 by Andrew Lawson, professor of geology at the University of California, Berkeley.

Commonly referred to as the San Francisco Earthquake, remembered as much for the fire it caused in that city as for the damage from shaking, the quake actually caused severe destruction all along the rupture line. It is estimated that more than 3,000 deaths were caused by the quake and the resulting fire. More than 225,000 people were left homeless; 28,000 buildings were destroyed. Monetary loss was estimated at least $480 million, in 1906 dollars.[29]

The quake prompted scientists, engineers, and public officials to study the potential for further earthquakes in the region and to seek ways to prepare for them and mitigate the potential for destruction.

Winds of War

While natural disasters of the early 20th century came with lessons in the value of preparing for whatever the elements might bring, wars that few could have imagined introduced new circumstances that demonstrated a need to be prepared. Sometimes the government, like a protective parent, led the way in helping the country and its citizens ready themselves for what lay ahead. But sometimes its actions gave rise to fears that led to deep-seated distrust of the government.

Americans did not expect to get caught up in the flames of war that engulfed Europe in late summer of 1914. President Woodrow Wilson had stated his desire to have the country remain neutral, a difficult proposition, given that staying neutral could further jeopardize an ailing American economy. The country was just starting to pull out of a recession that started sometime around January 1913, and the war set in motion an economic upturn, as Europeans started purchasing goods from the U.S. to support their war effort, and financial institutions started making extensive loans to France and Great Britain.[30]

But as the war spread in Europe, there was mounting pressure within the U.S. to strengthen the country's military forces, and in 1915 a movement led by General Leonard Wood, former president Theodore Roosevelt, and a number of other prominent national figures urged and campaigned for, a build-up of military forces.

Known as the "Preparedness Movement," the coalition was born in part out of a military training program for college men started by Wood in 1913. The program conducted 90-day training camps in California and Pennsylvania and later added one in Plattsburg, N.Y., for business professionals,[31] which was attended by Roosevelt's sons, Quentin and Theodore, Jr., as well as other notables like the mayor of New York City and the general manager of the *New York Times*. Camp attendees, who were eyed for future roles as wartime military officers, were drilled in physical fitness, shooting, marching, and other military disciplines. Preparedness Movement leaders proposed a military conscription program to further beef up the armed forces. Although this proposal was initially defeated, it ultimately inspired the passage of the Selective Service Act in 1917, which helped raise the manpower necessary for the military challenge presented by America's eventual entry into the war.

World War I brought with it alarming innovations in weaponry and warfare. Zeppelins — light, gas-lifted non-rigid airships — were used by the Germans to bomb Britain from the air, a strategy previously unknown in warfare.[32] Planes, initially equipped with only whatever weapons the pilots and crew could carry, evolved to also carry bombs, machine guns, and cannons.[33] Machine guns, which had been invented in the 19th century, were improved to be more efficient, with the firepower of 100 guns. Chemical weapons, in the form of poisonous gases, were used for the first time in modern history by both the French and Germans, some in grenades soldiers threw into enemy trenches. (Historians report that poisonous gases caused more than a million casualties during World War I.[34]) Submarines — known as "U-boats," from the German word for "under sea boat" — were equipped with torpedoes and were used heavily by the Germans to destroy ships at sea. It was a submarine that helped tip the scales toward the U.S. entry into the war.

Leaders in the United States recognized the psychological toll being taken on citizens in Europe as the Germans employed the use of aerial bombing raids — against both military and civilian targets — to demoralize and overcome their enemies. And although government officials did not believe the U.S. was vulnerable to these kinds of attacks because World War I aircraft lacked long-distance capabilities, they nevertheless saw, for the first time, a need to take steps to ensure protection of the public. On August 24, 1916, Wilson signed into law the Army Appropriation Act, which established the Council of National Defense. The council was staffed by the secretaries of War, the Navy, the Interior, Agriculture, Commerce, and Labor, and was charged with "coordinating resources and industries for national defense and stimulating civilian morale." [35,36] Wilson stated in his public announcement about the establishment of the council, "The country is best prepared for war when thoroughly prepared for peace."[37]

However, despite Wilson's intentions to stay out of the war, the U.S. did not remain untouched by it. On May 7, 1915 an escalating U-boat campaign by the Germans resulted in the sinking of the British ocean liner RMS *Lusitania*, killing 1,198 people—including 128 Americans. The Germans also launched a campaign of covert activity in the United States, designed to keep arms from flowing to the European Allies. Starting in 1915, a number of fires and explosions at key locations—such as the Robeling Steel foundry in Trenton, New Jersey—were attributed to German saboteurs.

One of the most outrageous acts of German sabotage was the attack on a major munitions shipping depot in Jersey City. The facility, which was a transportation hub for munitions manufactured in the Northeast, was located on Black Tom Island, a pier on a landfill in New York Harbor opposite the Statue of Liberty. (The pier, so named after an early African-American fisherman who resided there, is now part of Liberty Island.) On the night of July 30, 1916, German agents set fire to freight cars and barges at the munitions terminal, which were loaded with more than two million pounds of ordnance bound for Europe.[38] The explosion that resulted is said to have had the power of an earthquake measuring 5.0 to 5.5 on the Richter Scale. It broke windows within a 25-mile radius of the blast, rocked buildings as far away as Philadelphia, and damaged the skirt on the Statue of Liberty.[39] Seven people were killed, and hundreds were injured. Costs were estimated at $20 million, the equivalent of nearly half a billion dollars today. The Statue of Liberty sustained about $100,000 in damages.[40]

The government played down the incidents, leaving many residents of New York and New Jersey unaware that they were under siege, in spite of the recurring attacks on munitions facilities. In January 1917 fire was set at the Kingsland, New Jersey, munitions factory, destroying 1.3 million artillery shells. An explosion in March at the U.S Navy Shipyard at Mare Island, California, killed six people, injured 31, and destroyed a number of barges filled with ammunition.[41]

The U.S. was finally provoked to declare war on Germany in April 1917, after the Germans resumed a campaign of all-out, unrestricted submarine warfare on any vessels bound for Great Britain—despite its pledge in 1916 not to attack any other passenger ships after the sinking of the *Lusitania*.

With public opinion about the war splintered by the perspectives of the many first- and second-generation immigrants who hailed from countries that were involved in the conflict, Wilson's administration

23

created the Committee on Public Information in 1917 to control information about the war at home and abroad and to help win over public opinion.[42] The information campaign it waged at home was designed to fan the flames of patriotism where it existed and to spark those flames where it did not. Colorful posters were created to secure resources for the war effort and to justify U.S. involvement in the conflict. The posters urged people to join the military and to make sacrifices for the good of the country.

An important part of the country's mobilization effort centered around food. Feeding the military, maintaining food stocks at home, and providing food for the wartime humanitarian relief presented an extraordinary challenge. In August 1917 Congress ratified the Lever Food Act which, among other things, established the U.S. Food Administration. Wilson appointed Herbert Hoover to head the agency, and gave him the authority to set food prices, oversee food purchases and exports, to develop a strategy for conserving food at home — and to act against hoarding.

An extensive propaganda campaign appealed to citizens to voluntarily conserve and make wise use of food, in order to help win the war. Households were encouraged to consume less bread, meat, and sugar. They were urged to observe two "wheatless" days a week, two "porkless" days, and one "meatless." Although these suggestions were officially considered "voluntary guidelines," they were presented through the media as something more, in headlines such as, "Hoover Decrees 'Victory Bread' and Cut Rations" and "President Calls on Patriots to Observe New Regulations."[43]

Furthering the cause of citizen participation in ensuring food availability, wealthy conservationist Charles Lathrop Pack worked to establish the National War Garden Commission in 1917, and launched an initiative to encourage U.S. households to become more self-reliant, supporting the war effort by not only conserving food, but also by growing as much of their own produce as possible in backyard "Victory Gardens," also called "War Gardens."

The government's pro-war propaganda campaign was a success, but the widespread sense of patriotism it engendered, coupled with the psychological effects of the Germans' sabotage campaign, gave rise to paranoia and suspicions — about those who did not support the war, about immigrants who "might not" support the war, about anyone

24

whose behavior was perceived as a threat to America's ability to win the war — and a darker side of the government's involvement in life on the home front emerged.

Congress passed the Espionage Act of 1917 and later the Sedition Act of 1918, in an effort to set up a framework for punishment of both enemy activity and expression of doubts about U.S. involvement in the war. The Sedition Act in particular enforced severe penalties — up to $10,000 or 20 years in prison — on anyone found, during a time of war, to be making false statements with the intent of interfering with military operations; anyone found to be obstructing the sale of U.S. bonds or securities; or anyone using "disloyal, profane, scurrilous, or abusive language about the form of government of the United States or the Constitution of the United States, or the military or naval forces of the United States, or the flag...or the uniform of the Army or Navy...."[44]

Federal agencies expanded their use of intelligence operatives, creating an extensive network of domestic spies in a number of different departments, from the Office of Naval Intelligence to the Justice Department's Bureau of Investigation, the Treasury Department, and even the Railroad and Food administrations. Additionally, police departments in some of the country's bigger cities created their own intelligence units, which coordinated information with those at the federal level.

More ominous was the web of private, "patriotic" organizations that sprang up, eager to help government officials tasked with rooting out anyone who might pose a threat to the country. They included groups like the Anti-Yellow Dog League and the Boy Spies of America — both of which enlisted children as young as 10 to do their work — as well as the Liberty League, the Knights of Liberty, the American Defense Society, the Home Defense League, and the American Protective League (APL), to name but a few. The pervasive spy network was said to be larger than any country had ever assembled.[45]

Some of these groups, like the Home Defense League, were organized at a national level but extended their reach into cities and towns, where they intertwined with other patriotic groups. In New Brunswick, New Jersey, for example, delegates from the Home Defense League joined forces with representatives from 126 city-wide organizations that included the Women's Community Club, the Middlesex County Bar

25

Association, and the high school Parent-Teacher's Association, to create the Patriotic Force of New Brunswick.[46]

The most powerful of these home-grown organizations was the American Protective League, which organized in 1917, proclaiming its dedication to rooting out spies, anti-war groups, and draft-dodgers, whom they called "slackers." According to governmental records in the National Archives, the American Protective League organized with the approval of, and operated under the direction of, the U.S. Department of Justice Bureau of Investigation, and "functioned as a spy network for various law-enforcement organizations."[47] By late 1918, it had grown to a membership of some 300,000 people, with offices in 600 cities and a headquarters in Washington, D.C.[48] As author Ann Hagedorn says, in her book *Savage Peace: Hope and Fear in America, 1919*, the vigilantes of the APL were "hidden in the folds of American society, watching, trailing, and taping their bosses, colleagues, employees, neighbors, even the local butcher or their children's schoolteachers."[49] The APL was even sanctioned by the government to investigate people suspected of hoarding food. In a letter to the Food Administration on July 29, 1918, a leader of the APL's Berkeley, California, division reported the results of the group's investigation of a Berkeley resident reported to be hoarding food and itemized the foodstuffs its investigators found stored in the home.[50]

Despite a campaign by the APL to continue operations after the war, it was disbanded following the Armistice agreement in 1918. However, pockets of the organization survived, some serving as investigators of those considered political radicals or dissenters, some joining the Ku Klux Klan, and some continuing to provide the Federal Bureau of Investigation with information about radical activities.

Financial Storm Clouds Roll In

As the country struggled to recover after World War I, the economy experienced four recessions of varying lengths, which some economists characterize as "mild" recessions. Economic declines bring with them adversity that can be keenly felt across all strata of society. They are characterized by business slowdowns, layoffs, wage freezes, high unemployment, bankruptcies, loss of individual purchasing power, and soaring food prices. Those who have jobs live in fear of losing

26

them. But most of all, recessions bring with them fear of the future, because of what they take away in the present.

On the whole, however, the post-World War I economy was expanding, thanks to the industrial mobilization brought about by the war, and the worldwide cultural and economic renaissance known as the Roaring Twenties, which largely eclipsed in people's minds the periodic dips in business activity. The Roaring Twenties brought with them innovations in music, art, and entertainment, as well as technical innovations that enabled the increased use of electricity, cars, radios, televisions, and telephones. The expansion in communications facilitated the growth of the media industry, which brought news, sports, and advertising to more people than ever before. Industry was booming, driven by consumer demand for the things people heard about on the radio or saw in magazines, newspapers, television, and movie theaters.

By the middle of the 1920s, prosperity was widespread. More people than ever were buying on credit, and an increasing number took a chance on speculating in the stock market. Enjoying the good life, people were unprepared for what happened next.

The Worst of Hard Times

Although economists still debate the details of what, exactly, started the Great Depression, most agree that this devastating worldwide economic period was triggered by stock prices that started an ominous drop beginning about September 4, 1929, then fell through the floor in the stock market crash of October 29, 1929, known as Black Tuesday.

The crash precipitated a chain reaction that wiped out the wealth of many and caused a spike in unemployment, with a corresponding downward spiral in corporate profits and tax revenue. Cities dependent on manufacturing were hit especially hard. The unemployment rate in the U.S. topped 24 percent, with upwards of 12 million people out of work. By 1933, nearly two million Americans were homeless,[51] and the economies of other major countries were pulled into the downslide.

Those homesteading on the Great Plains, flush with cash from the success of wheat crops in the late 1920s, thought that a stock market

27

crash would only hurt the "rich city slickers." At that time, only about 3 percent of the country's population had ventured to take a chance in the stock market,[52] and none of those were among the sodbusters trying to coax just one more crop of wheat from the prairies to keep the good times rolling. But the price of wheat and other crops soon began to follow the path of the equities market. Farmers all over the country saw crop prices fall by nearly 60 percent.

The Depression made no distinction between rich and poor or farmer and city clicker, and laid all equally low. Writing in his book, *A Secret Gift,* about his grandfather's life during the Depression, author Ted Gup says: "… the bright line that separated the favored class from those below them could dissolve almost overnight, exposing the fragile divide between the haves and have-nots."[53]

Just as the Great Depression was tightening its hold on the country, two natural disasters added to the collective misery. First, the so-called Dust Bowl of the American Midwest began to manifest itself. Then there was the Ohio-Mississippi Valley flood.

The Dust Bowl is the name that characterizes what has been called the largest manmade ecological disaster in history.[54,55] Over a span of six to ten years, starting around 1930, vast regions of land in the Midwest were literally turned to dust, a result of severe drought and extreme soil erosion. The years of homesteaders trying to grow grains on the Great Plains—known to some as a "No Man's Land" that was never meant to be farmed in the first place—had taken their toll on the land. Instead of resting the soil or replenishing it between crops of wheat, the homesteaders of the prairies planted crop after crop of it, cultivating more and more of the land as they went. Farming methods that did not preserve the health or integrity of the soil left it vulnerable.

A prolonged lack of rain eventually dried out the soil, and with no organic matter or even roots of weeds and grasses to hold it together, it turned to dust, and the prevailing winds of the prairies blew it away in black clouds that reached all the way to the East Coast. The dust whipped away buildings and buried towns on the Great Plains in black storms that rained down off and on for nearly ten years. Families on the plains prepared for "dusters", as they were called, by putting wet towels at the bottom of their doors and covering the windows with bed sheets. In schools, the Red Cross handed out respiratory masks, and the schools conducted dust drills.[56] The worst of the dusters happened on what is called Black Sunday, April 14, 1935, when more than 300,000 *tons* of Great Plains topsoil was lifted into the air.[57]

Altogether, the Dust Bowl affected 100 million acres of land in parts of Kansas, Colorado, New Mexico, Texas, and Oklahoma.[58] It also affected hundreds of thousands of people, who were left homeless after their livelihoods or homes—or both—were devastated by the disaster. Those displaced sought refuge in surrounding regions, adding to the suffering and despair that were already under way courtesy of the Great Depression.[59] It was what author Timothy Egan calls the "Worst Hard Time," in his book by that name.[60]

While drought ravaged one part of the country during the Great Depression, a great flood laid waste to another. In January 1937 melting snow and heavy rains from unusual weather patterns caused the Ohio and Mississippi rivers to rise above previous record levels, flooding more than 200,000 square miles in four states—Ohio, Indiana, Kentucky, and Illinois—and leaving behind property losses estimated at more than $500 million ($8 billion in today's dollars). Three hundred eighty-five people were killed, and more than one million people were left homeless.[61],[62]

Those knocked down by the Hard Times endured privations unprecedented in modern history. Malnutrition and starvation were constant companions for millions. Some families had only pennies a day to spend on food. People who could, grew backyard gardens. Soup kitchens were unable to feed all those who waited in long lines for something to eat; bread was the mainstay of many.

Everyone in the family was expected to help put food on the table. Gup, in *A Secret Gift*, tells of a 7-year-old boy who regularly took a bus to the edges of the Ohio city where he lived, bringing with him a 16-gauge shotgun and a .22-caliber pistol, and went into the countryside looking for squirrels, rabbits, and pheasants—anything to bring home to his family.[63]

Some of those left homeless by the hardships of the times left the U.S., rather than endure living in makeshift, primitive wooden or stone shanties or cardboard boxes, or rummaging through garbage for food, as many did. Some went to Canada. Some, who had immigrated to America hoping for a better life, returned to their native countries.

Most of those who stayed struggled. In a 2009 interview with writer Joyce Wadler for the *New York Times,* a Florida woman said, "My mother never threw anything away. If a sheet got worn, she would cut it up and put it together with another sheet."

When sheets got so old that they became worn in the middle, she added, they were cut into narrow strips and put on a loom to weave blankets.

"They recycled everything, I tell you, everything," she said.[64]

Not everyone in America was brought completely down by the Great Depression. Some people were lucky enough to hold onto their jobs. Others, particularly in rural areas, already lived lives of self-reliance that minimized the impact of the Hard Times on them, growing and preserving their own food, hunting and fishing, and otherwise observing a lifestyle that kept them prepared for when times got tough. But no one was unaware of the widespread suffering, and all took whatever steps they could to minimize its effect on their own lives. And while some people remained hopeful that there was light at the end of the tunnel, others thought it would never end.

Depression-era humorist Will Rogers offered this observation in a 1933 New Year's question-and-answer column in the *New York Times*:

> "Do you think we will get out of this depression just because we got out of all the others? Lots of folks drown that's been in the water before. . . . Won't 1933 see a change for the better? I don't think so. We haven't suffered enough; the Lord is repaying us for our foolishness during prosperous days."

The Great Depression left its mark on the collective American psyche. Many people alive today may recall a mantra from that time in our history, passed on by parents or grandparents: "Use it up, wear it out, make it do, or do without."

Although the lessons of the Hard Times may have dimmed, there are still people around today who remember. Gup recounts in *A Secret Gift* that, in 2010, he followed up with descendants of Depression-era acquaintances of his grandfather, and saw clearly that the effects of the Great Depression were still being felt, three generations later. A 58-year old woman told him, "Though I do shop, sometimes I feel so wasteful, that we indulge ourselves a lot."[65]

Dawn of the Nuclear Age

Natural disasters, World War I, and the Great Depression brought with them hardships that taught both citizens and the government about the need to be prepared. And it was during World War I and the Great Depression that the seeds were planted for World War II and beyond, on a continuum that brought escalating levels of danger and violence into the world.

By World War II, people were taking national defense very seriously, and at both the grassroots and government levels, actions were taken to protect the country against threats from outside and within. Meanwhile, advances in communications made the world a smaller place, and advances in technology gave foreign enemies a greater reach and inspired the creation of the most terrible weapons the world had ever seen.

Run-Up to War

World War I had been the costliest war in human history, not only because of the heavy loss of life and the degree of material destruction it caused, but also because of the industrial expansion that helped speed up production for the war effort.[66] Even years after the war, people questioned whether the war had been a "just and necessary" war, and considered it to be "the war to end all wars."[67] The idea that any conflict of that scale could happen again was unthinkable, and the terror the next one unleashed was unimaginable.

In the 1930s, the country was still struggling to free itself from the grip of the Great Depression. Under the leadership of President Herbert Hoover, followed by President Franklin Roosevelt, a number of different programs and laws were enacted to help, including the Hoover initiatives that raised tariffs on imports and resulted in the Federal Home Loan Bank Act, and Roosevelt's well-known New Deal legislation that created programs to provide relief for the poor, stimulate the economy, and reform the financial system to prevent another depression. However, it wasn't until war clouds once again appeared on the horizon that the economy started to turn around.

In Europe, the economic struggles brought about by the Depression, combined with the tensions left over from the end of World War I, created a breeding ground for political turmoil. The treaties that had brought an end to the war—the Treaty of Saint-Germain-en-Laye, the Treaty of Trianon, and most notably, the Treaty of Versailles—imposed harsh penalties on the losers in the global conflict—the Central Powers, which included the German Empire, the Austro-Hungarian Empire, the Ottoman Empire, and the Kingdom of Bulgaria. By way of these treaties, leaders of the Allied Powers—primarily Great Britain, France, and Russia—negotiated a settlement that carved up the territories of the Central Powers, compelled them to pay significant reparations, and required them to accept responsibility for causing the war, a condition the Powers—in particular, Germany—deeply resented. As a result of the treaties, Germany lost 13 percent of its pre-war territory and had its armed forces reduced to a fraction of what it once was. Few of the countries that made up the Central Powers were happy with their new borders.[68]

The conditions set the stage for a new campaign of imperialism in Europe, and for the rise to power of the likes of Adolf Hitler, Josef Stalin, and Benito Mussilini, men who, among other things, promised to return their countries to their former glory. A new political alliance was formed when Germany, Italy, and Japan signed the Tripartite Pact in 1941, setting up a spirit of cooperation among those countries as they pursued their various economic interests. The alliance eventually led to the United States' entry into yet another world war.

The first shots of World War II were fired in Poland in September 1939, where Hitler sought to expand German control. The war subsequently broke out on several fronts as Hitler continued his aggression, ultimately violating a pact he'd made with Stalin, and invading the Soviet Union in June 1941, as other countries pursued campaigns of imperialism.

Although the United States was not then part of the conflict, President Roosevelt declared a state of "limited emergency" as the war erupted in 1939, realizing it would fall to the Americans to help arm the British—and recognizing the need to ramp up American preparedness in the face of the growing German menace. Those preparations included an increase in production of military arms, legislation to increase troops, and legislation to protect the homeland.

The American government, keenly sensitive to threats from within on the heels of the Germans' World War I sabotage operations in the U.S., passed the Smith Act, also known as the Alien Registration Act, in June 1940 as a tool to combat subversion. The legislation required aliens to register with the government and established criminal penalties for anyone—alien or citizen—advocating or assisting the overthrow of the U.S. government. By January 1941, more than 4.7 million people had registered with the government as a result of this law.[69] By January 1942, 2,971 people had been taken into custody under this Act, and 1.1 million were being "watched."[70]

In September 1940, Congress passed the Burke-Wadworth Bill, known as the Selective Training and Service Act of 1940, to create the country's first peacetime selective service program. Thanks to volunteers and the new Selective Training and Service Act, there were three-quarters of a million soldiers in training camps by June 1941.[71]

The increased attention on military readiness helped lift the lingering effects of the Great Depression, as thousands found employment in the military and defense plants began hiring more workers.[72]

Throughout this national defense period, Americans saw their military arsenal grow to include new armaments like the B-19 bomber, said to be the world's largest; a fifty-seven-ton tank, thought to be the most powerful armored vehicle in existence; and a new Jeep that could tow guns powerful enough to take out a German Panzer tank.[73] By the end of 1941, the country had commissioned seventeen battleships and had fifteen more under construction.[74]

Meanwhile, Japan's imperialist aspirations, which had fomented its war with China, expanded in 1940 as the country embarked on a drive to establish a "Greater East Asia Co-Prosperity Sphere," the vision of Japan's premier, Prince Konoye Fumimaro. As part of this crusade, Japan wanted control of the British Dutch colonies in Malaysia and the East Indies,[75] and the United States stood in its way. Emboldened by its Tripartite Pact alliance with Germany and Italy, Japan attacked the U.S. Naval fleet at Pearl Harbor, Hawaii, on December 7, 1941.

U.S. intelligence in the weeks leading up to the attack had suggested that a strike by Japan was imminent, but government officials thought that it would take place in the Philippines. The attack on Pearl Harbor, completely unexpected, caught the U.S. Navy unprepared and resulted in the loss of more than 2,400 American lives and the destruction of six battleships and 188 aircraft.[76] The United States declared war on Japan the next day. Four days later, under pressure from Japanese Ambassador Oshima to uphold his promise to join in a war against the United States if necessary, Hitler declared war on the U.S.

The New Face of War

In his "Fireside Chat" address to the nation on December 9, 1941, President Roosevelt described Japan's attack on the U.S. as being "all of one pattern" in the collaboration among the three Axis Powers—Japan, Italy, and Germany. He offered examples of the path of aggression the three nations had pursued since 1931, and said of the brutal attack on Pearl Harbor: "No honest person, today or a thousand years hence, will be able to suppress a sense of indignation and horror at the treachery committed by the military dictators of Japan."

Roosevelt assured the country that the government was ready to meet the challenge of arming for the war, and in fact had been making preparations for the previous year-and-a-half. He warned of coming hardships and characterized them not as "sacrifices," but as "privileges."

> "It is not a sacrifice to do without many things to which we are accustomed if the national defense calls for doing without," he said, adding, "Yes, we shall have to give up many things entirely."

In this fireside call to arms, Roosevelt told Americans: "We are now in this war. We are all in it—all the way. Every single man, woman, and child is a partner in the most tremendous undertaking of our American history." And he talked about how warfare had changed since the last "war to end all wars":

> "There is no such thing as security for any nation—or any individual—in a world ruled by the principles of gangsterism. There is no such thing as impregnable defense against powerful aggressors who sneak up in the dark and strike without warning. We have learned that our ocean-girt hemisphere is not immune from severe attack—that we cannot measure our safety in terms of miles on any map anymore."[77]

Warfare had, indeed, changed in many ways. With the mechanization and industrialization of the war-machine production process during World War I, a Pandora's box of new weaponry and weapons improvements was unleashed upon the world. Wartime equipment could now be made in a greater quantity, at greater speed, and with a higher quality, than ever before. And new strategies in how war was conducted took the horrors of war to a new level.

Where World War I saw bombs dropped from the air by way of dirigibles and airplanes, terrorizing both military troops and civilians, World War II saw planes used also to deploy paratroopers to specific locations to advance military operations. And those planes could travel longer distances, thanks to the wide use of aircraft carriers, which are sometimes credited with having been the "decisive weapons" of the naval contribution to the war.[78] Planes could, in fact, now reach the U.S. mainland.

Where World War I saw the introduction of tanks to trump the trench-style combat previously carried out by troops on the ground, World War II saw the development of stronger, more technically advanced tanks, along with powerful weapons to overcome them. Field artillery in various sizes was designed to be versatile enough to take out tanks, to take down planes, or to inflict damage on ground troops. According to authors Donald Sommerville and Ian Westwell, in their book, *The Complete Illustrated History of the First and Second World Wars,* more than half of all battle-related casualties in the war came from the "ever-more-deadly concentrations of artillery fire."[79]

And where World War I saw the use of poison gas-filled grenades in trench warfare, World War II brought with it the possibility that chemicals and poisons could be dropped from the sky, inside bombs, despite the prohibition in the Geneva Protocol of 1925 against the use of poisonous gas.[80]

Smaller ships that were lighter and faster and armed with long-range guns were ever-present in the battles at sea.[81] Improvements in torpedoes and sensing technologies made submarines more deadly than ever, and advancements in depth-charge technology were introduced to combat them.

The Germans, in particular, added formidable new weapons to the conflict, including ancestors of today's cruise missiles, ballistic missiles—and drones. They were collectively referred to as "V-weapons" (for the German word for "retaliation," *vergeltungswaffe*). The Germans' "drone," known as the V-1 flying bomb, was a small aircraft with a pulse-jet engine and an auto-pilot that could home in on its target. Their V-2 rocket could carry its payload 50 miles into the atmosphere, where it could be dropped to fall at supersonic speed. Fighter jets could not intercept the V-2, and it could not be taken down by anti-aircraft gunfire.[82]

The Advent of Civil Defense

Changing styles of warfare since World War I changed preparations during World War II. During WWI, the aviation industry hadn't been advanced enough to send bomber planes from Europe to the U.S.; during WWII, it was. News reporting about the war by the likes of legendary broadcaster Edward R. Murrow brought the worldwide conflict into people's living rooms, and people were transfixed as they listened to him detail the Luftwaffe's barrage on London. People, especially on the East Coast, began to envision the very real possibility of suffering a similar ordeal at the hands of the Germans.

Initially, the U.S. government took the approach of the British, who at first believed that civilians would panic under the threat of an attack and be unable to cope; they believed that the less the public knew, the better. Nevertheless, independent, grassroots organizations began to spring up all over the U.S.—the Northeast, in particular—acting as local civil-defense groups. In 1939, the governor of New Jersey appointed an Emergency Committee; Massachusetts established a Committee of Public Safety; Maine created a Military Defense Commission. The first local civil defense unit in the country is believed to be the Gloucester Civil Patrol, formed by three Gloucester, Massachusetts, women in December 1939.[83]

The activities of the local defense groups were varied. Some created blackout drills to help, presuming that the enemy couldn't bomb what it couldn't see; some developed air-raid drills as a means of protection from airborne attacks.

Some communities printed their own civil defense manuals for the public, offering an assortment of locally conceived advice: one recommendation was that people lock and immobilize their cars every time they were not in use, so as not to provide a possible means of transportation to paratroopers who might drop from the sky. Another recommendation was to use umbrellas for protection against mustard gas.[84]

The American Legion in New York offered to help civil defense efforts by proposing in June 1940 its "Service of Security" plan, which would have the Legion act as an auxiliary unit of the Army, directing blackout drills, training civil defense workers, and fighting spies. Even though the War Department turned down the offer, the organization continued to study how civil defense could be implemented in the U.S., going so far as sending a delegation to England to learn about that country's civil defense measures.[85]

In response to growing concern about the lack of an organized civil defense program in the country, President Roosevelt created the Division of State and Local Cooperation in August 1940. The goal of the new department was to coordinate the efforts of the myriad civil defense groups that had come into being and to create a foundation for a national system that could be launched in a unified way if needed.[86]

However, because the department's role was one of coordination only, it had no authority to create or direct any of the local civil defense groups, and the response from state to state was spotty. By April 1941, forty-four out of forty-eight states had local civil defense councils, but some had only a handful, while others, such as Massachusetts, had one in nearly every municipality. Some states, like Virginia, "actively discouraged the creation of local councils" because it was believed that the local councils tended to adopt measures that were poorly planned and executed.[87]

In May, under pressure from East Coast mayors who didn't believe the government was being aggressive enough to protect their cities, Roosevelt issued Executive Order No. 8757, which created the Office of Civilian Defense, and turned over to that agency the responsibility for coordinating civil defense efforts.[88] The OCD organized and trained volunteers to fight fires, provide first aid, and conduct blackout and air-raid drills. They also did their part to uphold morale.

Even with the OCD making inroads into organizing nationwide civil-defense activities, government officials still wondered how the

American people would react if the war came to their doorstep. They had an opportunity to find out on December 9, two days after the attack on Pearl Harbor, when false reports of hostile planes approaching the Eastern seaboard prompted air-raid alerts throughout the Northeast. In New York, two alarms sounded within one hour; in Boston, the alarms sounded for more than an hour. Hundreds of schools all over the Northeast were evacuated; in New York alone, a million schoolchildren were sent home. During the alert, the government saw its fears about mass hysteria borne out in places like Boston, where the master switches to the city's power were pulled to effect a blackout, creating traffic jams at intersections that now lacked traffic lights, and leaving fire engines stuck inside firehouses with electric-powered doors.[89]

It became evident that local defense councils were woefully unorganized and were often staffed with untrained volunteers; the trained volunteers often lacked the equipment they needed, such as armbands and whistles for air-raid wardens, or gas masks. Most towns and small cities had no air-raid sirens; those that did had no procedures in place to signal a raid or an all-clear. In large cities, the sirens were not powerful enough to alert the entire population.[90]

Nevertheless, millions of volunteers got on the bandwagon to help the civil defense effort. The patchwork of grass-roots civil defense-oriented organizations continued to spread across the country, bringing to life groups like the Grayson County Bicycle Defense Company, the Minute Boys, the Highland Hereford Rough Riders, and the Tillamook County Guerilla Rifle Club. A bartender in Chicago even launched a nationwide initiative to organize 200,000 tavern-keepers for tasks like administering first aid, fire-fighting, and looking out for saboteurs and anti-war propaganda.[91]

The local groups remained pretty independent, making it difficult for the OCD to organize and deploy consistent civil defense measures across the country. However, by mid-1942, the OCD had created a semblance of order among the volunteers, who stood ready to warn their communities about impending air raids, but who were actually called to action more often to help during natural disasters.

Life on the Home Front

As the war broke out, people at home quickly fell back on preparedness practices that helped them get through World War I and the Great Depression.

After the Japanese attack on Pearl Harbor, Americans were more than willing to make the sacrifices called for by President Roosevelt in his December 9, 1941, fireside chat, and considered it their patriotic duty to do what they could to support the war effort. They submitted readily to rationing programs set up to ensure that resources were available to citizens while the government fed, clothed, armed, and outfitted troops. Ration stamps were issued to people for the purchase of food, gasoline, clothing, tires, and heating oil. Posters released by the United States Office of War Information urged, "Do with less — so they'll have enough."[92] Scrap drives were organized to collect aluminum, metal, and rubber that could be recycled and used in the production of military equipment.

The concept of Victory Gardens introduced during World War I gained renewed popularity. Having one was considered one of the most patriotic things a family could do, since by families producing some of their own food, more of what was grown on large farms could go to the troops. Resources began to emerge to help people seeking to grow their own food. In 1942, Rodale, Inc. began publishing *Organic Farming and Gardening* magazine, offering an education on how people could grow healthier food by using natural methods and by paying attention to the health of the soil.[93]

Canning and other food preservation practices also became popular as a way of extending the life of a family's food supply. In his book, *World War II in Mid-America,* author Robert C. Daniels offers the recollections of a woman from Waupun, Wisconsin, whose family had a Victory Garden:

> "Everybody was expected to have a Victory Garden," she said. "Of course, we did anyway. We grew everything that we could, and my mother would can it. We had giant gardens."[94]

People made use of attics and basements to dry harvested produce, and cool cellars were used to store cabbages and root crops like potatoes and beets. People lucky enough to have an excess of produce were able to make some extra money by selling it at roadside stands.[95]

Abrogation of Rights

Besides having limits set on the things they could buy after the onset of World War II, people at home saw other limits imposed by the government, by way of legislation that intruded on civil liberties on a scale never seen before. This legislation had far-reaching consequences that were not finally resolved until 1989.

Even with the Smith Act of 1940 in place to keep track of foreigners, the attack on Pearl Harbor prompted the government to take additional steps to protect the country from subversion, and its attention turned to Japanese-Americans as potential saboteurs.

Japanese immigrants, who had come to this country between 1861 and 1940 and settled primarily on the West Coast, had grouped themselves in neighborhoods that became tight-knit ethnic communities. These areas became the target for Executive Order 9066, which was signed by President Roosevelt on February 19, 1942. Giving in to pressure from West Coast lobbyists and members of Congress, Roosevelt authorized the Secretary of War and military commanders appointed by the Secretary to designate any areas they deemed necessary as restricted military areas, and further authorized them to exclude people at their discretion—"any or all persons"—from those areas.[96]

Military zones were subsequently set up along the West Coast, and in March evacuation of those areas started. Military commanders began relocating anyone of Japanese descent—not only recent immigrants, but also people whose forebears had lived in the U.S. for two generations—by at first encouraging voluntary evacuation, then eventually resorting to involuntary relocation. Although most of those removed were of Japanese descent, others perceived to be a risk were also relocated, including citizens of Italian and German ancestry. Military leaders, with the authorization of EO9066, provided those evacuees with "other accommodations"—at fenced, guarded "relocation centers," or internment camps, at ten remote locations in Arizona, Arkansas, California, Colorado, Idaho, Utah, and Wyoming. By September, nearly 122,000 people had been evacuated to relocation camps, losing personal liberty, homes, and property in the process. The internment ended after Major General Henry C. Pratt issued a proclamation on December 17, 1944, stating that the Japanese-American detainees could return to their homes as of January 2, 1945.

Over the ensuing decades, former camp detainees and their families sought redress for their losses through the U.S. court system. Some were given token payments as a result of the Japanese American Evacuation Claims act of 1948 and the amendments to it enacted in 1951 and 1965, but final resolution did not come for another twenty-six years.

Executive Order 9066 was finally officially rescinded by President Gerald Ford on February 19, 1976. Four years later, President Jimmy Carter appointed a commission to study the order and its impact on Japanese-Americans. The Commission on Wartime Relocation and Internment of Civilians issued its findings in 1982, in a 467-page report titled "Personal Justice Denied." The report stated that the program of exclusion and removal was "conducted by the U.S. government despite the fact that no documented evidence of espionage or sabotage was shown, and there was no direct military necessity for detention."[97] It went on to say that the basis for the program was "race prejudice, war hysteria and a failure of political leadership."[98] The commission recommended that the government give Japanese-Americans survivors a public apology and that each one be given a tax-free redress payment of $20,000. The Civil Liberties Act of 1988 provided the apology and the approval for restitution. President George H.W. Bush signed the appropriations bill for the payments on November 21, 1989, authorizing payments to be made between 1990 and 1998 — starting a full forty-five years after the end of World War II.

The Ultimate Weapon of Mass Destruction

President Roosevelt's was the hand that guided the country through nearly twelve years of its darkest days. He served an unprecedented three terms in office and was elected to a fourth term in 1944. However, as World War II raged on, his health began to fail, and he died of a cerebral hemorrhage on April 12, 1945, three months after his inauguration. It fell to Vice President Harry Truman to lead the country

41

toward a successful conclusion to the war, which he did by making one of the most momentous decisions in history — to use the atom bomb.

Scientists in Britain, Denmark, and Germany were already exploring nuclear fission as early as the late 1930s. Two scientists who escaped the persecution of the Nazis and Italian Fascists, respectively — Albert Einstein and Enrico Firmi — were acutely aware of the power of this technology, and in 1939, fearing a breakthrough by the Germans, urged President Roosevelt to begin an atomic research program. The U.S. allocated $6,000 in 1940 to explore the feasibility of such a project, and in 1941 Roosevelt agreed to move forward with the development of an atomic bomb.[99]

The U.S. assembled an international team of scientists, and work on the program — dubbed the "Manhattan Project" — began. In September 1942 Roosevelt assigned responsibility for it to General Leslie Groves, who, under the direction of Secretary of War Henry L. Stimson, oversaw the construction of more than thirty sites for use in the research, development, and testing of components for the bomb.[100]

As Vice President, Truman had known nothing about the Manhattan Project,[101] but twelve days after Roosevelt's death, Stimson informed him about it and told him that the atom bomb would be "the most terrible weapon ever known in human history."[102] Truman wrote in his diary that night that the country was perfecting "an explosive great enough to destroy the whole world."[103]

Stimson became extremely influential with the president in subsequent military strategy about use of the weapon being developed. Both men were driven to uphold the legacy of Roosevelt, who had insisted early in 1943 that Germany, Italy, and Japan "surrender without condition."[104] April 1945 saw the defeat of Italy, brought about by Mussolini's capture and subsequent execution, and the defeat of Germany through the sheer military might of the Allied Forces, capped by Hitler's suicide. But Japan continued to hang on.

Stimson, Truman, and others considered that the nuclear bomb, if development was successful, could be the thing that would finally win Japan's unconditional surrender. Although there was much discussion about the bomb among the powers-that-be, discussions always centered on *how* to use it, not *whether* to use it.[105] The resources committed to its development made its use almost inevitable. The project employed about 120,000 people at thirty locations, and in a cost study completed in 1998, costs for the project were estimated at $20 billion in 1996 dollars; which would be close to $30 billion today.[106] As author Andrew J. Rotter says in his book, *Hiroshima: The World's Bomb*, "Once under way, the Manhattan Project became a means that required an end, a force of logic that could be satisfied only by resolution in the cause of battle—that is, against people."[107]

Meanwhile, those in the scientific community working on the project began to have grave reservations about using the weapon. In June 1945 a report from eight leading scientists on the Manhattan Project recommended against using nuclear bombs against Japan. The Franck Report was submitted to an "Interim Committee" created by Stimson to advise on matters relating to nuclear energy. The preamble to the report stated:

> *"The scientists on this project do not presume to speak authoritatively on problems of national and international policy. However, we find ourselves, by the force of events, the last five years in the position of a small group of citizens cognizant of a grave danger for the safety of this country as well as for the future of all other nations, of which the rest of mankind is unaware."[108]*

The report cautioned that use of nuclear weapons would precipitate an arms race that could ultimately lead to war. It stated, "In the war to which such an armaments race is likely to lead, the United States, with its agglomeration of population and industry in comparatively few metropolitan districts, will be at a disadvantage compared to the nations whose population and industry are scattered over large areas."

It went on to say that taking all things into account, "the use of nuclear bombs for an early, unannounced attack against Japan" was inadvisable, and concluded that if the United States were the first country to make use of such weapons, it would "sacrifice public support throughout the world" and would "prejudice the possibility of reaching an international agreement on the future control of such weapons."

After reviewing the report, the Interim Committee stood by its earlier conclusion—that there was no alternative but to use the bomb against Japan.[109]

By the summer of 1945, the Manhattan Project had one atomic bomb ready to test. The test bomb, code-named "Gadget," was detonated at a site in Alamogordo, New Mexico, on July 16, 1945. The bomb exploded in a blinding flash that could be seen nearly 200 miles away, blowing out windows in buildings close to 100 miles away. The temperature at its core was said to be four times greater than the temperature at the center of the sun.[110] With the power of about 20,000 tons of TNT, the blast left a crater about half a mile wide, in the process transforming 800 yards of desert sand to glass.[111]

Among the officials who witnessed the test was Brigadier General Thomas F. Farrell. In a memo he wrote to Stimson about it afterward he said:

> *"Thirty seconds after the explosion came first, the air blast pressing hard against people and things, to be followed almost immediately by the strong, sustained, awesome roar which warned of doomsday and made us feel that we puny things were blasphemous to dare tamper with the forces heretofore reserved to The Almighty. Words are inadequate tools for the job of acquainting those not present with the physical, mental, and psychological effects. It had to be witnessed to be realized."*

Meanwhile, during the run-up to the July 16 test, Truman and Stimson were meeting with other Allied leaders in Potsdam, Germany, to determine an end-game to the war—including territorial boundaries, dismantling of the collective war machine, reparations, prosecution of war criminals—and the surrender of Japan. They were notified about the success of the nuclear test, and in his diary on July 25, 1945, Truman wrote: "We have discovered the most terrible bomb in the history of the world. It may be the fire destruction prophesied in the Euphrates Valley era, after Noah and his fabulous ark. ... This weapon is to be used against Japan between now and August 10. I have told the secretary of war, Mr. Stimson, to use it so that military objectives and soldiers and sailors are the target and not women and children. The target will be a purely military one and we will issue a warning statement asking the Japs to surrender and save lives."[112]

The next day, the Potsdam Declaration, defining the terms of Japan's surrender, was presented to the Japanese Prime Minister, Admiral Suzuki Kantaro. It made no mention about the weapon now at the disposal of the United States, but called for Japan's complete and unconditional surrender, offering as an alternative "prompt and utter destruction."[113]

Some historians believe that Kantaro rejected the proposal outright, prompting Truman to authorize the use of the nuclear bomb. Other historians believe that Kantaro's response was misunderstood, that he had actually said we would not comment on it yet.[114] But based on the entry in Truman's diary, it appears his mind was already made up to use the weapon.

By early August, the Manhattan Project had produced two more nuclear bombs. The first was dropped on Hiroshima, Japan, on August 6, 1945. The second was dropped on Nagasaki on August 9, 1945. It is estimated that 150,000 people in both cities were killed instantly and 100,000 more later died from radiation burns and radiation poisoning.[115]

The Nuclear Age had begun, and the world was changed forever. Those who lived through World War I, the Great Depression, and the most terrible war—World War II, experienced hardships against which ancient prophesies cautioned, and they saw firsthand the possibility that mankind's own actions could bring about the end times that the prophecies foretold.

For people already practicing lifestyles of preparedness, these dark periods in American history reinforced their beliefs about being prepared. Spencer W. Kimball, twelfth president of The Church of Jesus Christ of Latter-day Saints, lived through all of them, and used his experiences to inform the teachings he passed on to his church. Among them was this:

> *"What I have seen with my own eyes makes me afraid not to do what I can to protect against calamities."*[116]

45

Part One:

The History of Preparedness

Chapter Two: Postwar Years to 1960s

It seems that every era in human history has seen societal and political upheavals that people have believed heralded the end of the world. Yet at the same time, every age has brought with it innovations in thought, technology, and culture that have held out exciting possibilities for the future. The years after the "greatest war" were no different.

The 1950s and 1960s were rife with political turmoil, and technology provided advances in military weaponry that created the most terrifying weapons in human history—and also landed a man on the moon. The assassination of a president left the country—and the world—stunned. The threat of Communism that raised its head during the'50s and'60s created fear and mistrust within the government and among citizens, led to two more wars, and shaped the political landscape for generations. The American government and the population grappled with the idea of preparedness—and survivability—in the presence of the most horrific weapons ever known.

But those years also saw a blossoming of awareness about myriad risks to the wellbeing of the human condition beyond war: civil rights, the environment, a burgeoning world population, the finite resources of the planet, natural disasters, and even economics. People protested the weapons that threatened the annihilation of humanity and protested wars waged by a government that had lost much public trust.

A youthful counter-culture that questioned authority and rebelled against conformity emerged, reviving the spirit of self-reliance expressed and made famous by 19th-century philosopher Ralph Waldo Emerson in his essay, "Self-Reliance." The term "generation gap" came to refer to ideological divisions between the youth of the 1950s/1960s—"baby boomers"—and their elders, as young people challenged long-

47

held cultural norms around sexuality, women's rights, and race relations. The advances in media and communications that helped make the Beatles a household name also expanded the reach of innovative music that offered America's youth a platform for expressions of protest, rebellion, and teenage angst.

The society that emerged from the 1960s was one that had been shaken by war and uncertainty, transformed by challenges and changes to the status quo, and poised to pursue the American Dream described by historian James Truslow Adams in his 1931 book *The Epic of America:*

> *"The American Dream is that dream of a land in which life should be better and richer and fuller for everyone, with opportunity for each according to ability or achievement. ... It is not a dream of motor cars and high wages merely, but a dream of social order in which each man and each woman shall be able to attain to the fullest stature of which they are innately capable, and be recognized by others for what they are, regardless of the fortuitous circumstances of birth or position."*

The Cold War

Like a phoenix rising from the ashes of its predecessor, the Cold War quickly grew out of the embers of World War II and colored the international political landscape for decades to come. Not fought on the battlefield, this ideological war between democratic and Communist world superpowers, led by the United States and the Soviet Union, was fought by way of propaganda, espionage, menacing rhetoric, and saber-rattling that raised the specter of "mutually assured destruction" among countries that had added nuclear weapons to their military arsenals. The threat of nuclear attack from the Soviet Union was a driving factor in political decision-making as well as federal, state, and private preparedness thinking for the duration of the Cold War.

Background

Throughout World War II there had been a growing mistrust among the Allies. The British and Americans in particular became suspicious of Soviet motives which, some historians say, was at the heart of Truman's decision to make use of the atomic bomb. [117],[118] The theory is that with Japan on the verge of surrender, Truman had feared a Soviet advance on Japan and subsequent claim to Japanese territory in post-war negotiations. Besides devastating Japan's ability to wage war and provoking an end to the war, the use of the bomb short-circuited Soviet ambitions in Eastern Asia.[119]

Holding fundamentally different beliefs about how the world should operate, the Soviets and other Allies maintained an uneasy alliance throughout the war. For its part, the worldview of the United States was firmly rooted in the notion of freedom instilled by its Founding Fathers, and in constraining power to let liberty flourish. In this view, everyone had an equal opportunity for success, enjoyed through hard work and determination; all were free to profit from the fruits of their labors.

Soviet philosophy was grounded in the teachings of Karl Marx, who posited that communism represented the epitome of social order, a classless, moneyless society where property and resources are owned collectively, where wealth is redistributed according to need, and no individual has an advantage over another. Marx believed that this new society would be achieved when the working class, exploited by capitalists, revolted and established the new order, a democracy ruled by the workers. Communism as the Soviets practiced it, however, was characterized by power concentrated in a central government seeking to bring about Marx's social order by force. The government imposed mass industrialization and collectivization of peasant farms — and employed imprisonment, torture, and execution against those who stood in opposition.

As World War II waged on, actions by one side or the other in the troubled alliance were either prompted by, or served to agitate, the suspicions that each inherently brought to the conflict. Fearing that the Soviets might fall to the Nazis and later align with them, the British and Americans reached out to give them support in the form of armaments, food, and clothing.[120] After the invasion of France, Stalin came to believe that the British and Americans had deliberately delayed the assault, leaving a disproportionate amount of the fighting ahead of it to the Russians. And, he was angry to discover that the Americans had secretly developed an atomic weapon.

Following the deployment of the atomic bomb at Hiroshima, Stalin commented, "War is barbaric, but using the A-bomb is a superbarbarity."[121] He subsequently approved a Soviet nuclear arms program, believing that the U.S. would use the threat of another bomb to gain postwar concessions from the U.S.S.R. In his view, "A-bomb blackmail" was American policy.[122] Stalin told his scientists, "Hiroshima has shaken the whole world. ...The balance has been destroyed. ...That cannot be."[123]

The nuclear arms race had begun.·

It Starts

George F. Kennan, U.S. Deputy Chief of Mission in Moscow from 1944 to 1946, gained a valuable understanding of the Soviet mindset during his tenure there, and in February 1946 the State Department asked for his insights into Soviet behavior. In response, Kennan penned the "Long Telegram," which served as the basis for the U.S. postwar policy of "containment" in Soviet matters and helped set the tone for the Cold War.[124]

In his telegram, Kennan said that the Soviets were "ignorant of the outside world" and held a "neurotic view of world affairs." They had a "traditional and instinctive" sense of insecurity, he said, and sought to advance their own influence in the world by "deepening and exploiting ...differences and conflicts between capitalist powers." For the Soviets, Kennan wrote, "It is desirable and necessary that the internal harmony of our society be disrupted, our traditional way of life be destroyed, the international authority of our state be broken" in order for Soviet power to be secure."

After laying out in the memo the background of Soviet thinking, Kennan followed with words that may have been what coalesced the U.S. position toward them for the duration of the Cold War. He said that the Soviets were "highly sensitive to [the] logic of force." If an adversary has sufficient force and shows his readiness to use it, Kennan said, he rarely has to do so. He said that staving off communism depended on the "health and vigor" of American society, warning, "World communism is like malignant parasite which feeds only on diseased tissue."

Britain's Prime Minister, Winston Churchill, who led that country from 1940 to 1945 and again from 1951 to 1955, brought the Cold War into clear view in a speech he gave at Westminster College in Fulton, Missouri, on March 5 1946.[125] In that speech, Churchill introduced the term "Iron Curtain," which came to be used throughout the Cold War to characterize the great division of philosophy between Communist countries and the Free World. He told his audience of his admiration and respect for Stalin, but went on to say:

> "It is my duty ... to place before you certain facts about the present position in Europe. From Stettin in the Baltic to Trieste in the Adriatic an iron curtain has descended across the Continent. Behind that line lie all the capitals of the ancient states of Central and Eastern Europe. ... All these famous cities and the populations around them lie in what I must call the Soviet sphere, and all are subject, in one form or another, not only to Soviet influence but to a very high and in some cases increasing measure of control from Moscow."

Churchill stated his belief that Communists "constitute a growing challenge and peril to Christian civilization." He said, "I do not believe that Soviet Russia desires war. What they desire is the fruits of war and the indefinite expansion of their power and doctrines."

This, ironically, was similar to what the Soviets believed about the United States. Soviet Ambassador to the United States, Nikolai Novikov, wrote a response to the Kennan telegram in September for his superiors.[126] In his telegram, which helped set the tone for the Soviet posture throughout the Cold War, Novikov depicted the U.S. policy as one bent on achieving world supremacy, driven by capitalists seeking to expand their influence in the world, and he accused the American press of waging an anti-Soviet campaign to win support from a war-weary public for a military confrontation against the U.S.S.R., a conflict in which, the Soviets believed, the atomic bomb would be used against them.

Speaking before Congress in 1947, President Truman introduced what became known as the Truman Doctrine, a doctrine that formed the basis of the U.S. international relations policy for the duration of the Cold War.[127] In his appearance before Congress, Truman made an appeal for $400 million in aid to Greece and Turkey, in response to pleas from both countries for financial assistance that Truman saw as essential in order for them to survive as free nations. His rationale for this request is what formed the basis for the Truman Doctrine. He saw both Greece and Turkey as being vulnerable to Communist takeover, and believed it was incumbent upon the U.S. to stop the spread of the "malignant parasite" described by Kennan. He told Congress:

> *"The very existence of the Greek state is today threatened by the terrorist activities of several thousand armed men, led by Communists ... I believe it must be the policy of the United States to support free peoples who are resisting attempted subjugation by armed minorities or by outside pressure."*

The State of Civil Defense

By 1945, the Office of Civil Defense (OCD) had started developing tangible civil defense plans that included air-raid drills, blackouts, and the stocking of sandbags. But as World War II wound down, government officials came to believe that the threat of an attack on the U.S. homeland had receded, and in June, President Truman signed Executive Order 9562, closing down the OCD. However, that sense of security was short-lived, with increasing tensions between the U.S. and the U.S.S.R. providing the impetus for a reevaluation of programs to protect U.S. citizens from military attack.[128]

In 1946 Secretary of War Henry Stimson established a board to study the effects of strategic bombing of Nazi Germany during the war and of the use of the atomic bomb against Japan, in an effort to identify lessons learned that could be applied to the U.S. homeland. The report concluded that civil defense plans "could significantly mitigate the effects of strategic bombing" in the U.S. It stated that components of a workable civil defense plan would include mass evacuation for people living in urban areas and the presence of shelters for those not able to leave.[129]

However, the following year, a report by the War Department's Civil Defense Board, which was chaired by Major General Harold Bull, concluded that "civil defense is the responsibility of civilians, and the military should not be expected to get involved in such matters."[130] The report reasoned that "civil defense was best implemented locally, a concept referred to as 'self-help'."

With each ensuing change in presidential administration for years to come, emphasis on civil defense shifted back and forth between the idea that it should be a federal responsibility and the notion that it should be locally planned, controlled, and implemented.[131]

Similarly, presidential administrations differed in their ideas of what civil defense should actually be, vacillating between protection from military attack and protection from natural disasters — several of which occurred in the 1950s and 1960s.

The most disastrous hurricane season in history, until 2005, occurred in 1955, a year that saw 10 hurricanes and three tropical storms. According to a December 1955 report published by the Weather Bureau Office in Miami, Florida, the hurricanes of 1955 "broke all previous records for damage."[132] The report called Hurricane Diane, which struck North Carolina in August, "the greatest natural catastrophe in the history of the United States." Collectively, the hurricanes of 1955 caused more than 1,518 deaths and over $1 billion in damage.

In 1961, President Kennedy split the Office of Civil Defense into two organizations — the Office of Emergency Planning (OEP), responsible for advising the president on nonmilitary emergency readiness plans, and the Office of Civil Defense, which was charged with administering the military civil defense program.

After Congress passed legislation in 1966 to grant Federal loan assistance to victims, the focus of civil defense began to shift from preparedness for military attack to preparedness for all hazards — whether manmade or natural.[133]

Smoldering Embers

The conflicts that consumed so much of our country's resources, attention, and spirit over the years never seemed to be quite over when they ended. There was always unfinished business on one side or the other that served as the spark for the next firestorm.

Super Bombs

In the international arena, the nuclear arms program fast-tracked by Stalin culminated in the Soviet Union's first nuclear test on August 29, 1949, prompting concern and reaction from Washington. On September 23, Truman released a statement to the public stating that the U. S. had detected an atomic explosion in the U.S.S.R.[134] The announcement caused a panic among scientists and government officials, who scrambled to formulate an American response.[135] The Department of Defense decided the time was right to test the country's air-defense plans and initiated the "Operation Lookout" exercise that was held in ten northeastern states.[136]

For their part, scientists began to argue in favor of building a "super bomb" — a hydrogen bomb 700 times more powerful than the bomb that destroyed Hiroshima.[137] In October, the Atomic Energy Commission (AEC) sought advice from its advisory panel, made up of a number of scientists who, after two days of discussion and evaluation, recommended the expansion of the nuclear weapons program. However, regarding the H-bomb, the panel concluded that it was not "a weapon which can be used exclusively for the destruction of material installations of military or semi-military purposes. Its use therefore carries much further than the atomic bomb itself the policy of exterminating civilian populations." The advisory panel unanimously recommended against a program to build the H-bomb.

Within the AEC, opinions were divided on how to proceed. AEC Chairman David Lilienthal reiterated the recommendations contained in a March 1946 report issued by a panel he had chaired, which had been commissioned by Secretary of State Dean Acheson to evaluate the position of the United States with regard to the threat of nuclear weapons: Lilienthal said that the U.S. should work within the international community to develop controls of nuclear weapons, and he recommended against a program to build the H-bomb.

Lilienthal's concerns stemmed from what he learned during his service on the 1946 panel, during which he wrote in his journal:

> No fairy tale that I read in utter rapture and enchantment as a child, no spy mystery, no "horror" story, can remotely compare with the scientific recital I listened to for six or seven hours today. ...I feel that I have been admitted, through the strangest accident of fate, behind the scenes in the most awful and inspiring drama since some primitive man looked for the very first time upon fire.[138]

However, AEC Commissioner Lewis Strauss disagreed with the recommendation of the AEC advisory panel and said in a November 25 letter to Truman, "I believe that the United States must be as completely armed as any possible enemy." Keenly aware that the successful Soviet test meant the U.S. had lost its military advantage over the Russians, the Joint Chiefs of Staff concurred, saying, "The United States would be in an intolerable position if a possible enemy possessed the bomb and the United States did not."[139]

After much thought and discussion with members of his National Security Council, Truman agreed with recommendations in favor of the project and on January 31, 1950, announced his decision to proceed with development of the H-bomb. The Soviets had already begun exploring the new technology that could produce such a bomb, and in early February Soviet Deputy Premier Lavrenti Beria requested a progress report from scientists working on the project, to hurry it along.

Meanwhile, as development of the new H-bomb progressed, manufacture of "conventional" nuclear weapons continued, and by the end of 1950, the United States had 369 of them in its arsenal; the Soviets had five.[140] Both the U.S. and the U.S.S.R. invested heavily in not only weapons, but also delivery systems, including submarines and long-range inter-continental ballistic missiles (ICBMs) that had a range of 5,500 miles.

The U.S. H-bomb project culminated in a successful test of the world's first hydrogen bomb, dubbed "Mike," in the Pacific Marshall Islands on November 1, 1952. The bomb vaporized the island of Elugelab and destroyed parts of islands nearby; it produced a fireball three miles wide and left a mile-wide crater in its wake.[141],[142]

Following closely on the heels of the U.S. test, the U.S.S.R H-bomb project ended in success with the detonation of its first H-bomb on August 20, 1953. According to reports, the bomb was 30 times more powerful than the Hiroshima bomb. And, unlike the U.S. "Mike" bomb, it was small enough to fit in a plane.[143]

The race for nuclear supremacy saw the U.S. and the U.S.S.R. testing weapons of ever-increasing power throughout the Cold War. On March 1, 1954, the U.S. conducted a nuclear test which, due to a design error, turned out to be its largest test ever.[144] The test, conducted on the Marshall Island of Bikini Atoll, created an explosion more than twice as large as expected — over 1,000 times as powerful as the Hiroshima bomb. Radioactive fallout from the test was spread over nearly 7,000 square miles. The radiation affected people living on the islands of Rongelap and Utrik—100 miles and 300 miles east of the test site, respectively—and was also detected in the United States, Europe, Australia, India, and Japan. Two hours after the test, radioactive ash began to fall on a Japanese fishing boat located 90 miles from Bikini Atoll. Crew members began to suffer the effects of radiation poisoning within days; one eventually died.

The residents of Rongelap were evacuated one day after the blast; the residents of Utrik, within two days. They exhibited symptoms of radiation poisoning after their evacuation and, for many, the effects lasted for years. Ten years after the test, 90 percent of those who had been living on the islands as children began to develop cancerous thyroid tumors. The government finally took responsibility for exposing the islanders to radiation and appropriated funds as compensation in 1964.[145]

Bikini and other islands in that chain of atolls have been uninhabitable since the explosion. The people who were evacuated from Bikini to facilitate the island's use as a nuclear proving ground were, in March 2001, awarded $563 million by a Nuclear Claims Tribunal, for cleanup and repair of the physical damage to the island.[146] The current plan is to return the island to descendants of the original islanders, if it ever becomes habitable.

Not to be outdone by the U.S. March 1954 test, the Soviets, on October 30, 1961, detonated the most powerful nuclear weapon ever constructed—3,300 times more powerful than the Hiroshima bomb— over Novaya Zemlya, a chain of islands in the Russian Arctic Sea. The blast created a seismic shock wave equivalent to an earthquake measuring more than 5.0 on the Richter Scale—a shock that could be felt around the world. The mushroom cloud it created extended upward for 37 miles.[147]

In the meantime, other countries were also making plans to enter the nuclear arms race. Great Britain conducted its first nuclear test on October 3, 1952.[148] On February 13, 1960, France detonated its first atomic bomb.[149] And on October 16, 1964, Communist China conducted its first nuclear test, earning its membership in the growing "A-bomb club."[150]

Duck and Cover

Following the successful Soviet test of its first nuclear weapon in 1949, state governments in the U.S. began to demand more support from the federal government in formulating civil defense plans.[151] In response, the National Security Resources Board created an outline of civil defense roles and responsibilities and how they should be implemented, contained in a proposal called the *Blue Book*. Among the recommendations in the proposal was the formation of an independent federal civil defense organization, whose role would be to establish national policy that would guide local civil defense efforts. In response to the recommendation, Congress passed the Federal Civil Defense Act of 1950, which created the Federal Civil Defense Administration (FCDA).[152] A centerpiece to plans for the FCDA was to be the creation of air-raid shelters. In his speech to the nation announcing passage of the Act, President Truman said:

> *"The Act will permit the Federal Government to provide matching grants of funds to the States for constructing air-raid shelters. The Act also allows certain measures to be taken by the Federal Government directly, such as the procurement and stockpiling of necessary medical and other materials and supplies and the provision of suitable warning systems."*[153]

As they attempted to define what was meant by national security, those working to develop FCDA policy realized that a top-down effort by the Federal government in a time of crisis had the potential to lead to a "garrison state" as people surrendered freedoms in exchange for security. Thus, they strongly favored self-help as a basis for local civil defense programs.[154] However, as Truman promised, the FCDA did lead shelter-building programs, established an attack warning system, and embarked on a national civil-defense education campaign.

A primary focus of the FCDA education campaign was teaching schoolchildren about attack preparedness and offering instruction for teachers in leading students in civil defense drills. Those who grew up in the 1950s will likely remember the cartoon character Bert the Turtle who, in a short film released by the FCDA in 1951, showed children in classrooms all across the country how to "duck and cover!"—hiding under their desks or in some other nearby shelter—in the event of an air raid during school hours.

Recording her recollections for a Michigan history project, one woman who grew up under the nuclear shadow told a *Detroit News* reporter that in her school, students and teachers were sent to "the steam tunnels in the bowels of the school building" during air-raid drills. She said, "We marched quietly down into the basement and lined up against the cement walls, hoping that the sirens meant just another safety test, and not the real thing."[155]

Although Truman was a supporter of shelters, he was reluctant to commit government funds to a full-blown shelter program. Congress was equally unenthused, and despite funding proposals from many quarters, approved only 10 percent of what was requested.[156] However, Congress and Truman agreed on the wisdom of providing for continuity of government operations in the event of an attack, and in 1951, Truman authorized the construction of "Site R" in Raven Rock Mountain, Pennsylvania, to be used as a command center in the event that command centers in Washington, D.C., were destroyed.

President Dwight Eisenhower, Truman's successor in 1953, had a different idea about civil defense, favoring a federally supported "bug-out plan"—a policy of mass evacuation from cities to rural areas. His view helped fuel support of a substantial federal highway program—the means by which such massive evacuations would happen.[157]

After information about the destructive power of H-bombs was released to the public following the U.S. and Soviet H-bomb tests in 1952 and 1953, FCDA Director Frederick Peterson argued against a shelter program, since it was evident that no shelter could withstand the effects of an H-bomb blast. Congress agreed, and continued to support mass evacuation over sheltering programs, with the exception of members like Congressman Chet Holifield of California, who argued vigorously in favor of federally funded shelter-building.[158]

Following the 1954 detonation of the massive bomb that devastated Bikini Atoll, the public—and Congress—became alarmed at the widespread effects of radioactive fallout from the blast, and attention turned once again to the state of civil defense, with a focus on shelters as a means of protection from fallout.

Four months after the Bikini Atoll test, the government authorized a nationwide civil-defense drill, to assess the country's readiness to withstand a nuclear attack. The drill was organized by the FCDA and included operations not only in 54 U.S. cities, but also in Canada, Puerto Rico, the Virgin Islands, and Alaska and Hawaii (which had not yet become states). The 10-minute exercise started with the sounding of alarms in chosen cities, after which citizens were expected to immediately seek cover wherever they could—in fallout shelters, if available, or in places like subway tunnels and basements. Although officials declared the test a success, citing only minor communications problems, the Civil Defense Administration estimated that such an attack would have killed more than 12 million people.[159]

Congress and Eisenhower continued to disagree on the value of shelters vs. mass evacuations, and the FCDA, slow to make any progress on an organized evacuation plan, drew heavy criticism from many quarters. Holifield became a vocal critic and in 1956 called for hearings to determine the FCDA's value to the country.

To counter the criticism, the FCDA developed a National Shelter Policy, proposing $32 billion in funding to support tax incentives and special mortgage rates to encourage private shelter-building. Stunned by the cost of the proposal, Eisenhower put the brakes on it and asked his Science Advisory Committee to evaluate both the "active and passive measures to protect the civilian population in case of nuclear attack and its aftermath," in the context of existing and "probable new" weapons systems in conjunction with the "deterrent value" of the country's existing retaliatory forces.[160] The panel, chaired by H. Rowan Gaither, an administrator of the Ford Foundation, concluded that the U.S. could not defend itself from a surprise Soviet attack.[161]

The Gaither Report, released in 1957, recommended more funding for military programs, saying that a federal fallout shelter system should rank only second in priority to military deterrence and readiness. This recommendation took on a sense of urgency with Russia's successful launch of *Sputnik I*, the world's first manmade satellite, a month before the panel published its report, since *Sputnik I* presented the possibility of nuclear attack from space.[162]

The report by the Gaither panel also recommended support of the FCDA's proposed private shelter-subsidy program, but Eisenhower dragged his feet on moving ahead with the program, opting instead for extensive research on shelters and existing structures that could be used as shelters, as well as keeping the public informed about shelters. He eventually dissolved the FCDA.[163] However, like Truman, he saw the value in providing for continuity of government operations, and in the mid-1950s he authorized construction of a bunker, similar to Truman's, under the Greenbrier Resort in West Virginia.[164]

Some states, meanwhile, took matters into their own hands in advancing plans to protect the public by way of bomb shelters. States like Alabama and New Jersey still have on their books tax exemptions for fallout shelters, enacted in the 1960s. New Jersey's Title 54, Chapter 4, subsection 54:4-3.48 offers up to $1,000 in exemptions to individuals who erect on their property fallout shelters for up to two families.[165] Similarly, in Alabama, Title 40: Section 40-18-15 offers up to $1,000 in exemptions to individuals who build a "community fallout shelter" on their property.[166]

In Washington State, a 200-person public bomb shelter was built underneath Interstate Highway 5 in the 1950s, along with a shelter in the Seattle branch of the Federal Reserve Bank of San Francisco, designed to protect not only a handful of people, but also the bank's portion of the U.S. money supply.[167]

President John F. Kennedy, Eisenhower's successor, supported creation of a nationwide shelter system and made civil defense a greater priority than at any other time in U.S. history[168]—because, unlike any other president in U.S. history, Kennedy faced and navigated the country through crises that brought it to the brink of nuclear war. He talked openly during his administration about the importance of civil defense and urged every man in the country to provide protection for his family. He said it would be "a failure of responsibility" if a man didn't know what to do or where to go in the event of a nuclear attack.[169]

The Berlin crisis in August 1961 strengthened Kennedy's resolve to pursue a shelter system, and he approached Congress for funding, requesting more than $200 million— twice as much as Eisenhower had ever sought for civil defense.[170] Congress approved, and work on the shelter program began. The first task was to survey all existing shelters and determine which ones were suitable as public shelters. The Department of Defense Supply Agency was charged with furnishing shelter supplies to local governments, in order for them to stock the shelters in their areas.

More than 104 million individual shelter spaces had been identified by 1963[171], and by some estimates, nearly 200,000 private bomb shelters were built through 1965.[172]

During the administration of President Lyndon B. Johnson, who took office after the assassination of President Kennedy, Secretary of State Robert McNamara advanced the notion of "mutual assured destruction," or MAD, which meant that both the U.S. and the Soviets possessed weapons that could annihilate the other, and this alone was an effective deterrent to nuclear war: "Whoever shoots first dies second."[173] MAD put a damper on the government's perceived need for shelters.

While the friendly cartoon character from the "Duck and Cover" campaign had given the impression that surviving a nuclear attack was as simple as finding shelter, and booklets provided by the FCDA offered advice on how to survive an atomic attack, news reports painted a different picture. The scenarios discussed in the media, along with emerging information about the effects of radioactive fallout, offered little hope about the survivability of a nuclear attack. The children who experienced bomb shelters at home and "duck and cover" at school grappled with this stark reality as they grew up.

Suspicion Reigns

In 1950, the country was stunned by the discovery of two major espionage cases involving highly placed Soviet agents. The discovery sparked one of the most repressive periods in 20th-century America, which offered added incentive to those considering pursuit of a survivalist lifestyle.[174]

With the U.S. on the lookout for spies and saboteurs since World War I, the U.S. House of Representatives had created the House Committee on Un-American Activities (HUAC) in 1938 to investigate cases of suspected subversive activity, including individuals or organizations with Communist ties.[175] Between 1950 and 1953, the committee's investigations revealed an extensive "atomic spy network" that had been responsible for funneling information on the U.S. nuclear weapons program to the Russians.[176],[177]

On January 21, 1950, former State Department official Alger Hiss was revealed as a spy when the HUAC convicted him of perjury for having lied in previous testimony stating that he had not been a Soviet agent during the late 1930s and early 1940s. Within days of the Hiss conviction, the British government disclosed that German scientist Klaus Fuchs, who had fled Nazi Germany in 1933 and subsequently worked on the Manhattan Project, had admitted spying for the Russians during his tenure on the top-secret project.[178]

In February, Republican Senator Joseph McCarthy fanned the flames of suspicion and paranoia about Communist infiltrators during a speech before the Women's Republican Club of Wheeling, West Virginia. He told his audience that the very reason the Soviet Union was able to develop an atomic bomb so quickly on the heels of the United States was because of the secrets that had been passed to them by spies. He alleged that there were more than 200 members of the Communist Party "working and shaping policy in the State Department," and urged President Truman to launch investigations.[179]

McCarthy subsequently inspired an anti-Communist campaign obsessed with the search for Communist infiltrators, which some likened to a witch hunt. "McCarthyism," as it came to be known, was characterized by sometimes baseless, unsubstantiated accusations, especially against political adversaries.

The McCarthy-led crusade, which lasted until about 1954, fed public hysteria about perceived Communist threats to the country. Federal, state, and local governments instituted "loyalty review boards" to investigate the loyalties of government employees, and in industry, private companies were hired to ensure there were no Communists in the work force. McCarthyism ruined careers and called into question the loyalties of well-known Americans, many of whom were bold enough to speak out against McCarthy's tactics. Among them were people in the fields of entertainment and journalism, such as mystery writer Dashiell Hammett, singer Lena Horne, film producer and director Elia Kazan, playwright and essayist Arthur Miller, composer and conductor Leonard Bernstein, silent film star Charlie Chaplin, comedian Mort Sahl, and broadcast journalist Edward R. Murrow.[180]

Many in Hollywood who were suspected of having Communist ties, but who refused to cooperate with the investigations of the HUAC, were blacklisted and banned from employment at major movie studios for years.[181] Those in Hollywood who did testify before the committee were shunned by their industry, which protested the committee's intrusive approach. Elia Kazan, one of the most influential and accomplished directors in Hollywood in the 1950s and 1960s, was recognized for his career achievements only in 2000, because of the film industry guilds' fifty-year grudge.[182]

The experience of those who lived through or witnessed the bullying and intimidation that typified the McCarthy years left many unsettled, unsure about placing their trust in their government—or their neighbors.

Wars Flare

Just as Americans thought that they had seen the last of war and all its horrors, two wars grew out of the remnants of World War II: the Korean War in 1950, and the Vietnam War in 1959. Both wars ended in a stalemate; both took their toll on American lives.

Until the fall of Japan in 1945, the Korean peninsula had been part of the Empire of Japan. As the Japanese resistance fell apart in the summer of 1945, the Soviet Red Army found an opportunity to advance into North Korea. American troops, following their original mission to invade the home islands of the Japanese empire, advanced into South Korea. Washington and Moscow agreed that the 38th parallel, which split the peninsula in half, would serve as the dividing line between the Soviet and American occupations until a Korean government was put in place and troops could withdraw.[183] The forces ultimately withdrew by 1949, but the peninsula remained divided, with the Soviets retaining influence in the north, and the Americans in the south.

Seeing the opportunity ripe for possible Communist expansion in East Asia, Stalin supported the ambitions of North Korea's dictator Kim Il-sung, who authorized an invasion of the South on June 25, 1950, violating the boundary that had been sanctioned by the United Nations. The United States quickly came to the aid of South Korea, not only in the spirit of Communist containment, but also in defense of U.N. authority. The war lasted until 1953, with neither side prevailing over the other. The stalemate ended with the signing of the Armistice

63

agreement on July 25, 1953. By its end, it had cost the Koreans and Chinese millions of lives; more than 50,000 American lives were lost in the conflict.[184] Thousands of American troops were reported missing, and although the U.S. conducted a 10-year search operation starting around 1995, more than 5,300 remained missing as of 2012.[185]

Meanwhile, keeping his eye on East Asia, Stalin saw another opportunity for Communist expansion, this time in Vietnam. Vietnam had been part of the French empire until it was overrun by the Japanese during World War II. The Vietnamese independence movement, a militia of 10,000 guerilla fighters led by Ho Chi Minh, conducted successful campaigns against the Japanese throughout the war. After the war, the Allies returned South Vietnam to the French, and left the North to the non-Communist Chinese. The Viet Minh, backed by Stalin, launched a campaign to regain control of the whole country and continued to battle the French, in a bid for the South.

The Geneva Agreement of 1954 ended the eight-year-long war between the French and the Communist-backed militia, and divided Vietnam at the 17th parallel, leaving the north in the hands of Ho Chi Minh and the Viet Minh, and the south under the control of Ngo Dinh Diem's non-Communist government.[186] However, the agreement did not stop Minh's ambitions, and in 1959 the Viet Cong, reinvented Viet Minh loyalists that comprised the militia of the National Liberation Front, began a guerilla campaign to regain control of the south. Seeking to stop the spread of Communism to the south, the U.S. began supplying aid to Diem's regime, although limiting its involvement to this between 1961 and 1963.

However, in 1963, U.S. leaders became alarmed at Diem's increasingly dictatorial rule and brutal oppression of his opponents and gave South Vietnamese military leaders encouragement in their plot to overthrow him.[187] Diem was assassinated on Nov. 12, 1963, just three weeks before President Kennedy himself was killed by an assassin.

The U.S. was drawn more directly into the war in 1964, when the North Vietnamese launched an attack on a U.S. warship in the Gulf of Tonkin. Following the attack, the U.S. Congress approved the Tonkin Gulf Resolution (P.L. 88-408), authorizing President Johnson to engage in conventional military operations in Vietnam even though there had been no formal declaration of war. Expansion of the military draft swelled the ranks of U.S. ground troops sent to fight in Vietnam. More than 8.7 million GIs were on active duty from August 1964 to March 1973.[188]

As the war continued without measurable progress toward a successful conclusion, and as American casualties mounted, American sentiment against it grew. The nightly news kept the American body count in front of the public, and reports of atrocities by American soldiers sparked outrage. The voices in the antiwar movement that formed in the mid-1960s saw the war as immoral — American lives were being lost in a battle many felt should be left to the Vietnamese. Protestors vented their anger at returning troops, hurling insults at them and blaming them for the war. Many soldiers felt betrayed and rejected by the very people for whom they had done their duty. Many turned to drugs and alcohol for comfort, and some withdrew from society in search of a survivalist-type lifestyle where they were dependent on no one but themselves.

With antiwar sentiment mounting in Congress and among the public, the war finally ended during the administration of President Richard Nixon, when all parties involved — the U.S., North Vietnam, South Vietnam and the Viet Cong — agreed to the terms of the Paris Peace Accords. Under the conditions of that agreement, the U.S. agreed to halt military operations immediately and withdraw troops within 60 days. Vietnam, it was agreed, would remain a divided country until both sides with claims to the south — the government of Nguyen Van Thieu and the National Liberation Front — negotiated a settlement and organized elections.[189]

By the time the last U.S. troops were withdrawn on March 1973, 58,282 American soldiers had lost their lives and another 303,644 had been wounded.[190] In addition, more than 1,500 troops were missing in action, giving rise to a belief by nearly two-thirds of the American public — for years — that hundreds of prisoners-of-war (POWs) were being held captive in Vietnamese jungle prisons. Many people were angry at the government for its lack of visible effort to search for the missing until the 1980s.[191]

What had started as a civil war in Vietnam in the late 1950s turned into a complicated quagmire that drew the United States in deeper and deeper during the ensuing 20 years, in the name of stopping the Communist menace from expanding any farther across the globe, and left in its wake widespread death and destruction. Between 1965 and

1968 alone, the U.S. dropped more than 643,000 tons of bombs on North Vietnam—a country slightly larger than half the state of Tennessee.[192]

In addition, the countryside was devastated by the defoliant "Agent Orange," used by the U.S. in its "Operation Ranch Hand" between 1961 and 1971 to denude jungles that were concealing enemy guerillas and to defoliate agricultural lands that provided the enemy's food supply. During the operation, the U.S. sprayed more than 19 million gallons of chemicals over 4.5 million acres of the country.[193] The use of Agent Orange was discontinued in 1971, after the National Institutes of Health discovered that it contained a chemical responsible for birth defects in lab animals.[194] The chemical, dioxin TCDD, is believed to be one of the most deadly chemicals ever created.

Agent Orange left lingering effects among U.S. veterans and the estimated 5 million Vietnamese who were exposed to it. Although soldiers had been assured by the U.S. government that the use of Agent Orange posed no risks to them, thousands who were exposed to the chemical later developed serious health issues—including cancers, birth defects, rashes, and psychological disorders. During the war, Vietnamese doctors began delivering babies that exhibited horrific birth defects, including missing limbs, missing eyes, and even missing brains.

The U.S. government was slow to acknowledge any link between the reported health conditions and Agent Orange; its position was supported by information supplied by the chemical's manufacturers— Dow Chemical, Monsanto Corporation, Hercules, Northwest Industries, Diamond Shamrock, and North American Phillips. Veterans turned to the legal system for help, and in 1978 launched the first of several lawsuits against the chemical companies. A judge awarded a $180 million settlement in 1984, which was invested while the details of the distribution were worked out and ultimately grew to $330 million; the first checks were mailed out in 1989. Those deemed 100 percent disabled were eligible to receive up to $12,800—paid out over 10 years. Those who developed symptoms later and were not part of the 1984 settlement continue to pursue their claims in court today. Fifty-eight percent of the half-million Vietnam veterans who died between the years 2000 and 2007 were younger than age 60.

In his book *The Fifty-Year Wound*, Derek Leebaert writes of the war:

66

"As the greatest single Cold War outlay of lives and money, Vietnam has become the most painful episode of these years in the memories of many Americans. Some of us still regard it with shame and guilt; others view it with pride as one terribly lost battle. The war marked a defining passage for America — from a power perhaps too ready to seek control without thinking into one unprepared even to contemplate the range of disorder that still afflicted the world."

Painful Truths Revealed

The Cold War era was one in which Americans learned not only to fear Communists and nuclear weapons, but also to look at their own government in a new way. While the public may have rallied around the government during World War II, seeing it as a benefactor that would save them and then help improve their lives after the war, many came to realize that they had been naïve to view it as a benevolent parent that would always take care of them — especially the Vietnam veterans whose health claims for exposure to Agent Orange lingered, unanswered, into the 21st century.

Documents declassified in the late 20th century revealed more government cover-ups that served to fuel public suspicion. In 1959 declassified documents revealed new details about a surprise German attack on the port of Bari, Italy, on December 2, 1943, an incident that has been likened to the attack on Pearl Harbor for its stealth and the scale of death and destruction left in its wake. During the attack, the United States lost a ship, the SS *John Harvey*, which, documents revealed, had been carrying a secret cargo of mustard gas bombs — 1,350 tons' worth.[195]

The Allies had maintained large chemical depots near Oran, Algeria, during World War II, and acting on intelligence that the Germans might be preparing for a chemical assault, the U.S. quietly began to stockpile a reserve of chemical weapons in the Mediterranean, in order to prepare for a swift response. Part of the chemical cache was to be stored at Foggia, Italy, just over an hour from the port of Bari, which was a key supply route for the Allied forces in Italy. While the SS *John Harvey* sat in its berth at Bari waiting to have its deadly cargo unloaded, more than 100 German bombers attacked, and in less than two hours sank 28 ships, severed an oil pipeline, and killed thousands of servicemen and civilians.

Doctors treating patients after the disaster began to notice symptoms consistent with mustard gas poisoning. Hundreds of military and civilian casualties died from exposure to the toxic chemical, yet military hospitals were instructed by Allied Force Headquarters to identify those cases as "not yet diagnosed" dermatitis.[196] Kept in the dark about the cause of the symptoms they were seeing, doctors were unable to provide proper treatment for those affected.

Rumors surfaced that the Germans had used mustard gas during the attack, but an investigation in late December by a chemicals expert concluded that the cargo of the *John Harvey* was to blame for the presence of the poison. Then-General Dwight Eisenhower instructed a top-secret panel to investigate the incident, and in March 1944 the panel concurred with the findings of the chemicals expert: the deadly toxin had come from the *John Harvey*. However, even in his postwar memoir, Eisenhower did not acknowledge the extent of the disaster, instead recording for history that the gas had caused no casualties.[197]

Drawing on the documents released in 1959 and a related scholarly article published by the U.S. Naval institute in 1967, author Glenn B. Infield revealed details about the chemical weapons dispersed during the Bari attack in his 1971 book, *Disaster at Bari*. And although British military leaders had denied any knowledge about the cargo of the *John Harvey*, a 1986 report in *The Times* of London stated that there had been an official admission that 600 British seamen at Bari had been gassed in the infamous attack and would be awarded backdated war pensions for their suffering.[198]

Culture in Crisis

The life experiences of those who grew up in the 1950s and 1960s helped shape their values, which became expressed in literature, music, art, and behavior that included rebellion and protest. Protests and alternative lifestyles espoused by prominent figures in society began to influence people in viewing escape and going "back to the land" as a means of dealing with the crises of the times.

Among those influencing the "back-to-the-land" movement were Helen and Scott Nearing who, during the Great Depression, had moved to rural Vermont to live a life of self-reliance. In the early 1950s they relocated to Cape Rosier, Maine, where on "Forest Farm" they continued their self-reliant life. In 1954, the couple wrote and published *Living the Good Life,* championing the values of simple living. In the 1960s, they joined close to 500 writers and editors in protesting the Vietnam War by refusing to pay taxes to support it, declaring their intentions in a full-page ad in the *New York Post.*[199] The back-to-the-land movement, exemplified by the lifestyle of the Nearings, drew adherents bent on leaving urban areas for the perceived safety of the "simple life."[200]

During the 1950s and 1960s there was no lack of things to offer inspiration for living a simpler life. Besides the Vietnam War, the 1960s in particular saw crises that shook the country to its core.

International Bully

When Nikita Khruschev came to power as First Secretary of the Soviet Union Communist Party 1953 and then Soviet Premier in 1958, he upped the ante on Cold War nuclear saber-rattling, and in the 1960s played a role in bringing the world the closest it's ever come to all-out nuclear war. As John Lewis Gaddis put it in his book *The Cold War: A New History*, Khruschev "... openly, repeatedly, and bloodcurdlingly threatened the West with nuclear annihilation."[201] Khruschev frequently boasted about the superiority of the Soviet nuclear arsenal and claimed that the soviets could "wipe out any American or European city."

In 1955, seeking to reduce international tensions, leaders of the countries that were the major players in the Cold War—the U.S., France, Great Britain, and the Soviet Union—met in Geneva to discuss a number of topics that could lead to improved East-West relations, including the arms race, international security, and trade agreements.[202] At the conference, President Eisenhower proposed an "open skies" plan that would allow the U.S. and the Soviet Union to execute reconnaissance flights over each other's countries. Khruschev rejected the idea, but Eisenhower pursued it for the U.S. nevertheless, and in 1956 the first of the country's U-2 spy planes conducted a mission over major cities in the Soviet Union. The surveillance confirmed that the Soviet nuclear stockpiles were not as great as those of the United States. That, however, did not keep Khruschev from his bullying, and in 1961 he precipitated a crisis that many believed would end in war.

The city of Berlin, Germany, had been divided after World War II, with the Communists in control of East Berlin, and the Western Allies — Americans, French, and British — in control of West Berlin. In the early 1950s, East Berliners began to notice that those in West Berlin enjoyed a better quality of life, and began to flee to the West. Between 1949 and 1961, the population of East Berlin had declined by more than 2 million people, and those who left there predominantly the ones who were the most highly educated.[203]

Khruschev tried repeatedly to get the Western Allies out of West Berlin, with a goal of having a unified Germany under Communist control. He issued an ultimatum in 1958 that led to a conference in Geneva in 1959 to discuss the Berlin problem and possibly negotiate a new agreement. However, relations between the U.S. and U.S.S.R. deteriorated after the Soviets shot down an American U-2 spy plane over Soviet territory.

In 1961 Khruchev issued another ultimatum for the western powers to leave Berlin, and in response, and in preparation for a possible confrontation, President Kennedy authorized a troop buildup, activating 150,000 reservists.[204] Not willing to risk escalating the standoff into a nuclear conflict, but still determined to limit western influence in Berlin, Khruschev authorized the erection of a barbed-wire fence to separate the East and West sections of the city. The fence went up in the middle of August 1961, and later became more permanent with the addition of concrete blocks and guard towers. Soviet guards were ordered to shoot anyone who tried to cross. When the guards began stopping western diplomats traveling between the two sectors to examine their travel documents, the United States posted tanks on the western side of the wall, aimed at the East. In response, the Soviets moved their own tanks to the eastern side of the wall, aimed at the West. Through intermediaries, President Kennedy was able to persuade Khruschev to remove the tanks, agreeing that if he did, the U.S. would do the same. The confrontation eventually ended peacefully.[205]

Communists Close to Home

The Communist threat that was the bane of existence during the Cold War for the West, and the United States in particular, materialized 90 miles from the shores of America when, in 1959, pro-communist Fidel Castro seized power in Cuba, ousting American-backed dictator Fulgencio Batista.[206]

Castro immediately acted to reduce American influence in the country, and his speeches became filled with anti-American rhetoric. Relations between the U.S. and Cuba quickly deteriorated, and in 1960, the U.S. broke off trade relations—the same year Cuba established diplomatic relations with the Soviet Union.[207] Castro seized control of and nationalized $850 million in American assets in Cuba, prompting the U.S. to institute a trade embargo, which remains in place today.[208]

Seeking to restore American interests in Cuba, outgoing President Eisenhower authorized the Central Intelligence Agency to recruit and train 1,400 Cuban expatriates in a covert scheme to overthrow the Castro government.[209] Before leaving office, Eisenhower closed down the American embassy in Cuba and broke off diplomatic ties with the country. Incoming President Kennedy continued support for the plan, seeing it as a way to make a statement to the Soviets and the world that the United States was determined to win the Cold War. The invasion was launched April 17, 1961, on the shores of Cuba's Bay of Pigs, but the invaders were quickly and soundly defeated by Castro's military. More than 100 of them were killed, and 1,200 were taken prisoner.[210] The incident helped set the stage for the most dramatic crisis of the 1960s, a year later.

During a U-2 reconnaissance flight over Cuba in 1962, it was discovered that the Soviet Union had installed nuclear-armed missiles there, a discovery that sparked the crisis that had Americans checking for the locations of the nearest fallout shelters. President Kennedy authorized a naval blockade around the island and told the American public—and the world— that the U.S. was ready to use force to remove this threat to America's national security. Khruschev ultimately backed down and agreed to remove the missiles if the U.S. agreed not to invade Cuba.[211]

The Nation Mourns

People who came of age in the 1960s can tell you exactly where they were on Friday, November 22, 1963, when they first learned of the assassination of President Kennedy. It was a defining moment in the country that left people shaken and feeling a vulnerability they hadn't known before.

Kennedy had been traveling in a motorcade in an open convertible with his wife, Jacqueline, and Texas Governor John Connally, when shots rang out as the convertible passed by the Texas School Book Depository Building at 12:30 p.m. Connally and Kennedy were both struck. Kennedy, who had been struck twice, was pronounced dead 30 minutes later at Parkland Hospital.[212]

The sniper, Lee Harvey Oswald, was apprehended two hours later, and the next day was arraigned for the murder of the president. Hungry for details about exactly what had happened, and why, people in the nation sat transfixed before their television sets for days, as live news broadcasts carried interviews and covered details of every related event. On November 24, a crowd of reporters with live cameras waited at Dallas police headquarters to capture, live, the transfer of Oswald to the County jail. As Oswald stepped into the room, a gunman suddenly stepped out of the crowd and shot him with a .38 revolver — as millions watched in horror on live TV. The gunman, Jack Ruby, was immediately arrested. He was later found guilty and sentenced to death. (Years later, while awaiting execution, he died in prison of lung cancer.)

Six years later, the assassinations of two more prominent American leaders shook the country. Martin Luther King, Jr., the African-American Baptist minister from Georgia who had been an icon in the Civil Rights movement, was shot to death on April 4, 1968, in Memphis, Tennessee. Two months later, on June 6, 1968, Senator Robert F. Kennedy, brother of the slain president, was shot in Los Angeles, California, while campaigning for the Democratic nomination for president of the United States.

Protests, Conspiracies, and Revelations

The 1960s marked a period of civil unrest in the U.S. that was among the worst such periods in the 20th century. An undercurrent of mistrust of government helped fuel protests and also fed the belief in governmental conspiracies on many fronts. The Civil Rights movement, which came to life in the 1950s and gained ground in the 1960s, led to dozens of riots that in some cases required the intervention of the National Guard. Opposition to the Vietnam War brought out thousands of protesters in cities all over the country, in demonstrations that were at times peaceful and at times violent, requiring the intervention of police and military troops.

From the perspective of the government, those who engaged in disobedience, civil or otherwise, were subversives out to undermine governmental authority, as were those whose belief in governmental conspiracies and collusion served to stir up suspicion and discontent.

The uncertainty and suspicion that pervaded the United States in the 1950s and 1960s gave rise to conspiracy theories that stirred people's feelings of vulnerability and fueled a desire among many to turn to self-reliance as a way of coping.

Demonstrations Flare

The death of Martin Luther King Jr. precipitated five days of rioting in Washington, D.C. More than 6,000 troops, including Army and National Guard, were called in to quell the violence. Thirteen people died and thousands were injured.[213],[214] Violence also erupted in more than 100 cities across the country, including Baltimore and Chicago, resulting in looting, destruction of property, and hundreds of injuries and arrests.

In 1966 a coalition of anti-war activists organized as the National Mobilization Committee to End the War in Vietnam (the MOBE), to help organize large-scale protests against the war. In April 1967 they helped organize a massive protest in New York City, where an estimated 400,000 protesters marched to the United Nations from Central Park.[215] The MOBE organized a march on the Pentagon on October 21, 1967, which saw more than 150,000 people gathered in the nation's capitol to protest the war and the draft. Hundreds were arrested in a confrontation with National Guardsmen and U.S. marshals. The "Moratorium Rally" the MOBE organized in 1969 drew more than 250,000 people to Washington to demonstrate for an end to the war.

Possible Plots

Following the death of President Kennedy, the murder of the prime suspect left many questions unanswered about why Kennedy had been killed, and whether his killer had been acting alone. As investigators soon discovered, Lee Harvey Oswald had a checkered past that included three years residing in the Soviet Union, where he tried, unsuccessfully, to become a citizen. He married a Russian woman and later moved to the United States with her and their infant daughter. In early 1963 he founded a branch of a pro-Castro organization, the Fair Play for Cuba Committee.

Speculation, rumors, and conspiracy theories arose about Kennedy's assassination. Some people blamed Soviet KGB operatives, saying that it was part of a Communist plot. Some believed Cuba was behind it, in retaliation for the Bay of Pigs invasion. Some people believed it was a mob hit, and that Jack Ruby, who was reputed to have connections with the Mafia, killed Oswald to ensure he couldn't implicate anyone else.

Vice President Lyndon B. Johnson, Kennedy's successor, established a commission a week after Kennedy's death to investigate the assassination. The commission, headed by Chief Justice Earl Warren, spent nearly a year interviewing witnesses, reviewing evidence, and conducting their own research, and in September 1964 released an 888-page report, stating its conclusion that Oswald had acted completely alone. The report said:

> *"The Commission has found no credible evidence that he [Oswald] was a member of a foreign or domestic conspiracy of any kind. Nor was there any evidence that he was involved with any criminal or underworld elements or that he had any association with his slayer, Jack Ruby, except as his victim."*[216]

However, this didn't satisfy those who couldn't believe that a single gunman, in the person of someone like Oswald, could have taken down the president of the United States. Conspiracies persist today about who killed Kennedy and why, and although they are wildly different in many ways, they all seem to be fed by a belief that the government engineered or participated in a cover-up. Dozens of books have been written and a number of movies and documentaries have been produced about "what really happened."

Martin Luther King Jr.'s death similarly inspired conspiracy theories. His killer, James Earl Ray, was apprehended two months after King's death, following a two-month manhunt that ended at London's Heathrow Airport. Ray, a racist who was on the run after escaping from the Missouri State Penitentiary, initially proclaimed his innocence, but in March, 1969, confessed to the crime and was sentenced to 99 years in the Tennessee State Penitentiary. He later tried to recant his testimony, and continued to assert his innocence until his death in 1998. King's own family never believed Ray was the killer, and in 1997 King's son, Dexter, met with Ray in prison. He came away from the meeting convinced that Ray was innocent. Other prominent African-American leaders agreed.

The Rev. Jesse Jackson, a Baptist minister and Civil Rights activist, claimed the assassination was a plot by more than the likes of James Earl Ray. In a 2008 interview with the BBC, Jackson said:

> "I'm convinced Ray was not the lone shooter. He didn't have the money, the mobility nor the motive to have done it. The fact that James Earl Ray was able to get out of the city and out of the country means he was a hired hand. The government seems to have had the most motive for attacking Dr. King."[217]

In another 2008 interview, former U.N. Ambassador and Atlanta Mayor Andrew Young said he had always believed the FBI might have been involved somehow in King's death. He said:

> "You have to remember this was a time when the politics of assassination was acceptable in this country. ... I think it's naïve to assume these institutions were not capable of doing the same thing at home or to say each of these deaths (King and the two Kennedys) was an isolated incident by 'a single assassin.' It was government policy."[218]

A conspiracy theory of another sort surfaced in 1964 and has persisted even until today. That was the year that Phyllis Schlafly, a leader in the conservative movement in the 1960s, published her best-selling book, *A Choice, Not an Echo: The Inside Story of how American Presidents Are Chosen.* In it, Schlafly alleges that American elections are bought and sold by the rich power brokers of the world, and that the objective of selected candidates is to pursue the goals of the Council on Foreign Relations (CFR). (The CFR, which still exists today, describes itself as "an independent, nonpartisan membership organization, think tank, and publisher."[219]) In her book, Schlafly says that those who call the shots in the world are a group of elitists made up predominantly of members of the Bilderberg group, an association of the world's most rich and famous that meets in secret annually to discuss world issues. Many believe that what they're up to is conspiring to form a communist world government.

Discoveries and Dangers

Before the assassinations that rocked the country and gave rise to conspiracy theories, there were people in the scientific community who began to raise public awareness about issues that were troubling at the least, and alarming at worst. Certain of these findings called into question assumptions about the future of our energy resources, raised the possibility of a tainted food supply, and pointed out structural flaws in the Earth's surface that could make some parts of the country dangerous places to live. All of these discoveries offered new considerations for those seeking to secure their future.

Fueling the Future?

Geologist M. King Hubbert, who worked in the oil industry from the 1930s to the early 1960s, studied and became an expert in the patterns of oil-well discovery and oil-well depletion in the world. In 1949 he made a prediction that the era of fossil fuels would be a relatively short one, and in 1956 he specifically predicted that U.S. oil production would reach a peak around 1970 and would then begin a steady decline. It is important to note that he did not predict that the U.S. — or the world—would run out of oil. His prediction was based on a basic cost-benefit analysis he explained to a friend in 1982:

> *"So long as oil is used as a source of energy, when the energy cost of recovering a barrel of oil becomes greater than the energy content of the oil, production will cease no matter what the monetary price may be."*[220]

Experts agreed with Hubbert that there would be a peak in recovery of the finite fuel source left behind by the dinosaurs—someday. But many disagreed about when. Today there are experts who believe the peak has already been reached. Others believe it will not happen for another 30 to 40 years. However, according to a 2004 article in the *Washington Post*, many experts believe that nearly half of the oil available in the world has already been extracted.[221]

Those who were paying attention to Hubbert's predictions became alarmed early on at the ramifications of a decline in the supply of oil, a fuel serving a world population that was not only growing in numbers, but was also pursuing the life offered by an industrialized society. Every industry in the world was—and is—dependent on petroleum in some way; the gravest concerns—then and now—center around food production and transportation, medicines, and power generation.

Toxic Times

In 1962, marine biologist and nature author Rachel Carson caused a revolution in the environmental movement with her book *Silent Spring*. The book raised public awareness about manmade dangers to the environment and also caused people to question big industry and its ties to the government. It has been credited with altering the course of history.[222]

In her book, Carson revealed the effects of the uncontrolled use of pesticides—particularly DDT—on animals and birds, and ultimately on humans. She alleged that chemical pesticides had irreversibly harmed animals and birds, and further, that it had tainted the entire world food supply.[223] She charged that chemical companies—and our "industrialized, technological society"—were behaving irresponsibly toward the natural world, and explained the price humans might

77

ultimately pay. She also accused public officials of protecting industry interests by not scrutinizing the use of these chemicals more closely.

Her book drew an outpouring of support among the public, which began to press for change, and also drew criticism from the chemical industry, which launched an "education campaign" to assure the public about the benefits of pesticides. Concerned about revelations in the book, President Kennedy appointed a committee to study the use of pesticides, and in 1963, Carson was called to testify before Congress.

Carson died of cancer in 1964, but her warnings helped prompt the later public outcry about the use of Agent Orange and other chemicals during the Vietnam War. In response, the government established the Environmental Protection Agency (EPA) in 1970; DDT was ultimately banned in 1972.[224]

Faulted

After years of studying the San Andreas Fault after the disastrous 1906 California earthquake, scientists learned that the "fault" is actually a system of fractures in the Earth's crust that have occurred over millions of years. They established that the entire system is more than 800 miles long, running nearly the entire length of California, and that the fractures reach at least 10 miles into the depths of the Earth.[225]

In 1953, geologist Thomas Dibblee identified that more than 350 miles of displacement, or shifting, had already occurred along the fault. Scientists subsequently established that the tectonic plates — sections of the Earth's shell — along the fault line "drift" apart at up to 2 inches per year, and have collected data to help forecast future earthquakes along the San Andreas Fault. Studies have shown that large earthquakes have occurred along the southern portion of the fault every 150 years or so, and since the last large quake to occur along that segment happened in 1857, scientist believe there is potential of another one there at any time. This "potential" has given rise to much speculation about when "the big one" will happen.

Time to Retreat

Economically, the turmoil-plagued 1950s and 1960s saw a level of expansion that gave many Americans confidence in a future that seemed to promise peace and prosperity. The gross national product grew by more than double, from $200 billion to greater than $500 billion.[226] More people than ever enjoyed the fruits of this prosperity — cars, homes in the suburbs, TVs in nearly every living room, disposable income for the purchase of myriad consumer goods, and money for their children's education. But an incident in 1965 cast brief a shadow on the good life, just as Americans were getting used to the electricity-powered convenience of modern living, and rumblings in the economy started many people thinking about the need to become more self-reliant.

Blacked Out

Those in the Northeast got a taste of what life would be like without the electricity that framed their existence when the lights suddenly went out on November 9, 1965. Shortly after 5 p.m., just at rush hour, power was cut over 80,000 square miles in parts of Canada as well as the New England states, New Jersey, and New York.[227] Close to 25 million people were left without electricity for about twelve hours; nearly 800,000 people were trapped in subways, and thousands more were stranded in trains, buildings, and elevators.

Fifteen thousand troops, including 10,000 National Guardsmen and 5,000 police officers, were called to the city to help prevent looting and other violence.[228] President Johnson immediately called upon the Federal Power Commission to investigate the incident. In a memo to the commission he said:

> *"Today's failure is a dramatic reminder of the importance of the uninterrupted flow of power to the health, safety, and wellbeing of our citizens and the defense of our country. This failure should be immediately and carefully investigated in order to prevent a recurrence."*[229]

Johnson offered the commission the "full resources of the federal government," including the Federal Bureau of Investigation and the Department of Defense, to help with the investigation.

The cause of the power disruption was determined to be human error, after it was found that an incorrect setting had allowed an overload that tripped one of the major transmission lines in Canada. Most Americans forgot about the incident shortly after it was over and life returned to normal. Three years later, the government created the North American Electric Reliability Council (NERC) to monitor operational compliance along the national electric grid.[230]

Planning for Collapse

A recession in the early 1960s lasted for about a year, bringing a cloud over the economy, but it gave way to a period of economic growth whose length was second only to that of the 1990s.[231] However, as the decade ended, a recession once again loomed on the horizon, prompting concerns among some about a monetary collapse, even as others were hell-bent on pursuing the American Dream.

In 1967, investment adviser Harry Browne started offering seminars with financial advice on how to survive a monetary collapse. Architect Don Stephens, who saw how a monetary collapse could lead to a collapse of society, soon joined Browne at his seminars and offered participants a copy of his book, *Retreater's Bibliography*.

Stephens used the term "retreater" to described people who were making plans to relocate to a remote hideaway in the event of a societal collapse,[232] and offered in his book practical advice about how to live a survivalist life successfully. Influenced by the environmental movement, Stephens designed systems that could be maintained indefinitely, such as solar power, and introduced the idea of resource renewability as a component of a self-sufficient lifestyle. He employed building techniques that made use of natural and recycled materials, and incorporated some of his ideas into *Retreater's Bibliography*, as well as other related books he wrote in the ensuing years, including *Personal Protection, Here and Now* (1975), *Retreating on a Shoestring* (1975), *The Survivor's Primer & Updated Retreater's Bibliography* (1976), and *Green Papers* (1987). He contributed a chapter on "Safe Shelter & Independent Energy" to *The Complete Survival Guide* (1983), edited by Mark Thiffault.

The ideas of self reliance and living off the land were attractive to many in the youthful 1960s counterculture that largely rejected the status quo. They believed in the possibilities of the future and believed they could change the world. And some of them did. Stewart Brand, a biologist/author who was at the heart of the 1960s counterculture, was someone committed to inspiring a retooling of American society to be ecologically sound and self-sustaining. Catering to what he saw as a groundswell of interest in self-reliance, sustainability, and protection of the natural world, Brand in 1968 started publishing the popular *Whole Earth Catalog*.

The catalog listed sundry products that would be helpful to people pursuing a sustainable lifestyle, including books, machinery, tools, clothes, and even seeds. (The catalog did not offer these things for sale, but listed vendors that did sell them, along with prices.) According to the opening page of a 1969 edition of the catalog, products worthy of entry into the compendium had to be "useful as a tool, relevant to independent education, high quality or low cost, not already common knowledge, and easily available by mail."

The catalog influenced a generation of creative thinkers, among them Steve Jobs, the genius behind Apple, Inc. Jobs gave the commencement address at Stanford University in 2005, and told the audience:

> *"When I was young, there was an amazing publication called* The Whole Earth Catalog, *which was one of the bibles of my generation.... It was sort of like Google in paperback form, 35 years before Google came along. It was idealistic and overflowing with neat tools and great notions." During the commencement speech, Jobs also quoted the farewell message on the back cover of the 1974 edition of the catalog: "Stay hungry. Stay foolish."*[233]

Part One:

The History of Preparedness

Chapter Three: 1970s to 1990s

The society that emerged from the 1960s had been shaken by war and uncertainty. Many people were suspicious of government and angry about a continuing war in the Far East that was widely considered to be illegal and continued to claim American lives.

The ongoing Cold War provided the backdrop for life in the world from the 1970s to 1991, when it was declared "over," and the nuclear menace that hung like a cloud over civilization from the time it was first unleashed upon the world spread, as more countries joined the nuclear club and worldwide stockpiles of nuclear weapons grew.

Changes in technology grew exponentially in the years between 1970 and 1999, bringing Americans marvels that changed the way they lived—from how they spent their leisure time to how they shopped, how they traveled, how they acquired information, how they connected with one another, and even how they made supper. But the pursuit of the American Dream that offered temptations at every turn, compliments of technology, electricity, and industry, was marred by events that called into question the future of the country—from its prosperity to its faith in government, its ability to defend itself, its resilience in the face of disaster, and its very quality of life.

In the largest-ever transformation of the country's civil defense program, FEMA was created by Executive Order 12148, issued by President Jimmy Carter in 1979.[234] But with each new presidential administration, the agency continued to struggle with what its mission should be and how it should be accomplished. Many people, concerned about world events, decided to take emergency planning into their own hands, and sought out resources to help them live more prepared lives.

Preparedness Rising

The unsettling times fostered a new interest in self-reliance and living off the land. Demographic studies show that in the 1970s, more people moved to rural areas than to cities, ending a trend that had, for most of the 20th century, seen millions of people forgoing life in the country to pursue the opportunities of city life.[235] The trend spurred the development—and popularity—of newsletters, books, and magazines about survival and self-reliance.

Following closely on the heels of Stewart Brand's *Whole Earth Catalog*, the *Mother Earth News*, a magazine launched in 1970, offered readers information, advice, and tips on living a more self-sufficient lifestyle. It covered a broad range of topics, from farming and gardening to do-it-yourself projects and alternative energy. It had appeal across a wide spectrum of people pursuing self-sufficiency, including back-to-the-landers, survivalists, "retreaters," and city dwellers dreaming of a simpler life in the country. The focus of the magazine was not so much on preparedness as an activity focused on risk as it was on a lifestyle that enabled resilience.

People pursuing the simple life—and the skills to live it—were drawn to Eliot Wigginton's *Foxfire Book*, a 1972 compendium of information about things like building a log cabin, slaughtering hogs, handcrafts, food preservation, and mountain lore. Topics in the book were taken from a magazine Wigginton and some students created in the 1960s to preserve some of the folk-culture traditions of the Southern Appalachians.

Similarly, *The Yankee Magazine Book of Forgotten Arts* (Richard M. Bacon, 1978), promised to help "recreate the simplicity and warmth of yesteryear's lifestyle" by reviving old-time skills. It offered instruction, drawings, diagrams, recipes, remedies, and formulas to help, all selected from among the "best of the best" articles published in *Yankee Magazine*.[236]

Economic concerns inspired Robert L. Preston's 1972 book *How to Prepare for the Coming Crash*, in which he not only predicted an economic collapse, but also offered a picture of how such a collapse might lead to a disintegration of civilized society. Howard Ruff authored the 1974 entry *Famine and Survival in America*, which, he says in the book, was inspired by Preston. Ruff's book focused on food, offering would-be preppers a wealth of information on food chemistry to help inform choices about what a long-term food-storage plan should include.

Making the Best of Basics, by James Talmage Stevens, was published in 1974, in the middle of the U.S. energy crisis. More than 800,000 copies have sold since then. Considered a "preparedness bible," it enjoys continuing popularity, and in 2013 its tenth edition ranked among the top 5 percent of sales online at Amazon.com.[237]

Another 1974 publication—*How to Grow More Vegetables Than You Ever Thought Possible on Less Land Than You Can Imagine,* by John Jeavons—offered inspiration to those looking to live off the land, wherever they might live. The eighth edition of the book was released in 2012, to inspire a whole new generation of rural and urban farmers.

John Seymour's 1976 book, *The Self-Sufficient Life and How to Live It: The Complete Back-to-Basics Guide,* was an inspiration to many, especially those who experienced the 1970s oil crisis and came to believe that the days of life powered by fossil fuels were numbered. Maria Rodale, CEO of Rodale, Inc., once met Seymour and called the meeting a "pivotal moment" in her life. She credits Seymour with being "the recognized leader of the self-sufficiency movement."[238]

Between 1977 and 1982 Mel Tappan published the *Personal Survival Letter,* a newsletter devoted to providing information about survival in the face of a major catastrophe. Tappan, who has been called "the godfather" of the preparedness movement, believed civilization was "hopelessly doomed."[239] He favored relocation to a remote retreat as a means of escaping whatever might be coming, and equipping oneself with the resources to live sustainably—including the means for self defense. Tappan wrote two books that are considered classics in the preparedness movement—*Survival Guns* (1979) and *Tappan on Survival* (1981). Both books were re-released years later—*Survival Guns* in 2009 and *Tappan on Survival* in 2006—and rank in the top 15 percent of online sales at Amazon.com.

John Pugsley's *The Alpha: The Ultimate Plan of Financial Self-Defense,* offering advice on insulating finances in an uncertain economy, was a best-seller for weeks in 1981.[240] Ragnar Benson's *Live Off the Land in the City and Country,* offering practical advice on self-reliant living, was published the same year, and remains a classic today, ranking among

85

the top 25 percent of sales on Amazon. Despite enjoying a certain amount of anonymity through the pen name "Ragnar Benson," the author went on to write a number of other popular survival-related books, including *Survivalist's Medicine Chest* (1982), *The Survival Retreat: A Total Plan For Retreat Defense* (1983), and *Ragnar's Guide To The Underground Economy* (1999), to name a few.

Backwoods Home Magazine was started in 1989 by publisher Dave Duffy, as a way to promote a book he wrote about building a cabin in the woods. Duffy says that his book didn't sell, but the magazine took off. In a 2013 interview, Duffy said *Backwoods Home* is about "being your own person ... totally self-reliant. It's about personal freedom and being your own boss ... getting away from the chains of Corporate America." He said that the magazine was first associated with the environmental movement, which had originally been identified with *Mother Earth News*. He noted that about five to ten years after he started *Backwoods Home*, it seemed to be "part of a preparedness/self-sufficiency movement."

The magazine remains popular today, with 37,000 paid subscribers to the print magazine, 6,300 Kindle subscribers; and another 12,000 or so in newsstand sales. [241] Duffy said the magazine is popular because "it offers a lot of in-depth advice about specific ways to be more self-sufficient and has a lot of experts to provide that information." He noted that *Backwoods Home* "doesn't particularly target preppers, but there's certainly a lot of interest from people who consider themselves to be preppers."

Besides books, magazines, and workshops on self-reliance and survivalism, the times introduced a new source of information—and information sharing—for those interested in survivalism: online computer forums. The September 18, 1985 issue of *InfoWorld*, a weekly news magazine for information technology professionals, announced the creation of an online bulletin board called the Survival Communication Forum, where survivalists and would-be survivalists could share their thoughts on emergency preparedness. Participants discussed everything from sourcing food to weaponry, the rebirth of society after a calamity, and even ethical questions about what level of responsibility well-prepared people had after a disaster toward those who had made no preparations.

James Wesley Rawles, survivalist author and owner of SurvivalBlog.com, was one of those posting to the early online boards. In a 2013 interview, he said he first started posting survival information to Usenet groups, such as Misc.Survivalism, in the late 1980s. He said that people using those groups posted about "the usual stuff — food storage, first aid, training — typical survivalist chit chat."

"It's all about beans, bullets, and BAND-AIDs®," he said.

Energy-Challenged

During the 1970s through 1990s Americans started to become aware of the downside to their country's reliance on fossil fuels, and gained glimpses into what life would be like without them. The specter of M. King Hubbert's 1949 and 1956 predictions haunted those who experienced two U.S. energy crises and saw the U.S. embark on a war that was ostensibly about defending Kuwait after it was invaded by Iraq, but seemed to be more about protecting U.S. oil interests in the Middle East. The events sparked a surge in the number of people seeking to build lifestyles that were less dependent on fossil fuels, lifestyles that offered resiliency if those fuels should disappear.

Life Without Oil

On October 6, 1973, a coalition of Syrian and Egyptian forces launched a surprise attack on Israeli forces in the Sinai Peninsula and the Golan Heights, sparking a war that lasted nineteen days and drew in the two Cold War super-powers — the United States and the Soviet Union — to aid their respective allies. For its part, the U.S. went to the aid of Israel by resupplying its military, while the Soviets kept the forces of the Syria-Egypt coalition supplied with arms.

In retaliation for the U.S. support of Israel, the alliance of oil-producing nations in the Middle East imposed an oil embargo on the United States and other countries that had supported Israel.[242] The embargo came at a time when U.S. domestic oil reserves were low, U.S. oil production was at a peak, and U.S. consumption of oil continued on an upward spiral.[243] At the same time, the Organization of Petroleum Exporting Countries (OPEC) cut back on overall oil production in an

87

effort to increase the price per barrel. Worldwide economies were sent reeling when the per-barrel price of oil climbed from $3 to $12.[244]

In the U.S., the price of gasoline jumped from about 32 cents a gallon to 84 cents a gallon. Gas rationing was imposed, and Americans waited in long lines at the gas pumps to refuel their cars and trucks. Some gas stations served customers only by appointment, or served only "regular" customers; some set limits on the amount of gas they sold to each customer; some reduced their hours of operation; others went out of business altogether. Fuel thefts from cars were common, giving rise to the need for locking gas caps.

Around the country people were asked to do whatever they could to help conserve energy. People, businesses, and towns turned off or turned down the lights; some towns banned the use of decorative lights during the holidays. People and businesses in northern states were urged to lower the setting on their thermostats by two degrees in winter; people were encouraged to dress in layers.

The auto industry started to suffer, as large vehicles, quickly recognized as "gas-guzzlers," fell out of favor. Automakers were forced to regroup and retool to produce smaller, more fuel-efficient cars.

The oil embargo was finally lifted in March 1974, after lengthy negotiations by the Nixon administration.[245] However, oil prices never went back to 32 cents a gallon, and the world learned how dependent it was on oil production in the Middle East. People came to realize how dependent they were on this fossil fuel—no matter what its source, and how their lives could be turned upside down without it.

Another oil crisis raised its head in 1979, a result of instability and warring between the oil-producing nations of Iran and Iraq. The crisis was compounded by another OPEC price increase and a hostage crisis that prompted a U.S. embargo against Iranian oil after Iranian students kidnapped fifty-two Americans from the American embassy.[246]

Even as he dealt with a delicate hostage situation, President Jimmy Carter embarked on plans to reduce U.S. dependence on foreign oil, which included deregulating oil price controls to spur more domestic production. He also worked with state governors to set gasoline conservation goals for all 50 states and lowered the maximum highway speed limits across the nation to 55 miles per hour.

However, realizing that the U.S. could not depend solely on its own oil production, and in response to Middle-East turmoil and Soviet aggression in Afghanistan, Carter issued a warning in his State of the Union address to Congress on January 23, 1980, a warning that became known as the Carter Doctrine.[247] He told Congress:

> *"Let our position be absolutely clear: An attempt by any outside force to gain control of the Persian Gulf region will be regarded as an assault on the vital interests of the United States of America, and such an assault will be repelled by any means necessary, including military force."*

He continued:

> *"Our excessive dependence on foreign oil is a clear and present danger to our Nation's security. The need has never been more urgent. At long last, we must have a clear, comprehensive energy policy for the United States."*

Ten years later, during the administration of President George H.W. Bush, the Iraqi invasion of the oil-producing nation of Kuwait was met with force by the United States, some say in the spirit of the Carter Doctrine.

In August 1990, Iraqi leader Saddam Hussein launched an attack on Kuwait, after accusing the country of siphoning oil from the Ar-Rumaylah oil fields on the border Kuwait shared with Iraq. He asserted that the country was catering to Western interests by keeping oil prices low, and with his country holding significant debt to other nations, sought a takeover of Kuwait as a way to leverage relief from that debt.

Alarmed at Hussein's aggression, leaders in Egypt and Saudi Arabia called on the United States and its Western allies for intervention. After Hussein refused demands by the United Nations Security Council to withdraw his forces from Kuwait by mid-January 1991, the U.S. led an offensive against his positions there with a coalition of troops from nearly thirty countries that included Great Britain, Egypt, France, Germany, Japan, Saudi Arabia, and the Soviet Union.

On the surface, the U.S. response appeared to be about defending Kuwait, but it stirred anti-war sentiment in the United States, with protesters crying, "No blood for oil!" And in an interview for the August 1990 issue of *Time Magazine*, an unnamed adviser to President

Bush said that the U.S. decision to go to the aid of Kuwait had been "an easy call." He went on to say:

> "*Even a dolt understands the principle. We need the oil. It's nice to talk about standing up for freedom, but Kuwait and Saudi Arabia are not exactly democracies, and if their principal export were oranges, a mid-level State Department official would have issued a statement and we would have closed Washington down for August.*"[248]

Well aware of what the U.S. was after, Hussein used the precious commodity against the Allied forces. Iraqi troops opened valves on oil tankers docked at Kuwait's Sea Island terminal, releasing 240 million gallons of crude oil into the ocean, in an effort to thwart a landing of U.S. marines on Kuwaiti shores.[249,250]

The assault on Iraq lasted 42 days. Approximately 750,000 Coalition troops served in the war, including 540,000 from the United States; only 300 troops were lost.[251] The conflict ended when President George H.W. Bush declared a cease-fire in February 1991, after Iraqi forces had been driven from Kuwait. But as the defeated Iraqis made their retreat, they blew up and set fire to more than 650 oil wells and damaged more than 70 more.[252]

Despite the war, the oil spill, and the oil-well fires, there was hardly a blip in the American oil supply. Analysts' predictions that the war would cause the price of crude to jump to $60 per barrel were proved wrong. It hovered at just above its pre-war price of $21 — nearly $10 more than the price during the 1973 oil shock.[253]

In January 1991, right after the war's end, Americans were paying an average of $1.17 per gallon at the gas pumps.[254]

The Pursuit of Power

The Gulf War and the oil shocks of the 1970s motivated a reinvigorated exploration of alternative power sources in the U.S. and around the world, including nuclear, solar, and wind.

As early as the late 1950s, countries had already begun to consider how nuclear energy might be harnessed for something besides weapons, and sometime between 1954 and 1956 the Soviet Union became the first country to generate electricity by way of a nuclear power plant. The United States followed suit in 1957, opening an experimental reactor in Shippingsport, Pennsylvania.[255] Starting in the late 1960s, the U.S. began work on a number of nuclear power plants, and between 1973 and 1996 had brought 104 of them online. Construction on more than half of those started in the 1970s.[256]

Exploration of solar power was slower to catch on. After years of experimentation in private laboratories and at the National Aeronautics and Space Administration (NASA), the U.S. finally committed to researching solar technology when the Department of Energy opened the Solar Energy Research Institute in 1977 and created the National Renewable Energy Laboratory to explore ways to harness the power of the sun.[257]

Investigation into wind technology spiked in popularity after the 1970s oil crises, but its implementation has been slower, primarily due to costs.

As promising as these new technologies were, people soon discovered that some came with costs that went far beyond dollars and cents and offered new reasons to focus on preparedness.

Nuclear Nightmares

In the new age of nuclear power, the word "meltdown" entered the modern lexicon and became synonymous with horrific nuclear disaster. "Meltdown" is the informal term used to describe the overheating of a nuclear reactor core, a situation with the potential for reactions that could lead to radiation leaks—poisoning the atmosphere as well as people, animals, and plants—and with a potential for devastating hydrogen explosions.

The world witnessed two dangerous meltdowns in the 1970s and 1980s, one in the United States, and one in Russia. The incidents prompted an international convention of experts in 1989 to establish a means of communicating to the public the scale and significance of nuclear accidents. The result of their efforts was the International Nuclear and Radiological Event Scale (INES), which provides a way to rate accidents on a scale from 1 to 7, identified as follows:

91

1 = anomaly with no safety significance

2 = incident

3 = serious incident

4 = accident with local consequences

5 = accident with wider consequences

6 = serious accident

7 = major accident

According to International Atomic Energy Agency, a United Nations organization, the panel of experts who developed the INES retrospectively rated the U.S. incident a 5, and the Russian incident a 7.[258,259]

Meanwhile, as the world watched these civilian nuclear disasters unfold, global stockpiles of nuclear weapons continued to grow, and the dangerous dance of military posturing between the United States and the Soviet Union led the world once more to the brink of disaster. Later, the breakup of the Soviet Union raised the specter of a free-for-all to claim the weapons in its nuclear arsenal.

In the U.S.: Three Mile Island

One of the early nuclear power plants in the United States, the Three Mile Island facility in Pennsylvania, was the scene of the worst nuclear accident in U.S. history in 1979, after only three months of operation.[260] The partial meltdown of TMI-2, one of the facility's two reactors, was caused, according to the U.S. Nuclear Regulatory Commission, by "a combination of equipment malfunctions, design-related problems and worker errors."[261]

The accident started around 4 a.m. on March 28, 1979, with an equipment failure in a section of the plant that prevented water from reaching the steam generators responsible for removing heat from the reactor core, resulting in the shutdown of the reactor. Actions taken by plant operators failed to correct or improve the situation, and at about 8 a.m. the Nuclear Regulatory Commission sent inspectors and a response team to the site. At 11 a.m., all non-essential personnel were evacuated from the plant.

Two days later, it was discovered that some radioactive gases had leaked out. The status of the radiation and ongoing concern about the condition of the plant prompted Pennsylvania Governor Richard L. Thornburgh to order an evacuation of people living within a 5-mile radius of the plant. Fears of an explosion mounted as a large hydrogen bubble was discovered in the dome of the container that held the reactor core. As technicians worked to reduce the size of the bubble, the absence of oxygen in the container finally caused it to dissipate, and the crisis ended on April 1. It was later discovered that there were no adverse effects from the gas leak; the crisis ended with no injuries.

Cleanup of the damaged reactor took close to twelve years, at a cost of nearly $973 million.[262]

In Russia: Chernobyl

The accident in Russia was far more serious. The Chernobyl power plant, located in the Ukraine, consisted of four nuclear reactors; a fifth was under construction at the time of the accident. On April 26, 1986, the power station's Unit 4 was destroyed in an explosion and fire that resulted from a power surge during a test of the reactor systems.[263]

The fire, which burned for ten days, released nearly 190 tons of radioactive material into the air, and ejected a massive cloud of radiation high into the atmosphere.[264] The radiation spread over large areas of the Soviet Union and parts of Asia; low levels of radiation from the accident were eventually detected all around the world, including the United States. According to a Reuters report published in the *Los Angeles Times* on August 17, 1986, the Chernobyl disaster "released 30 to 40 times as much lethal ash as the atomic bombs dropped over the Japanese cities of Hiroshima and Nagasaki in 1945."[265]

Emergency workers finally extinguished the toxic fire by dropping sand and boron over the area by helicopter. Several weeks after the fire was extinguished, workers encapsulated the site with a cement "sarcophagus" to prevent any additional radioactive material from escaping. Additionally, the Soviet government clear-cut nearly a square mile of forest near the plant and buried it, to further reduce contamination around the scene of the accident.

The original explosion at the nuclear plant killed two people. The scale of the disaster was initially downplayed by the Soviet government, which attempted to cover it up. The government finally began evacuating over 115,000 people from the immediate area a few days after the accident, and in the ensuing years eventually relocated an estimated 200,000 to 400,000 more.[266] More than twenty-eight workers and responders died in the first four months after the accident, and 106 workers developed acute radiation sickness.

It has been estimated that about 155,000 square kilometers — nearly 60,000 square miles — in the former Soviet Union were contaminated by the accident, affecting close to 9 million people either directly or indirectly.[267] The world is still dealing with the aftermath.

Eleven years after the accident, the United Nations Department of Humanitarian Affairs convened an international meeting on Chernobyl to launch an assistance program aimed at mitigating the ongoing consequences of the disaster. The Department reported high rates of cancers among the population in the region and higher-than-normal incidences of sickness among recovery workers. It also pointed to other problems that needed to be addressed, including continuing economic hardship in the area, problems with food production, agricultural and forestry management, and a need to address future environmental and nuclear safety. The Department announced plans for a number of projects planned to deal with these issues and appealed to the international community for financial aid and other assistance.[268]

With little information about the accident forthcoming from the Russian government, it's difficult to assess the human toll taken by the accident. According to a 2011 report in *The Atlantic Magazine,* some people estimate that cancer-related deaths attributable to the Chernobyl accident number from 4,000 to more than 200,000.[269] The U.S. Nuclear Regulatory Commission reported in 2013 that about 6,000 cases of thyroid cancer have been detected in people who lived in the area of the accident as children and had consumed milk tainted with radioactive iodine. Ninety percent were treated successfully; 15 had died by 2005.[270]

Estimates for future deaths related to the disaster vary. The Chernobyl Forum, a group of United Nations agencies organized in 2003 for scientific study of the nuclear accident and its impact on health and the environment, estimates that the final death toll from radiation exposure will be about 4,000. However, the environmental organization Greenpeace says it expects the total number of deaths could reach 93,000 worldwide. And the Chernobyl Union of the Ukraine, a non-governmental group that supports survivors of the disaster, says that 140,000 recovery works have died in the last twenty-five years. It puts the current death toll at more than 700,000.[271],[272]

Experts have blamed the nuclear accident on faulty system design and human error.[273],[274] In subsequent years, all of the Chernobyl reactors were shut down, with collaboration among the world's seven industrialized nations (the "G-7")—the United States, the United Kingdom, Canada, France, Germany, Italy, and Japan. As of 2013, a long-term project to build a permanent, 20,000-ton steel containment structure for the plant—called the New Safe Confinement (NSC)—remained under construction.[275]

In Stock: Formidable Weapons

As the people of the world bore witness to the terrifying nuclear disasters at Three Mile Island and Chernobyl, they were ever mindful of the nuclear technology still being applied to weaponry. In the spirit of "mutual assured destruction," world superpowers continued to work at keeping their nuclear stockpiles at least even. The estimated worldwide stores of nuclear weapons in 1970 were just over 38,000. At the time of the Chernobyl accident, the global inventory stood at 63,638, the highest number ever.[276] This included so-called "tactical" weapons, designed to be used for smaller-scale destruction on the battlefield rather than for wholesale obliteration of the enemy.

In 1982, an increasingly worried public began to push for a freeze on the development of nuclear weapons, and a grassroots campaign led to nine U.S. states passing referenda supporting a halt to nuclear weapons programs.[277] Even as the Cold War superpowers continued with nuclear weapons development and testing, public pressure prodded the leaders of the U.S. and U.S.S.R. to pursue arms-reduction talks. By the end of the 1990s, the tally of worldwide nuclear armaments had dropped to just over 33,000.[278]

Loose Nukes

At the time of the Soviet Union's collapse, the Soviet nuclear arsenal stood at close to 27,000 weapons, along with enough nuclear raw materials to produce three times that number.[279] As the former super power disintegrated into fifteen separate entities, world leaders became alarmed about the prospect of those weapons being under the control of unstable, fledgling governments, or worse, falling into the hands of terrorists. At the time, there were 3,200 strategic warheads located in the Ukraine, Kazakhstan, and Belarus — on alert and aimed at targets in the United States. But of greatest concern were the 22,000 or so tactical weapons that were small enough to fit into a knapsack. After nearly four years of U.S.-led negotiations, all nuclear weapons of the former U.S.S.R. were purportedly turned over to Russia.[280]

However, according to a 2001 report for Boston University by Foreign Policy Research Institute Fellow Rensselaer Lee, many incidents of theft of nuclear material have been reported since the early 1990s. Most have involved "radioactive junk," but some have been thefts of weapons-grade plutonium and uranium. The report stated that large amounts of nuclear materials were removed from Russian labs in the early 1990s, and pointed to corruption in the Russian nuclear establishment as an ongoing cause for concern.[281]

The International Atomic Energy Agency tracks and reports on incidents of illicit trafficking in nuclear and radioactive material all over the world — regardless of its source. According to its records, there were 16 incidents of trafficking in highly enriched uranium and plutonium between 1993 and 2005, as well as 60 incidents involving high-risk radioactive substances.[282]

Killing the Planet

Environmental disasters began to infiltrate the decision-making of those seeking to live a more self-reliant existence and helped frame a growing awareness of how individual choices could affect the planet.

The health of the environment became a concern for individuals and academics alike. Back-to-the-landers, intent on getting their sustenance directly from the land and waters around them, began to see that their own survival depended on the survival and health of the planet. And from the 1970s to 1990s, there were many reasons to be concerned about the planet's health.

American journalist and educator Richard Heinberg gained recognition in the early 21st century for sounding an alarm about the world's finite resources, through books such as *The Party's Over: Oil, War & the Fate of Industrial Societies* (2003), *Peak Everything: Waking Up to the Century of Declines* (2007), and *The End of Growth* (2011). However, as early as 1995 he was working to raise awareness about ways in which styles of modern living were affecting life on Earth. In June 1995, he presented his paper, "The Primitivist Critique of Civilization," at the 24th annual meeting of the International Society for the Comparative Study of Civilizations. He told the audience, "We are, it seems, killing the planet." He explained:

> *"By most estimates, the oceans are dying, the human population is expanding far beyond the long-term carrying capacity of the land, the ozone layer is disappearing, and the global climate is showing worrisome signs of instability."*[283]

Tainted Ground

In the late 1970s, the words "Love Canal" became synonymous with an environmental disaster that resulted from hazardous wastes that had been disposed of by burial in the ground, a disposal method that had been deemed acceptable by both the City of Niagara Falls and the United States Army. The effects have persisted into the 21st century.

Love Canal was a "model city" envisioned in the late 1800s by Developer William T. Love. Love planned to power the city by hydroelectric power from a man-made waterfall that would be created by digging a canal to connect the Niagara River with Lake Ontario. The project progressed into the early 1900s, until Love lost his financial backing with only three thousand feet of the planned six- to seven-mile long, sixty-foot-wide canal completed, and the project was dropped. The land was sold at public auction in 1920, and became used by the

City of Niagara Falls and the United States Army as a dump site for municipal and chemical wastes.[284]

The site was acquired by Hooker Chemicals and Plastics Corporation in 1947, which continued to use it as a disposal site. By 1952, the company had buried a significant number of metal drums there, altogether containing more than 21,000 tons of toxic chemicals — on top of what had already been left behind by the city and the Army.[285] In 1953, the company filled in the canal with dirt and sold the property for one dollar to the Niagara Falls Board of Education — with a disclaimer on the deed against any injuries caused by chemicals.

Meanwhile, housing development had started next to the canal in 1951. After the School Board acquired the Love Canal property, it sold off lots for more housing, and also built a school there. The school, which opened its doors in 1955, serviced some 400 students.

From the late 1950s through the late 1970s, residents frequently complained about odors emanating from their yards and the school playgrounds, as well as strange substances oozing from the ground. The city responded by covering the offending areas with dirt, and eventually hired a consulting company to investigate the many complaints. The company, Calspan Corporation, completed its study of the canal area in 1976, and reported finding residues of toxic chemicals in the air and in the sump pumps of many homes near the canal. The company recommended that the canal be covered with clay and that home sump pumps be sealed off.

The State of New York's Department of Health started its own investigation in early 1978, and by August had identified a high incidence of reproductive problems among women in the 239 families living closest to the canal. The investigation also uncovered high levels of contaminants in the air and soil. The State Health Commissioner declared a health emergency and urged the evacuation of pregnant women and young children.[286] A year later, a report by the U.S. Department of Health put the odds of Love Canal residents developing cancer at one in ten.

Eventually, all 239 families living in the area were evacuated, and the state fenced in the abandoned properties. However, people living outside of the fenced area were also concerned about their health, and after they took their case to the streets in a number of public protests,

98

scientists conducted studies of people living outside the fence. A study completed in 1979 concluded that chemicals had been carried by underground water currents to a much larger area than originally thought, and revealed that more than seventy-five percent of the people living outside the fenced area showed increases in serious health problems that included miscarriages, still births, nervous breakdowns, and epilepsy. The study also found that 56 percent of the children born in the Love Canal neighborhood between 1974 and 1978 had been born with birth defects.

In 1980, President Jimmy Carter ordered the evacuation of the entire neighborhood. Close to 950 families were relocated, and 350 homes were torn down.[287] That same year, in response to the Love Canal disaster, Congress passed the Comprehensive Environmental Response, Compensation, and Liability Act of 1980. The law, also known as "Superfund," provides federal funds to clean up sites contaminated with hazardous materials.

Cleanup of Love Canal was completed in 1998, at a cost of more than $350 million[288]; the EPA removed the site from the Superfund list in 2004.[289] However, not everyone was convinced that the cleanup had made the area safe. In 2012, lawyers took up the cause of residents living outside the "containment zone," who claimed that toxic chemicals were showing up in their neighborhood. The group asserted that health problems many of them had been experiencing were linked to the chemicals, and brought suit against the City of Niagara Falls for $113 million.[290]

In a report she wrote for Boston University's School of Public Health in 1983, former Love Canal resident and activist Lois Gibbs said:

> *"Residents learned at Love Canal that even low levels of chemical exposure have an effect on the human body, and that the government will protect you from this only when you force them to. If you think you're safe, think again. We can count only on ourselves to safeguard our families' health through vigilance, knowledge and collective action."*[291]

Before the Love Canal disaster was uncovered, there was already a growing awareness in the U.S. about the need to manage the byproducts of our industrialized world. Congress enacted the Resource Conservation and Recovery Act (RCRA) in 1976 to protect the public and the environment from the hazards presented by waste disposal.[292] The Act banned open dumping and launched a program to promote recycling and reuse of disposed materials, sparking the rise of a whole new industry devoted to the buying, selling, and reuse of recyclable materials.

Hazardous wastes presented a more challenging problem. The RCRA had established a program to control hazardous materials "from the cradle to the grave," which included strict requirements around the treatment, storage, and disposal of hazardous waste. By 1984, Congress had amended the RCRA to require the phase-out of simple dumping and burial of hazardous waste in the ground. However, the use of underground storage tanks was—and continues to be—allowed. In 1985 the EPA established the Office of Underground Storage Tanks, which oversees the Underground Storage Tank System implemented by states and territories. The agency says that there are now 581,000 storage tanks in locations across the country, some on Indian reservations, storing petroleum and other hazardous substances. It acknowledges the potential dangers of the program: "The greatest potential threat from a leaking UST is contamination of groundwater, the source of drinking water for nearly half of all Americans."[293]

Such leaky sites have, indeed, been discovered, and are referred to by the EPA as "LUST" sites—Leaking Underground Storage Tanks. In an update on its website in August 2013, the agency states that 17,400 LUST sites have been identified in the Pacific Northwest alone. Cleanup of those sites has been going on for the past ten years; 13,550 have been cleaned up so far.[294]

The problem of nuclear waste disposal, which arrived on the scene hand-in-hand with nuclear weapons and nuclear energy, was not solved during the late 20th century, and continues to challenge the world today. Some nuclear wastes are known to break down over a relatively short period of time; some can be reclaimed. But others take thousands of years to break down, presenting a dilemma on where to put them and how to contain them.

In the United States, a location at Yucca Mountain in Nevada was chosen in the 1980s to be the storage site for all of the country's nuclear wastes, and in 1987 Congress passed a law requiring that it be up and running by 1998. Meanwhile, the wastes would be contained in protected areas at the sites where they were created. However, the project encountered many hurdles and opposition by Nevadans concerned about the long-term effects of the site on the environment and their health. Then, in the face of the national budget woes of 2013, funding for the project was cut significantly, putting the project — and the wastes it was meant to store — in limbo, despite the estimated $15 billion already spent on it.[295]

In the meantime, thirteen other countries found an easy way to dispose of their nuclear waste — they dumped it at sea, from 1946 until 1993, when the practice was banned by international agreements.[296]

Toxic Waters

Festering nuclear waste wasn't the only manmade substance to contaminate the planet's oceans. Some of the worst oil spills in history took place from the 1970s to 1990s, leaving behind widespread damage to oceans, wildlife, and ecosystems. These incidents, along with oil shortages and world conflict that seemed centered around oil, caused many Americans — especially those concerned with self-sufficient living — to rethink how they used oil as well as how much of it they used, and prompted a U.S. ban on offshore oil drilling in 1990.[297]

History records the worst spill in the world during that period as the one left behind by the Gulf War in 1991. The sabotage of oil tankers by Iraqi troops released an estimated 380 to 520 million gallons of crude oil into the Persian Gulf, resulting in an oil slick four inches thick across about 4,000 square miles of open water and decimating thousands of sea birds and aquatic animals.[298] In an August 1991 interview with the *Chicago Sun-Times,* Greenpeace activist Paul Horsman, who had visited the area with a Greenpeace inspection team, said that parts of the shoreline along the Persian Gulf were "beyond repair."[299] That seemed to be confirmed in 2010, when Dr. Jacqueline Michel, President of Research Planning, Inc., told an interviewer on RPI's *The World* that a survey done between 2002 and 2003 showed nearly 500 miles of Saudi Arabian shoreline still contaminated with a million cubic meters of oil sediment. She said that the oil had penetrated so far into the mud flats that it was now impossible to remove it.[300]

There were also four major oil spills in the United States that took place between 1970 and 1999, resulting in the release of millions of gallons of crude oil into the waters off America's shores. The worst of these was the *Exxon Valdez* accident, considered to be "the biggest environmental disaster since Three Mile Island."[301]

The *Exxon Valdez*, a tanker carrying close to 54 million gallons of crude oil extracted from the Prudhoe Bay oil field in Alaska, struck a reef in Prince William Sound on March 24, 1989, while en route to Long Beach, California, and spilled an estimated 11 million gallons into the bay.[302] The spill devastated the wildlife in the bay, and along with it, the livelihoods of those who depended on the ocean's bounty for a living. It also decimated a major source of sustenance for Alaskans living off the land and sea. Estimates say that more than 250,000 seabirds were killed as a result of the spill, as well as 2,800 sea otters, 300 harbor seals, 250 bald eagles, as many as 22 killer whales, and an untold number of fish and fish eggs. A cleanup that cost nearly $2.1 billion (paid for by Exxon) and involved 10,000 workers and a squadron of boats, planes, and helicopters, went on for four years before it was called off.

A 2001 report by the Alaska Fisheries Science Center said that some of the wildlife in the area, such as sea otters and sea ducks, had still not recovered, and stated that remaining oil in the region may have become "a chronic source of low-level oil pollution" within the area affected by the spill.[303] A 2003 report in *Scientific American* confirms that a "significant amount of oil" was persistent in the region, and goes on to say, "the long-term impacts of oil spills may be more devastating than previously thought."[304]

The notoriety of the *Exxon Valdez* spill may have eclipsed in the mind of the public other disastrous oil spills along the coastal U.S. Until the *Exxon Valdez* ran aground, the worst oil spill in U.S. history was one that occurred in 1976, just south of Nantucket Island in Massachusetts, when the Liberian tanker *Argo Merchant* ran aground during bad weather on December 15, 1976. Despite efforts to salvage the ship and its cargo, it sank on December 21, and in the process spilled close to 8 million gallons of oil into the waters of Nantucket Sound. However, because of a shift in wind direction, the prevailing currents carried the spill out to sea.[305] The shores of coastal Massachusetts were spared the devastation later seen in Prince William Sound — but that oil, unmitigated by cleanup efforts, landed *somewhere*.

In the 1990s, the Norwegian tanker *Mega Borg* suffered an explosion that sent more than 5 million gallons of oil into the Gulf of Mexico, off the coast of Galveston, Texas,[306] and a three-way collision off the coast of Florida, involving the barge *Bouchard 155*, a second barge, and a freighter, spilled 336,000 gallons of crude into the waters of Tampa Bay.[307]

As suggested by Dr. Michel in her 2010 interview, it may take years to understand the full impact of these oil spills on the environment.

Accidental oil spills and nuclear waste dumping are not the only manmade threats to the oceans. In 1974, scientists discovered a "dead zone" in the Gulf of Mexico, at the mouth of the Mississippi River. The "dead zone" is an area that lacks oxygen as a result of pollution from synthetic fertilizers that are washed by rains from crop fields in America's heartland into the Mississippi River and are carried into the Gulf. The resulting oxygen-deprived area can no longer support marine life. Fishermen reported in 1998 that they were already seeing the effects of the contamination, being forced to travel farther and farther into the Gulf to find fish.[308] The contaminated area expands and contracts with the seasons and conditions, and has been known to grow as large as 8,000 square miles in size. Scientists worry that the dead zone could collapse the Gulf's $26 billion fish and shellfish industry.[309]

Manmade pollution has also been identified as a contaminant in many fish and sea mammals, and has been found to persist in the environment much longer than expected. One such contaminant is mercury. Mercury is a naturally occurring element which, in people exposed to it, can cause damage to the nervous system, the immune system, the brain, heart, kidneys, and lungs. But it is also found in manmade hazardous wastes and in emissions from coal-burning power plants.

In 1970, scientists found that the pollution from the dumping of mercury waste into Japan's Minamata Bay in the mid-1950s had spread beyond the bay, and had persisted in the waters for ten years longer than the government had originally estimated.[310] The mercury contamination had been identified in the late 1960s as the source of pollution that had poisoned thousands of people living on Minamata Bay.

In the mid-1970s, American scientists discovered that native peoples living along the Alaskan coast were being poisoned by mercury in the seal livers they ate—a delicacy they had enjoyed for generations.[311]

According to the EPA, scientists have determined that "coal-burning power plants are the largest human-caused source of mercury emissions to the air in the United States, accounting for over 50 percent of all domestic human-caused mercury emissions."[312] However, much of that is not even within U.S. control. Emissions from burning coal—and hazardous wastes—*anywhere in the world* enter the air and are carried all over the globe and are deposited in the water, contaminating fish and other marine life. The EPA says, "less than half of all mercury deposition within the U.S. comes from U.S. sources."

According to a 2004 report by the EPA, traces of mercury can be found in nearly all ocean fish and shellfish, but are most predominant in shark, swordfish, mackerel, and tilefish, as well as canned albacore tuna which, the agency says, contains more mercury than canned "light" tuna. The report said that fish eaten in moderation doesn't pose health risks for most people, but it advised pregnant women and young children to avoid eating these fish.[313]

And it has been discovered that freshwater fish are not immune from mercury contamination by manmade pollution. A 2009 report released by the U.S. Geological Survey stated that mercury contamination had been found in all one thousand fish they tested over a seven-year period, from almost 300 freshwater streams across the country.[314]

A 2012 report in the *Huffington Post* underscored the impact of mercury in fish, saying that scientists have discovered it is more dangerous than previously believed.[315]

Government: The Dark Side

The presidents who led the country during the 1970s to 1990s navigated the nation through some of its most difficult times, creating new chapters in American history. Historic legislation ended segregation, ended the draft, provided a framework for protecting the environment, created a path to greater transparency in government, and guaranteed Americans the right to privacy.[316] However, Americans gradually learned that, while some of the presidential accomplishments of the period were worthy of high praise, others were cause for concern, if not alarm. And they discovered that presidents past had not been all they appeared to be. For some people, this fed a growing mistrust of government and fueled an argument for relying on the government less, and on themselves more.

Secrets Revealed

Protests over U.S. involvement in the Vietnam War continued from the 1960s to the early 1970s and grew increasingly violent, prompting the involvement of local and state police, as well as National Guard troops, in quelling the hostilities. In 1970, two college-campus protests turned to tragedy when the police presence sent to control them used deadly force, shooting into the crowds and killing five college students. Four were killed by National Guardsmen at Ohio's Kent State University, and one was killed by police at Jackson State University in Mississippi.[317] Then, after years of dissent over the moral and legal justification for U.S. involvement in the Vietnam War, Americans had their fears confirmed in 1971, after a classified, government-prepared history of the U.S. role in that war was turned over to the *New York Times* by Daniel Ellsberg, an MIT research associate and military analyst who had worked on the history project.

Highlights of the forty-seven-volume history, known as "the Pentagon Papers," were published in serial form by the *Times* starting in June of that year, exposing a growing U.S. involvement in Vietnam that took place over a period of thirty years and revealing a pattern of public deception that spanned four presidential administrations.

The papers disclosed that it was President Truman who first involved the U.S. in the Vietnam War by providing military aid to France as that country waged war against the communist-led Viet Minh. President Eisenhower acted to further entrench the U.S. in the conflict by acting militarily to prevent a takeover of South Vietnam by the Communist regime in the North. President Kennedy secretly expanded the U.S. role there, and after his death, President Johnson not only intensified the covert operations, but also made plans for outright war as early as 1964, a year before the government finally admitted to the public the extent of the country's involvement in the conflict. Further, even

105

though a study by U.S. intelligence agencies concluded that bombing North Vietnam would not stop its support for the ongoing Viet Cong insurgency in the South, Johnson ordered a bombing mission of the North in 1965.[318]

In an interview with United Press International following the publication of the Pentagon Papers, former Republican presidential candidate Barry Goldwater and Democratic Senator Birch Bayh shared their reactions to the disclosures. Goldwater said:

> *"During the [presidential] campaign, President Johnson kept reiterating that he would never send American boys to fight in Vietnam. ... he knew at the time that American boys were going to be sent. In fact, I knew about ten days before the Republican Convention. ... I was being called a trigger-happy, warmonger, bomb happy, and all the time Johnson was saying he would never send American boys, I knew damn well he would."*[319]

Bayh observed:

> *"The existence of these documents, and the fact that they said one thing and the people were led to believe something else, is a reason we have a credibility gap today, the reason people don't believe the government.*[320]

Embarrassed by the Pentagon Papers' disclosures in an election year, then-President Richard Nixon sought a court injunction to stop the *Times* from continuing to publish what the government claimed was "top secret" information after the third installment was released. However, less than two weeks after the *Times* series was launched, the U.S. Supreme Court ruled 6 to 3 that the government had failed to make its case, freeing the *Times*—and other publications—to publish the material.

Ellsberg told *TIME Magazine* in an interview on June 28, 1971:

> *"To see the conflict and our part in it as a tragedy without villains, war crimes without criminals, [and] lies without liars, espouses and promulgates a view of process, roles and motives that is not only grossly mistaken but which underwrites deceits that have served a succession of presidents."*[321]

After the court ruling, Nixon's administration brought criminal charges against Ellsberg for conspiracy, espionage, and stealing government property. The charges were dismissed during the trial in 1973, after prosecutors discovered that a team of burglars had been dispatched by the White House to break into the office of Ellsberg's psychiatrist, seeking information to discredit him.[322]

It turns out that Nixon used what were later called "dirty tricks" repeatedly to discredit political opponents. The most famous incident was the Watergate affair. During the 1972 presidential campaign, Nixon and his advisers plotted to spy on Democratic opponents by planting recording devices in the Watergate Hotel, the venue for the Democratic convention. After it was discovered that some of the planted microphones weren't working properly, a team was sent to the hotel to fix them, and in the process was discovered by a security guard, who called police and had them arrested. Some people suspected the burglars had connections in high places, but Nixon swore the White House wasn't involved, and was handily reelected by trusting voters.[323]

However, *Washington Post* reporters Carl Bernstein and Bob Woodward reported on October 10, 1972, that the Federal Bureau of Investigation (FBI) had determined the Watergate incident was part of a "massive campaign of political spying and sabotage conducted on behalf of President Nixon's re-election." Further, they alleged that direction for the operation had come from the top, from both White House officials and officials of the president's reelection committee.[324]

The ensuing investigation revealed that, not only was the president connected to the incident, but that he had later tried to cover it up, appropriating thousands of dollars in "hush money" for the burglars, and instructing the Central Intelligence Agency to hold up the FBI investigation.[325]

Ultimately, facing certain impeachment, Nixon resigned on August 8, 1974. Three years later, Nixon was interviewed by British television journalist David Frost, who asked him whether any of his actions had been illegal. He responded:

"Well, when the president does it, that means that it is not illegal."[326]

Power Unchecked

Twelve years after Nixon's resignation, a scandal unraveled in the administration of President Ronald Reagan, revealing covert operations and deceptions that had the United States embroiled in a war between Iran and Iraq as well as a revolution in Nicaragua.

A hallmark of the presidency of Ronald Reagan, who served as president from 1981 to 1989, was his passion for stopping the expansion of Communism. In his State of the Union address to the nation on February 6, 1985, Reagan outlined a foreign policy that came to be known as the Reagan Doctrine, a policy that set the stage for Reagan's worldwide anti-communism campaign. Key points of the policy were:

- Freedom is a universal, God-given right
- America's mission in the world is to defend freedom and democracy anywhere in the world where those values are threatened.

Reagan said:

> *"We must stand by our democratic allies. And we must not break faith with those who are risking their lives – on every continent, from Afghanistan to Nicaragua – to defy Soviet-supported aggression and secure rights which have been ours from birth. ... Support for freedom fighters is self-defense."*[327]

With this statement, Reagan justified covert actions by the U.S. Central Intelligence Agency to train and aid anti-Communist insurgencies all over the world. One of those was in Nicaragua, where a group of rebels known as the Contras were fighting to gain control of the country, which had fallen to the socialist Sandinista National Liberation Front in 1979.[328] Some of the funds used to support that effort came from another covert operation which, after its discovery – and the discovery of the elaborate scheme to cover it up – became known as the Iran-Contra Affair.

The complicated operation started with Reagan's approval in August 1985 of a secret program to sell arms to Iran, in spite of a U.S. embargo against selling weapons to either side in the war between Iran and Iraq.[329] The impetus for the sales was an attempt to win favor in the Middle East, with the hope of gaining the release of American hostages who had been taken prisoner by terrorists in Lebanon. Since Reagan had publicly condemned negotiating with terrorists, Israel was enlisted as the "middle man" in the Iran arms arrangement. Funds from the weapons sales were then diverted to the Nicaraguan Contras.[330]

The arms sales were halted in 1986 after the Lebanese newspaper "Al-Shiraa" broke the story about the secret arms deal that November.[331] An ensuing investigation by the Reagan-appointed Tower Commission and a subsequent eight-year investigation by Independent Counsel Lawrence Walsh resulted in resignations, firings, and fourteen people being charged with crimes related to the operation or the cover-up. Although there was widespread speculation about the direct involvement of Reagan and his vice president, George H.W. Bush, neither the commission nor Walsh found evidence linking the two to the affair.

Meanwhile, in 1984, the government of Nicaragua had brought suit against the United States in the United Nations' International Court of Justice, for its military and paramilitary operations in the country.[332] In June 1986 the twelve justices of the court issued a ruling consisting of sixteen findings, among them:

> "[The Court] Rejects the justification of collective self-defense maintained by the United States of America in connection with the military and paramilitary activities in and against Nicaragua the subject of this case. (By twelve votes to three)

> "[The Court] Decides that the United States of America, by training, arming, equipping, financing and supplying the Contra forces or otherwise encouraging, supporting and aiding military and paramilitary activities in and against Nicaragua, has acted, against the Republic of Nicaragua, in breach of its obligation under customary international law not to intervene in the affairs of another State." (By twelve votes to three.)

Years later, authors and editors at the National Security Archive, a private public interest organization, published a retrospective of the Iran-Contra Affair based on 100 previously classified documents that were released in the early 1990s. An editorial review of the 1993 publication— *The Iran-Contra Scandal: The Declassified History*, by author Peter Kornbluh and editor Byrne Malcolm — calls the Iran-Contra affair "one of the most important political scandals since Watergate."[333]

Finances, Food, and Foes

For the average American, the world economy and the principles that drive it are a complicated mystery. And for many, global politics are filled with incomprehensible nuances that keep the subject out of focus as they go about their daily lives — working, paying the bills, raising their children, and putting food on the table. Yet events and decisions made in all of these areas between 1970 and the end of the millennium affected daily life in America profoundly, providing an impetus for many to pursue a more self-sufficient lifestyle.

Navigating Financial Waters

Predictions of economic collapse cropped up repeatedly during this period, and although some people may have had difficulty understanding how such an event would affect them personally, others got a firsthand taste of it during recessions that cost them their jobs and stock market crashes that cost them their investments. Memories and stories about the Great Depression loomed large in the minds of many. And like their predecessors who served since the time of the Great Depression, presidents of the 1970s to 1990s worked to erase such possibilities from America's future.

When President Richard Nixon took office in 1969, the United States had been through six recessions since the Great Depression.[334] The country was facing a $7 billion deficit, and a faltering economy was poised to usher in yet another recession. The recession that unfolded in 1970 sparked a rise in U.S. unemployment to 6 percent, the highest it had been since 1960.[335]

Nixon and his advisers worked feverishly to get the country's economy back on an even keel, by implementing wage and price controls authorized by Congress, controlling interest rates and implementing strategies to bring down inflation, balance the budget, and create jobs. However, foreign economies were having their own share of economic troubles, and some countries began cashing in their American greenbacks for the gold by which their value was guaranteed. By 1971, America found its stock of gold bullion standing at half of what it had been in 1960, and found foreign banks holding more U.S. dollars than the country had to back them with gold. On August 12, a demand by

110

Great Britain for the U.S. to guarantee $750 million it held prompted a high-level meeting of Nixon and his advisers at Camp David, to discuss a course of action that would get the economy back on track and protect the country from a run on its gold reserves. Three days later, Nixon addressed the nation to announce a new economic policy embodied in Executive Order 11615, a policy whose ramifications are still being felt today, and is consequently referred to as "The Nixon Shock."

In his address, Nixon framed the policy as a way "to bring about a full generation of peace, and to create a new prosperity without war."[336] He told Americans that his goals were to create more jobs, to stop the rise in the cost of living, and to "protect the dollar from the attacks of international money speculators."

The specific actions he announced were:

- A ninety-day freeze on wages and prices
- A 10-percent duty on imported goods
- Appointment of a Cost of Living Council to work with business and labor leaders to set up a mechanism for maintaining price and wage stability
- Temporary suspension of the "convertibility of the dollar into gold or other reserve assets, except in amounts and conditions determined to be in the interest of monetary stability and in the best interests of the United States."

Forty years after Nixon's announcement, financial analysts with the benefit of hindsight have called the policy — particularly the removal of gold as the standard backing the U.S. dollar — a "colossal error."[337] What had started as a temporary change had become permanent. In an article marking the policy's fortieth anniversary, a writer for *Forbes Magazine* said:

> "No other single action by Nixon has had a more profound and deleterious effect on the American people. In the end, breaking the solemn promise that a dollar was worth 1/35th of an ounce of gold ... marked the beginning of the worst 40 years in American economic history."

The U.S. continued to battle economic woes for the rest of the millennium, suffering recessions from 1980 to 1982 and from 1990 to

111

1992, and enduring stock market crashes in 1973 and 1987. The country's ongoing struggles to balance the budget and reduce the deficit prompted Congress to pass several pieces of legislation between 1981 and 1997, designed to keep the finances in control. Yet disagreements between Congressional Democrats and Republicans on spending cuts resulted in government shutdowns between November 1995 and January 1996, and left people with growing concerns about the country's financial future.

'Frankenfood'?

In the 1970s, scientists were researching ways to use a ground-breaking 1953 discovery that gave them the ability to join together genes from one kind of organism into the DNA of another. The result of their work led to the creation of genetically engineered life forms, including an oil-eating organism that could be put to work in cleaning up oil spills, and genetically engineered drugs, such as insulin. And in a historic 1980 decision that would have far-reaching consequences, the U.S. Supreme Court ruled that genetically altered life forms could be patented.[338]

As scientists continued their work on the new technology, they turned their attention toward using it to improve food production, to help satisfy the hunger of an ever-growing world population. The first trials with genetically altered plants were with tobacco and tomatoes in 1987. The U.S. Department of Agriculture approved a genetically modified tomato for commercial use in 1992, the same year that Vice President Dan Quayle announced a new policy of the first Bush Administration, declaring that engineered foods were "substantially equivalent" to traditionally grown foods, and therefore needed no special regulation.[339] The policy was presented in the context of the Bush-Quayle initiative to reduce "burdensome regulations" for corporations.[340]

In 1989 a genetically engineered dietary supplement of L-tryptophan manufactured in Japan was released to the U.S. market. Within months, there was an outbreak of EMS (Eosinophilia–myalgia syndrome) among a number of people who had consumed the supplement. Thirty-seven people died; 1,500 were permanently disabled.[341] A subsequent investigation showed that the genetically engineered tryptophan contained a toxic contaminant never before seen in batches of the conventionally produced supplement. Although there was no decisive proof that genetic engineering had caused the EMS outbreak, the coordinator of the U.S. Food and Drug Administration's Biotechnology Working Group, Dr. James Maryanski, told government officials in 1991, when pressed, that bioengineering could not be ruled out.

During his 1999 testimony before the House Subcommittee on Basic Research, Maryanski explained that human tinkering with plant genetics is nothing new, noting that hybrid plants, which are in common use, are also created through breeding practices that require human intervention. Bioengineering, he said, was just another tool used to accomplish the same goal — plant improvement. He said:

> *"Today's techniques give breeders the power to cross biological boundaries that could not be crossed by traditional breeding. For example, they enable the transfer of traits from bacteria or animals into plants."*[342]

The World Health Organization offers further insights about genetically modified organisms (GMOs). It defines them as "organisms in which the genetic material (DNA) has been altered in a way that does not occur naturally," and points out that they are developed because "there is some perceived advantage either to the producer or consumer of these foods." For consumers, that might mean a food with a better taste, or longer shelf life, for example. For producers, it could mean improved resistance to insects or disease. On its website, the organization explains:

> *"The GM crops currently on the market are mainly aimed at an increased level of crop protection through the introduction of resistance against plant diseases caused by insects or viruses or through increased tolerance towards herbicides. Insect resistance is achieved by incorporating into the food plant the gene for toxin production from the bacterium Bacillus thuringiensis (BT). This toxin is currently used as a conventional insecticide in agriculture and is safe for human consumption."*[343]

Despite assurances by the FDA and by companies involved in the manufacture of GMO foods, the public became increasingly anxious about GMOs in the food supply, and concerns about this technology going against the natural order of things earned GMO foods the moniker "Frankenfood." Public concern also arose about the ability of

113

corporations to patent living organisms, raising the specter of monopolies and increasing corporate control of the food supply.

However, corporate control of seeds is not limited to companies that produce GMO seeds, contrary to popular belief. Hybrid seeds, which have been widely used for years, can also be patented, although not all are. The simplest difference between GMO plants and hybrids is that hybrids are created by interbreeding plants of different species, whereas GMOs are created by exposing plant cells to radiation or chemicals to splice them with DNA from a widely different source— including the animal kingdom.

More recent research about GMOs has provided additional evidence of their safety,[344],[345] however, many people, including doctors and scientists, remain unconvinced.[346] San Francisco pediatrician Dr. Michelle Perro, who was interviewed by CBS in December 2013 for a report on a grassroots effort to label foods containing GMOs, said:

> *"We have lots of clinical research that's showing us there are profound health effects in animals fed GMOs."*[347]

One of the concerns is that plants bred to resist pests—by actually creating their own pesticide—could be harmful to humans when consumed.

In addition to the serious concerns about the possible health effects of consuming GMO-laden foods, for those seeking a more self-sufficient lifestyle there are lingering concerns about two characteristics that GMO plants share with their hybrid counterparts:

- Attempting to grow and cross-breed seeds from either type of plant, if they are patented, is illegal.
- Neither hybrid nor GMO seeds can be saved for future production—they won't produce plants that are "true to type," i.e., like the parent plant.

In the "old days," people choosing a self-reliant lifestyle could grow their own fruits and vegetables simply by saving seed from a given year's crop to use in the following year's growing season. With the advent of GMO and hybrid seeds, those people became increasingly dependent upon corporations for the seeds needed to grow their own food—unless they sought out "heirloom" seeds: those that occur naturally, are not patented, and can be used to perpetuate crops from

114

year to year. With growing concerns about the disappearance of these heirlooms, people looking to become self-sufficient have made it a priority to seek them out and save seed from the resulting crops, in order to assure sustainable crop production.

Global Insecurity

During the Cold War, while those who paid attention to world affairs were largely preoccupied with the threat of a nuclear attack from the Soviet Union, another international threat emerged, bringing death and destruction to American interests all over the world. And while it may be easy for the average American to lose focus of what's happening "over there," Americans began to sit up and take notice when some of those attacks started happening *here*.

During the 1970s, militant groups in the Middle East began a worldwide campaign of terror in attacks that began with hostage crises and eventually grew to include acts of suicidal mass murder. Some of these groups were engaged in rebellion against governments in Middle Eastern countries, and used attacks against Western interests as a way to draw attention to, and gain leverage for, their causes. Others were engaged in a holy war against the world's "infidels" — primarily, people who were not followers of Islam. Their objective seemed to be to kill as many "nonbelievers" as they could.

The first attack by Middle Eastern radicals against Western interests *outside* the United States took place in September 1970, when four jetliners were hijacked and diverted to an airfield in Jordan by members of the Popular Front for the Liberation of Palestine.[348] The planes hailed from the United States, Switzerland, Great Britain, and Israel; in total, more than 400 people were on board the flights. Most were released by the Palestinian rebels on September 11; however, forty were detained, with the hope that they could be exchanged for Palestinian rebels being held in Israeli prisons.

Reacting to the situation, then-President Nixon released a statement condemning what he called "the menace of air piracy," and he outlined steps the United States would take to combat the threat. Those steps, he said, would include:

115

- Placing specially trained, armed United States government personnel on flights of U.S. commercial airliners
- Using electronic surveillance equipment and techniques at all "gateway airports and other appropriate airports in the United States"
- Developing new methods for detecting weapons and explosive devices
- Determining whether metal detectors and x-ray devices used by the military could be used in airport surveillance efforts.[349]

The day after Nixon's statement, the rebels, believing they were about to be attacked, blew up all four planes (minus the hostages), even though the announced deadline for the release of the prisoners had not yet been reached. Then, despite the position of the U.S. and its allies not to negotiate with terrorists, the Palestinian prisoners were ultimately released in exchange for the hostages.

A more significant hostage crisis unfolded nine years later, on November 4, 1979, when a gang of young Islamic revolutionaries stormed the U.S. Embassy in Tehran and took more than sixty Americans hostage.[350] The event that precipitated the attack was the decision of President Jimmy Carter to allow the former Shah of Iran, who had been ousted by revolutionaries in July, to come to the United States for cancer treatment; however, it had its roots in a history of U.S. intervention in Iran—roots that centered around oil.

Since the discovery of oil in Persia, now Iran, in 1908, British and American corporations had controlled most of the country's oil reserves. In 1951, Iranians elected a new prime minister, Muhammad Mossadegh, who announced plans to nationalize Iran's oil industry. In reaction, the American Central Intelligence Agency and Britain's Secret Intelligence Service launched covert operations to overthrow Mossadegh and replace him with a leader who would look more favorably on Western financial interests in the country. With the support of the king, Mohammad Reza Shah Pahlavi, who signed orders for the ouster of Mossadegh, the plan was executed, but initially failed, forcing the Shah to flee the country. However, he returned in 1953 with assistance from American and British operatives, who carried out a second coup d'état. This time the plan was successful, and General Fazlollah Zahedi—hand-picked by the American-British coalition and approved by the Shah—was named prime minister. The new government returned control of 80 percent of Iranian oil reserves to the British and Americans, and in return received tens of millions of dollars in foreign aid.

But the Shah's new regime proved to be a brutal dictatorship, which eventually sparked a revolution in the 1970s, led by the radical Islamist cleric Ayatollah Ruhollah Khomeini. Inspired by Khomeini's promise of independence and a break from the influence of the West, the Iranian people who had suffered under the Shah's rule rose up and forced him to flee the country in July 1979.

It was against this backdrop that the 1979 hostage crisis took place. After long and arduous negotiations, the hostages were finally released 444 days after they were taken.

The 1980s brought a wave of terrorist attacks against Americans and other Western interests by radical Islamists and similar factions in the Middle East, and included suicide bombings, hijackings of airliners and one cruise ship, the taking of more hostages, and the bombing of a U.S. commercial airplane. Some of those responsible for the attacks were caught; some were not. Hundreds of Americans lost their lives or were maimed in these incidents[351]:

- A suicide bombing on April 18, 1983, killed sixty-three people, including seventeen Americans, at the U.S. Embassy in Beirut, Lebanon.
- Two hundred forty-one U.S. Marines were killed and more than 100 were injured in a suicide bombing at the U.S. Marine barracks in Beirut on October 23, 1983.
- Six people were killed and more than eighty were injured in a bombing attack on the American Embassy in Kuwait on December 12, 1983.
- Thirty Westerners were kidnapped in the Middle East during a 10-year hostage-taking crisis that lasted from 1982 to 1992. Four were Americans, among them Beirut CIA Station Chief William Buckley, who was kidnapped on March 16, 1984, and later died in captivity; and journalist Terry Anderson, who was held captive for 2,454 days.
- A truck bomb killed twenty-four people as the U.S. Embassy annex in Beirut on September 20, 1984.
- Iranian militants hijacked a Kuwaiti airliner bound for Pakistan on December 3, 1984, and diverted the flight to Tehran, Iran.

Two Americans were killed; the remaining hostages were released when Iranian security forces rushed the plane.

- American airliner TWA flight 847 was hijacked while en route to Rome, Italy, from Athens, Greece, and was diverted to Beirut, Lebanon, on June 14, 1985. Hijackers demanded the release of seventeen people who had been imprisoned for the 1983 attack on the American Embassy in Kuwait, along with 700 Shiite Muslim prisoners who were being held in Israeli and Lebanese prisons. When the demands weren't met, the hijackers killed an American passenger, Robert Dean Stethem, a U.S. Navy diver, and dumped his body on the tarmac. After Israel began releasing some of the prisoners it held, the hijackers released their hostages.

- On October 7, 1985, the Italian cruiseliner *Achille Lauro* was hijacked by four gunmen off the coast of Egypt and diverted to the port of Tartus, in Syria. The gunmen demanded the release of certain Palestinian prisoners in the Middle East; however, their demands weren't met, and when the ship was refused permission to dock at Tartus, the gunmen killed a disabled American tourist and threw his body overboard. The hijackers directed the ship to return to Port Said, Egypt, and after its arrival they agreed to release the ship and its passengers in exchange for safe passage out of the area. U.S. fighter jets intercepted the plane on which the men had made their escape, and escorted it to a NATO base in Sicily, Italy, where the hijackers were arrested.

- Simultaneous bombings at airports in Rome and Vienna on Dec. 17, 1985, took the lives of twenty people, including five Americans.

- One American soldier and a woman from Turkey were killed on April 5, 1986, in a bombing at a discotheque in West Berlin known to be frequented by off-duty U.S. servicemen.

- Two hundred fifty-nine people on board U.S. Pan American flight 103, traveling from London to New York, were killed on December 21, 1988, when the plane exploded over Lockerbie, Scotland.

In the 1990s, terrorist attacks by Islamic radicals grew increasingly violent and destructive, and continued to target American interests all over the world:

118

- In November 1995, a large car bomb was set off in a parking lot next to a building in Riyadh, Saudi Arabia, which housed the Office of the Program Manager of the Saudi Arabian National Guard. Five Americans and two Indians were killed.[352]
- In 1996, a massive truck bomb was detonated next to an eight-story housing complex in Khobar, Saudi Arabia, a complex that housed U.S. Air Force and allied troops involved in Operation Southern Watch, a mission to monitor and control airspace in Iraq. Nineteen U.S. servicemen and 498 others were killed in the attack.[353]
- On August 7, 1998, simultaneous truck-bomb attacks took place against U.S. embassies in Kenya and Tanzania, killing 224 people and injuring 4,500.[354] The attacks provoked outrage from then-President Bill Clinton, who vowed to bring the bombers to justice "no matter what or how long it takes."[355] The investigation that followed identified the mastermind behind this attack as Saudi Arabian exile Osama bin Laden. Bin Laden was known to be the organizer of a global militant Islamist organization called Al-Qaeda, a stateless "army" devoted to promoting a "holy war" against non-Muslims. U.S. intelligence found that bin Laden had terrorist training camps in Afghanistan, and those became the target for the missile strike ordered by Clinton in retaliation for the embassy bombings. Four of bin Laden's operatives were apprehended and indicted for the bombings in February 2001. In October 1998 they were all sentenced to life in prison without parole. Another, who had been among those indicted for his involvement in the crime, remained at large. In October 2013, a team of Navy SEALs captured the man, Abdul-Hamed al-Ruqai, also known as Abu Anas al-Liby, ending a 15-year manhunt.[356]

Besides carrying out worldwide attacks against American interests, terrorists also set their sights on the U.S. homeland. However, it is important to note that, despite popular belief, terrorism was not a new phenomenon in the United States in the late 20th century, and radical Islamic terrorists were not the only perpetrators of terrorist attacks in this country. "Home-grown" terrorists have been visiting violence on this country since its earliest days, starting with Indian raids on Early American colonists.

119

During the 19th century, the deep feelings engendered by the anti-slavery movement led to violent attacks by people on both sides of the issue. Throughout the 20th century, there were war-related attacks by saboteurs, and political activists of all stripes used violence to underscore their beliefs. Some people with mental and emotional problems committed acts of violence for no apparent reason. Some of the most notable "home-grown" terror attacks in the 20th century included:

- The Bath School Disaster in 1927, which is widely considered to be the deadliest school mass murder in U.S. history. Andrew Kehoe, the school board treasurer in Bath Township, Michigan, set off bombs at three schools, after killing his wife and family and setting fire to his farm. Forty-four people were killed in the school explosions, including thirty-eight children. One other bomb failed to detonate.[357],[358]
- The reign of the "mad bomber," who terrorized New York City from 1940 to 1956, setting off more than thirty bombs in public places such as Grand Central Station, movie theaters, and phone booth, and injuring more than fifteen people.[359]
- A series of eight bombings at major New York City institutions in 1969, carried out by radical anti-war activists.[360]
- Attacks by the "Alphabet Bomber" in 1974, including a bombing at the Pan Am Terminal at Los Angeles International Airport, which killed three people and injured eight. The perpetrator, Yugoslavian Muharem Kurbegovich, also firebombed the houses of two police commissioners and a judge, and burned down two apartment buildings in Marina Del Rey, California.[361]
- The country's first known bioterrorism attack, in the fall of 1984. Members of a Buddhist cult called Rajneeshee, seeking an advantage for their candidate in a county election in Oregon by making residents too sick to vote, exposed more than 700 people to salmonella contamination by way of ingredients at a pizzeria salad bar, table-top coffee creamers and potato salad at ten restaurants, and more.[362]
- The bombing of the Alfred P. Murrah Federal Building in downtown Oklahoma City, Oklahoma, on April 19, 1995 — considered to be the worst act of "home-grown" terror in the country's history. The blast killed 168 people, including nineteen children, destroyed or damaged more than 300

buildings within 16 blocks of the explosion, and caused more than $650 million in damage. Two American right-wing radicals, one a former soldier in the U.S. Army, were convicted in the crime. One was executed; the other was sentenced to life in prison without parole.[363]

Radical Islamist-style terrorism first arrived in the United States in the guise of a "home-grown" terror incident on March 1, 1989, when the offices of the *Riverdale Press* newspaper were firebombed five days after the paper published an editorial that was critical of a bookseller for pulling from its shelves copies of *The Satanic Verses,* a novel by Salman Rushdie. The bookseller had pulled the books in reaction to statements by Iran's ruler and spiritual leader, Ayatollah Khomeini, calling for the death of Rushdie and anyone associated with publishing the book, which Khomeini said was blasphemous of the prophet Mohammed. Although no one was ever arrested in the incident, an FBI investigation concluded that the bombing was, in fact, related to the newspaper's defense of Rushdie's novel.[364]

A more serious attack on American soil occurred on February 26, 1993, when Islamic fundamentalists detonated a truck bomb in the parking garage of New York's World Trade Center, killing six people, injuring more than 1,000 people, and causing more than $500 million in damage. Most of those responsible were caught and convicted, and sentenced to life in prison. Ramzi Ahmed Yousef, the alleged mastermind of the plot, was arrested in Pakistan two years later; the driver of the truck, Eyad Ismoil, was apprehended in Jordan the same year. Another man believed to be directly involved in the attack, Abdul Rahman Yasin, remained at large.[365]

An FBI investigation found that all the men involved in the attack were connected with, and had been inspired by, Sheik Omar Abdel Rahman, a radical Muslim cleric who preached in the New York City area. Rahman was apprehended in Pakistan in 1995 and charged with seditious conspiracy against the United States and directing others to commit terrorist acts. He was convicted in 1996 and sentenced to life in prison for being behind plans for a series of bombings and assassinations in the U.S. that included a plan to blow up the United Nations headquarters. The judge who sentenced him said that if his plans for bombings had been carried out they would have caused devastation on a scale "not seen since the Civil War" and would have made the 1993 bombing of the World Trade Center "seem insignificant."[366]

By the time the 1990s neared an end, Americans had seen repeated examples of how terrorism from any source could disrupt life in this country as they knew it.

Nature Offers Its Worst

What nature had to offer kept preppers and non-preppers alike on their toes from the 1970s through the 1990s. While Americans had certainly endured ferocious storms in the 1800s and early 1900s, many of the storms nature dished out during the last thirty years of the 20th century were not only fierce, but were also memorable because of the devastation they caused in an expanding and increasingly industrialized society.

No matter how modern the world got, it remained as vulnerable as ever to the disturbances that had helped shape the planet and plagued mankind since the dawn of time: atmospheric tempests, upheavals from the depths of the earth, and even eruptions on the sun. But as of the early 1990s, one thing was different, thanks to the arrival of the Internet in households across the country: the ability of people to instantly communicate the horror that some of these events visited upon civilization. This alone offered ample inspiration for people to start thinking about preparedness, if that hadn't already crossed their minds.

Ravaging Gales

A number of record-breaking hurricanes struck the United States between 1970 and 1999:

- *Hurricane Agnes*, 1972: The storm seemed like nothing to worry about when it struck the Florida Panhandle as a Category 1 hurricane on June 19 and weakened to a tropical depression as it made its way northeast. However, it merged with a low pressure system over New York on June 23, and became a "super storm" that wrought havoc on the Northeast for two

122

days by way of record rains that killed 122 people and caused more than $2 billion in damages from flooding (more than $11 billion in today's dollars). It was, at the time, the costliest hurricane in U.S. history.[367]

- *Hurricane Allen*, 1980: This hurricane, which struck the United States in Texas, gained notoriety as one that sustained its Category 5 status longer than any other hurricane in the Atlantic. It killed nearly 300 people and caused more than $1.2 billion in damage (more than $3.5 billion in today's dollars). The storm was so ferocious that the name "Allen" was retired from use as a name for hurricanes by the World Meteorological Organization, an agency of the United Nations. As a matter of policy, the agency removes names from the hurricane-name list when "a storm is so deadly or costly that the future use of its name on a different storm would be inappropriate for reasons of sensitivity."[368]

- *Hurricane Gloria*, 1985: Anticipated by forecasters to be the "storm of the century," Hurricane Gloria prompted the evacuation of hundreds of thousands of people from South Carolina to Maine as it made its approach to the East Coast of the U.S. in late September. The storm achieved a Category 4 status as it neared the Bahamas, and although it weakened noticeably as it made landfall on the barrier islands off the coast of North Carolina, it also made landfall on Long Island, New York, and in Connecticut as it followed the coastline northward. More than 2 million people from the Carolinas to Maine were left without power, and some remained without it for more than a week. Fourteen people died in the storm, which left behind more than $900 million in damage ($1.9 billion in today's dollars) along the eastern seaboard as it made its way toward Canada and, eventually, out to sea. Hurricane Gloria was the biggest storm to strike the Northeast since Hurricane Agnes, and was the first significant storm to directly strike Long Island and New York since 1960.[369] "Gloria" was also removed from the list of names for future hurricanes.

- *Hurricane Hugo*, 1989: Not to be outdone by its predecessors, Hurricane Hugo earned the dubious distinction of being the most damaging hurricane in U.S. history at the time, after it brought its destructive power to the Caribbean and the eastern seaboard of the United States during the middle of September.[370] As it made its way to the Caribbean from the western coast of Africa, it briefly achieved Category 5 status, but then backed off to become a Category 4, where it remained as it struck the Leeward Islands and the east coast of Puerto Rico. Although it weakened to a Category 3 hurricane over Puerto Rico and then further weakened to a Category 2 as it churned out into the Atlantic, it gained momentum and strengthened back to a Category 4 as it made landfall in Charleston, South Carolina. More than fifty people were killed in the storm, 100,000 were left homeless, and tens of thousands were without electricity. Estimated damage was $7 billion in the United States and $1 billion in Puerto Rico and the Virgin Islands (More than $15 billion in today's dollars).[371]

- *Hurricane Andrew*, 1992: Three years after Hurricane Hugo left its mark on the eastern seaboard of the United States, Hurricane Andrew blew ashore in late August, and ultimately earned the reputation of being one of the most destructive hurricanes of the 20th century.[372] Anticipating its arrival, more than a million Floridians fled their homes to seek shelter away from the storm's wrath; more than 160,000 were eventually left homeless. The powerful storm had originated off the west coast of Africa and whipped across the Atlantic, making landfall in the Bahamas as a Category 4 hurricane, after which it regained strength and raged ashore in the Florida Keys as a Category 5. It weakened to a Category 4 as it wheeled out into the Gulf of Mexico to take aim at Lousiana, which it struck as a Category 3. Continuing its trek northeast, it finally dissipated over the Appalachian Mountains. By the time it was over, nearly thirty people had lost their lives as a result of the storm, and damage totaled in the billions. The Bahamas suffered $250 million in damage, but damage estimates for the U.S. — primarily along a 25-mile stretch from Homestead, Florida, to Kendall, Florida — were more than $26 billion — nearly $64 billion in today's dollars. A 2012 article in the *Huffington Post* marking the twentieth anniversary of the hurricane reported that, after the storm, an investigative report by the Miami-Dade Grand Jury had "slammed the community and officials for a lack of preparedness that turned South Florida into a 'third-world existence.'"[373] The investigative report warned: *"A major failing of all Floridians has been our apparent inability to learn and retain the important lessons previous hurricanes should have taught us."*

Hurricanes were not the only cyclonic storms to bring death and destruction to the country as the 20th century came to an end. One of the most memorable storms of the period was the "Great Blizzard of 1993," also known as the "'93 Superstorm" and "Storm of the Century."

The intense winter storm formed when three separate weather systems joined forces over the Gulf of Mexico and grew into a monster that stretched from Central America to Canada. It battered coastlines with hurricane-force winds that sank two freighters off the coast of Florida and downed power lines that left more than 10 million people without electricity. It dumped snow in amounts that shut down schools and halted travel in major cities for days—amounts ranging from a foot to more than 40 inches in northern regions. It even dropped as much as 6 inches as far south as the Florida Panhandle.

The storm left in its wake $9 billion in damage (today's dollars)[374]; its effects were felt across 40 percent of the nation.[375] One of the most notable things about it was the accuracy with which it was predicted — five days ahead of its arrival. A government assessment of the storm afterward credited the early warnings with prompting a response from the media and government organizations that was "unprecedented in preparing the public" for a winter storm of "incredible proportions." However, despite the advance warnings, more than 200 people still lost their lives as a result of the storm. The report states that, in the southern states, people's perceptions about the threat and their response to it were "uneven," due in part to a "lack of personal experience with severe non-tropical storms." As a result, it says, a large number of people and some emergency management organizations failed to "fully appreciate the seriousness of the threat." It concludes:

> *The subsequent lack of response led to difficulties for the populace in preparing properly for the approaching storm throughout the southeast U.S., particularly in Florida. Many people and some EMOs were simply unprepared for the event."*

However, people in the northern states, to whom blizzards were no stranger, fared much better. The government report says that the public "seemed to understand the potential magnitude and destructiveness of this severe winter storm." Individuals and emergency management organizations prepared accordingly. For the northern states, the storm was memorable, but for them, the report says, it was not quite the "Storm of the Century."[376]

125

Seismic Surprises

The exponential growth of technology and scientific understanding in the 20th century facilitated great strides in the ability of scientists to predict extreme natural events, and as the 20th century came to an end, some of those methods were better understood than others. Scientists who studied hurricanes, blizzards, and even tornadoes during this period were able to predict them with increasing accuracy, offering fair warning to populations in the paths of such disturbances and giving them ample time to prepare accordingly, if they chose. But tumults originating in the depths of the earth were another matter, and three notable events of that kind took place between 1980 and 1994: one volcanic eruption and two earthquakes.

On May 18, 1980, Mt. St. Helens in Washington State exploded in a blast that has been ranked among the top ten most significant volcanic eruptions in geologic history. Although its rumblings beforehand caught the attention of scientists, the general public was largely unaware of any potential threat.[377] Scientists had not yet determined — and still have not — how to accurately predict volcanic eruptions. However, two scientists with the U.S. Geological Survey did offer a prediction in 1978 that Mt. St. Helens would be the most likely of the fifteen active volcanoes on the U.S. side of the Pacific "Ring of Fire" to erupt during the 20th century. They based their prediction on the relatively young age of the volcano (less than 37,000 years old) and its believed frequency of eruption — about once every 100 years. The last known eruption of Mt. St. Helens had taken place nearly 130 years earlier, so they reasoned it was due.

The eruption that finally ensued let loose with a power equivalent to 500 Hiroshima bombs, spewing out ash and lava that killed 57 people, caused nearly $3 billion in damage (nearly $9 billion in today's dollars), and blasted 1,314 feet off the north face of the mountain in a landslide said to be the largest ever recorded on Earth.[378,379,380]

The initial eruption instantly wiped out everything within eight miles of the explosion and devastated an area 230 square miles in size. A second blast sent a plume of ash and gas 12 miles into the air. The resulting ash cloud darkened skies more than 300 miles away and temporarily shut down air traffic over the entire Northwest. An estimated 540 million tons of ash were carried by air currents across an estimated 2,200 square miles and deposited over seven states, where it damaged cars, buildings and even crops. Heat from the blast instantly melted snow and glacial ice on the mountain, sending a sizzling slurry of mud and volcanic matter gushing down the mountainside into three nearby river systems. The eruption resulted in the destruction of more than 200 homes and damage to over 185 miles of roads and 15 miles of railway.[381]

Geologist William "Willie" Scott, a lead scientist at the Cascades Volcano Observatory in Vancouver, Washington, told a *Seattle Times* reporter in May 2000 for a story on the state's historic eruption:

> *"Mount St. Helens having erupted made believers out of everybody. It was, 'OK, this can happen.' "*

The eruption prompted a concerted effort among scientists at the U.S. Geological Survey to develop methods of predicting possible future eruptions—not only at Mt. St. Helens, but also at the 168 other active volcanoes in the U.S. A study concluded by the agency in 2005 culminated in a report titled, "An Assessment of Volcanic Threat and Monitoring Capabilities in the United States: Framework for a National Volcano Early Warning System" (NVEWS). It identified 37 volcanoes that pose a "very high threat" of an eruption, and another 21 that were "under-monitored."[382]

The NVEWS plan proposed:

- Increasing partnerships among federal agencies, local governments and first responders
- Providing grants to universities and other groups to research volcano science and monitoring technologies
- Add staffing and automation to provide round-the-clock monitoring of volcanoes
- Develop computer systems to consolidate all volcano-monitoring systems and distribute information to scientists, local governments and the public.[383]

Today the USGS operates five volcano observatories—in Hawaii, the Cascade Mountains in Washington and Oregon, Alaska, Yellowstone National Park, and California—in conjunction with state universities and local authorities.[384] One of the most dangerous volcanoes under its watchful eyes is Washington State's Mt. Rainer.

Given the sizable population centers that are in close proximity to Mt. Rainier, scientists are most concerned about the potential impact of a lahar—a surge of hot, flowing mud resulting from landslides or snow and ice melted by a volcanic eruption, combined with volcanic matter and having the effect of poured concrete. Scientists who have studied the mountain have determined that at least one of the mountain's past lahars, which originated with a landslide, could have taken place at a time when the volcano was quiet, and thus fear that another could occur with little or no advance warning. Mt. Rainier last erupted sometime around 1894.[385]

With this in mind, government officials in Washington State have made plans that they believe will enable them to evacuate more than 100,000 people from the path of oncoming steaming lahars in about 40 minutes.[386]

Although volcanic eruptions are among nature's most devastating events—indeed, they have literally shaped the planet over its 4.5 billion-year lifetime—they haven't demonstrated their power in this country in modern times as frequently as earthquakes. During the 1990s alone there were more than 28,000 earthquakes in the U.S., of varying intensities.[387] About 630 of those quakes were intense enough to register more than 5.0 on the Richter scale, a numerical scale developed by seismologists in the 1930s to convey the power of the energy released during an earthquake. But there were also two potent and memorable earthquakes that happened in the late 20th century, both along the San Andreas Fault, which scientists had been watching as the source of "the next big one" since the massive 1857 quake in the Fort Tejon region of California.

One of the two quakes, which was among the most powerful earthquakes ever to hit a populated area of the United States, struck the San Francisco Bay area on October 17, 1989, registering a magnitude 6.9 on the Richter Scale. Sixty-seven people were killed, more than forty of them when an overpass on Interstate 880 collapsed onto the cars below. The upper deck of the Bay Bridge also collapsed onto its lower level, killing one person. Buildings collapsed all along the San Francisco Marina; fires were sparked by broken gas mains. In the end, the quake had caused more than $5 billion in damage (close to $10 billion in today's dollars).[388]

128

In an effort to prepare "for the next big one," San Francisco and surrounding communities enacted strict building codes to help structures withstand future temblors, even going so far as to require that unreinforced masonry buildings be retrofitted accordingly.

The next "big one" for California came along five years later, when a 6.7-magnitude quake struck a heavily populated area near Los Angeles on January 17, 1994. It claimed 57 lives and destroyed or damaged thousands of buildings. And although it didn't quite measure up to the magnitude of the 1989 earthquake, it caused more than $20 billion in damage (more than $31 billion in today's dollars), making it the costliest earthquake in U.S. history.[389]

Even though Los Angeles joined San Francisco in developing stricter, "quake-proof" building codes after the 1994 earthquake, A CBS News report in October 2013 reported that many California buildings remained vulnerable to destruction from earthquakes, and asserted that little was being done about it. According to the report, scientists in California say there is a 99.7 percent chance that a "massive quake" will strike California in the next thirty years.[390]

Storms from Space

Volcanic eruptions and ground-shakers are not the only sort with the power to wreak havoc on mankind. Eruptions on the sun — aka coronal mass ejections (CMEs), or solar flares — have, for millennia, put on light shows for earthlings, but modern scientists have come to realize that, like their earthly counterparts, these eruptions, too, carry destructive power — power that can jolt our planet.

The more intense flares observed by humans have resulted from sun storms that are thought to occur about every 11 years. These light shows may have inspired awe and fear of the gods in primitive man, but they pose an increasingly serious threat to a modern world that has become dependent on, and defined by, electricity.

The largest known CME event to impact the earth occurred in 1859, and was known as the "Carrington Event," named for the scientist who observed and recorded it, Richard C. Carrington. The event caused widespread disruption of communications around the world — which, at that time, largely meant telegraph communications. Lloyd's of

London has estimated that, with today's increased dependence on electricity, the cost of recovering from the same type of event today could be as much as $2.6 trillion.[391]

In the late 20th century, Northeastern Canada experienced the impact of a CME on March 15, 1989, when one of the strongest magnetic storms ever recorded tripped major distribution lines from Hydro-Quebec, the power station servicing Canada's Quebec province, and shut down power to 6 million people for more than 9 hours.[392,393]

Power stations across the U.S. were also affected, although, thanks to backup capabilities, there were no major blackouts. More than 200 power grid problems broke out all across the country, and in the Northeast, two major power suppliers lost a combined total of 1,560 megawatts of power.[394]

Could it happen again? In July 2012, the earth "barely missed taking a massive solar punch in the teeth," according to a report in the *Washington Examiner*. The paper reports that a huge coronal mass ejection from the sun crossed the path of Earth's orbit in July and "just missed us." It created an electromagnetic pulse (EMP) big enough to knock out electricity—including the power to cars and iPhones—all across the country. The article quoted CIA Director James Woolsey as saying that even if only 20 of the 2,000 to 3,000 major transformers in the country's power grid were knocked out, that electricity to parts of the nation would be out "for a long time."[395]

Meanwhile, Feds Prepare

World events and changing presidential administrations molded and shaped governmental civil defense and disaster preparedness strategies as the 20th century drew to a close. When each new disaster proved that government wasn't up to the task of responding adequately, studies were conducted, agencies were created, disbanded, and reformed, and programs were funded—or not—depending on the current geopolitical climate. Seeing this, many people took preparedness into their own hands, but many did not.

In 1969, President Nixon and his administration reacted to what they saw as inadequate government response to the destruction wrought by

Hurricane Camille in August of that year, by redefining civil defense to include preparations for natural disasters. A study subsequently commissioned by the president found that the country's readiness to respond to natural disasters was "minimal to nonexistent."[396] As a result, the Office of Civil Defense was replaced in 1970 with the Defense Civil Preparedness Agency, which ultimately fell under the auspices of the Department of Defense. This change allowed funds previously restricted for use in planning against military attacks to be shared with state and local governments for natural-disaster planning. The shift away from military civil defense planning was further reinforced in 1972 after the U.S. and Soviet Union reached an agreement that would limit their arsenal of nuclear weapons as well as their anti-ballistic missile defense sites. The Nixon administration believed that if the U.S. were in any way perceived by the Soviets to be stepping up its military civil defense programs, the Soviets might reason that this signaled a corresponding increase in its nuclear weapons development, and the agreement would collapse.

Later, during the administration of President Gerald Ford, U.S. intelligence operations uncovered continuing development of Soviet civil defense programs, prompting concerns that, not only were comparable U.S. programs lagging behind, but also that the level of Soviet readiness would prevent the U.S. from inflicting any serious damage on the Soviet Union if circumstances drew the two powers into an armed conflict. Subsequently, the focus of civil defense in the U.S. shifted away from preparedness for natural disasters and back to military civil defense.[397]

Also during the Ford administration, the doctrine of "mutually assured destruction" in a nuclear conflict fell out of favor and was superseded by a policy of "flexible response," whereby small-scale nuclear strikes could be launched against significant military and industrial facilities and could be countered in kind by the opposition, replacing the strategy of launching massive attacks against, and devastating, highly populated cities. With the new thinking — that nuclear attacks could be survivable if they were smaller — the U.S. created a new initiative, the "Crisis Relocation Plan," under which residents of urban areas that might be targeted in a "limited attack" would be relocated to "rural host counties," supported with federal funds for not only relocation, but also food distribution and medical care.[398] However, the plan was highly criticized in Congress, because the success of large-scale evacuations through transportation routes that would quickly become bottlenecked seemed unlikely, and the plan was dependent upon a one- to two-day warning time, which would be effective only if a missile strike against the country could be predicted. Congress therefore set up committees to investigate the civil defense quandary, but made little progress on solving the problem during Ford's administration.

The administration of President Jimmy Carter—which was of the opinion that it was unnecessary to keep its civil defense preparedness on a par with the Soviet Union[399]—put civil defense on the back burner, until the chaotic response to the Three Mile Island incident in 1979 revealed another source of nuclear disaster besides military conflict, for which the country was unprepared. As a result, Carter created the Federal Emergency Management Agency (FEMA) with Executive Order 12148 in July 1979. The order folded five civil-defense related agencies into FEMA, making it the largest merger of federal civil defense departments in history. However, the new agency struggled with its mission, and it received little funding to implement any programs.

During Ronald Reagan's presidency, there was a renewed focus on civil defense for both natural disasters and military attacks on the U.S., and influenced by Reagan's hard-line stance against the Soviet Union, nuclear preparedness became a priority. However, Congress was not supportive of Reagan's continued emphasis on evacuation as a viable civil defense strategy, and repeatedly blocked the administration's funding requests, allocating to FEMA only 58 percent of what it asked for.[400]

Congress instead favored more "all-hazards" preparedness, and pressured FEMA to plan accordingly; the agency developed the Integrated Emergency Management System to support this approach. However, Congress didn't believe FEMA's plan adequately addressed preparedness for *all* hazards, and never approved the funding requested by the agency.

Shortly after George H.W. Bush succeeded Reagan as president, some of the major disasters of the late 20th century struck the nation: the *Exxon Valdez* oil spill, Hurricane Hugo, and the San Francisco Earthquake. Federal response to all three disasters drew significant criticism.

132

In response to the March 1989 oil spill, Bush bypassed FEMA, and instead assigned responsibility for managing the federal response to the EPA and the U.S. Coast Guard, neither of which was equipped to handle such a crisis. Later that year, reacting to the devastation from Hurricane Hugo, Bush assigned responsibility to the Secretary of the Interior. FEMA participated in the response, but was hampered by a shortage of trained responders, communication problems, and a lack of coordination among the groups dealing with the disaster.[401] With lessons learned, FEMA went back to the drawing board and created a plan that defined how 27 federal agencies and the American Red Cross could work together to respond effectively in the face of overwhelming disasters.

In 1991, the collapse of the Soviet Union brought an abrupt end to the Cold War, and with it the compelling need for civil defense against a nuclear attack. In 1992, President Bush directed FEMA to develop a comprehensive all-hazards emergency management plan, encompassing both natural and manmade disasters.

Nevertheless, when the next disaster struck — Hurricane Andrew, in 1992 — FEMA was no better prepared to respond than it had been during earlier disasters, and was roundly criticized by Congress for poor performance that included slow response and lack of coordination in relief efforts. A study initiated by FEMA at the direction of Congress, using outside consultants, concluded that FEMA could be successful in responding to major natural disasters only if the White House and Congress took "significant steps to make it a viable institution."[402] However, with Bush's term winding down, it was too late for his administration to react; that was left to the incoming administration of President Bill Clinton.

During Clinton's administration, FEMA was reorganized, and the position of FEMA director was elevated to Cabinet level. Both changes helped strengthen the agency and focus its efforts. It was also during the Clinton administration that the terrorist threat to the country emerged, and Congress called upon FEMA to develop early warning systems and responses to such threats, along with plans for responding to disasters involving pandemic outbreaks or chemical spills.

However, in 1994, Congress made a change that further supported FEMA's response to natural disasters while reducing its responsibility for national security programs, and responsibility for protecting the nation took two divergent paths—one that had FEMA solidly responsible for natural disasters, and one with other evolving federal agencies in charge of terrorist threats.

Recognizing the threat from terrorists using "weapons of mass destruction" (WMD), Congress passed the Nunn-Lugar-Domenici Act in 1996, requiring that the Department of Defense (DOD) provide training and advice to civilian agencies regarding appropriate responses to WMD attacks. Initially, FEMA was expected to lead the training efforts, but FEMA officials pointed out that the DOD was the only agency with the knowledge and tools to do this. Later, WMD response was transferred from the DOD to the Office of Domestic Preparedness, under the auspices of the Department of Justice, while the DOD worked to establish "Rapid Assessment and Initial Detection" (RAID) teams within the National Guard for providing equipment and technical expertise in the event of a WMD attack.[403]

Clinton's administration recognized the serious threat posed by potential terrorist attacks, and assigned responsibility for protecting the country against those threats to a number of different agencies, depending on their areas of expertise. Clinton's Presidential Decision Directive number 63 chartered those agencies with developing systems for sharing and coordinating efforts with private-sector agencies and local governments.

By the end of the 20th century, the U.S. seemed more prepared than it had ever been.

Bugged Out

As the 1990s neared an end, computer experts began to realize the profound impact a change in century could have in computer programs that by now were controlling nearly every aspect of daily life, not only in the United States, but all over the world. The problem stemmed from the practice of programmers to use in programming code only two digits to represent the year. With the change of millennium, the numbers in those two places would both be "0," prompting fears about computing failures caused by invalid dates. The problem came to be known as the "Y2K" bug, the "Y2K" a representation of the Year 2000.

Threats of dire consequences from the Y2K bug came from everywhere, along with advice on how to prepare for an event that many believed would truly bring about an end to life as they knew it. And the dramatic century turn that would bring about a new millennium helped fan the flames of fear, sparking a concerted focus on preparedness.

Y2K doomsayers predicted that the "bug" would be responsible for everything from a failure of the country's electric grid to bank closures, failures of oil refineries and wastewater treatment facilities, economic collapse, and the eventual disintegration of civilized society.

A spate of books on the impending Y2K disaster appeared on store bookshelves—some were novels depicting how the disaster might unfold; others offered advice on how to survive it. Among them were:

- *The Y2K Personal Survival Guide,* by Michael S. Hyatt (Mar 15, 1998)
- *Y2K – It's Already Too Late,* by Jason Kelly (June 1998)
- *Y2K: The Millennium Bug-A Balanced Christian Response,* by Shaunti Feldhahn (November 1998)
- *Boston on Surviving Y2K,* by Kenneth W. Royce and Boston T. Party (Dec 1998)
- *The Y2K Survival Guide and Cookbook,* by Dorothy R. Bates and Albert K. Bates (Jan 15, 1999)
- *The Hippy Survival Guide to Y2K,* by Mike Oehler (Feb 1999)
- *Y2K for Women: How to Protect Your Home and Family in the Coming Crisis,* by Karen Anderson (May 1999)
- *Dutch Oven and Outdoor Cooking Y2K Edition,* by Larry Walker, Jeanie Walker and Robyn Heirtzler (Jul 1, 1999)

Packed with information on survival, the *Hippy Survival Guide* and *Boston on Y2K* remain popular resources among today's preppers.

A 1998 study commissioned by Cap Gemini America, a New York consulting firm, revealed that, of the thirteen economic sectors studied for Y2K readiness in the United States, the federal government was the least prepared.[404]

In October 1998, President Clinton formed the Council on Year 2000 Conversion to work with federal and state officials and industry leaders in charge of mission-critical systems on ensuring that the necessary code fixes were made ahead of the calendar's page turn from 1999 to 2000. Chairman of the Council, John Koskinen, was certain that these systems would be adequately prepared for the year change, but warned that the hoarding of food, fuel and money by millions of jittery Americans ahead of the Y2K arrival could create a bigger disaster than any potential computer malfunctions.

As the end of the year approached, members of the Council on Year 2000 Conversion were confident that the changes were on track, and that there would be no cause for concern when the new millennium arrived. However, many people were unconvinced that the changes would be made in time—or that they would be effective—and began making their own preparations, including buying generators and stocking up on food and fuel, as Koskinen feared.[405]

Federal, state, and local governments had emergency personnel standing by as the clock ticked toward midnight on New Year's Eve, 1999.[406] When light dawned on January 1, 2000, however, there were no major computer failures, giving rise to jokes about the "disaster that wasn't" and to criticism that the potential for problems had been overstated. But few people were aware of the feverish efforts that took place behind the scenes to stave off disaster, efforts that cost nearly $300 million, half of that in the U.S., in upgrades to make computer hardware and software Y2K-compliant.

With the Y2K worries behind them, Americans were ready for whatever exciting possibilities the new millennium might hold.

Part One:

The History of Preparedness

Chapter Four: 2000–Present

People had great expectations of the 21st century when it arrived on January 1, 2000. Y2K fears notwithstanding, people generally saw the new millennium filled with promise. Technology would improve our lives in ways never before imagined, and would connect countries and industries in ways that would foster a vibrant global economy. Maybe this would be the century where we ended war, poverty, and starvation. Maybe this would be the century when mankind traveled to Mars. The possibilities seemed endless.

But a dark cloud arrived early on, and changed American society—and the world—forever. The terrorist attacks that had been conducted against Americans all over the world in the late 20th century intensified, and to the horror of millions, climaxed in a series of coordinated attacks against the United States on September 11, 2001, that together made up the worst attack on American soil in history. The attacks demonstrated the vulnerabilities of a free society and prompted changes in government that many would argue made us a little less free. Americans' distrust of their government reached new heights as changes in laws allowed it to become more intrusive and less accountable, in the name of fighting terrorism. The 2001 attacks also changed the geopolitical landscape, where combating terrorism took front-and-center stage and guided much of the decision-making in global politics.

Meanwhile, natural disasters that eclipsed any seen before inflicted widespread damage all over the world, killing hundreds of thousands of people and leaving millions homeless. Inadequate response by the federal government to the disasters that happened in the United States provided a "wake-up call" to people who had relied so heavily on that government to rescue them in times of trouble. Technology offered people an unforgettable look at these catastrophes almost as they unfolded, by way of nearly nonstop television broadcasts and posts on the Internet.

The Internet exploded with preparedness-related websites that provided a platform for people to share their experiences and information about survival in the face of disaster, and also supported the growth of industries geared toward emergency preparedness and survivalism. However, technology also offered another vector by which calamity could be delivered, and those in charge of the nation's security began to focus on preparedness against cyber attacks and natural phenomena that could affect critical systems that were now so dependent on electronic communications. In online prepper forums, how to prepare against widespread failure of the country's electric grid became a frequent topic of discussion.

Terrorism and disasters, both manmade and natural, prompted another round of government reorganizations to address the new threats. And the declassification of government documents—now made readily available to the public, thanks to the World Wide Web—revealed, among other things, previously unknown nuclear close encounters, as well as the U.S. government's experimentation with chemical and biological weapons.

The economic collapse predicted for so long by so many seemed to once again loom large on the horizon. It came true for millions who lost their jobs in the Great Recession of 2008. And although the second Great Depression didn't materialize as many had predicted and the economy seemed to bounce back from the edge, the possibility of economic collapse remained an ominous presence throughout the next five years, and people who focused on preparedness became concerned about the societal collapse it could bring with it.

Meanwhile, activists began to sound the alarm about dwindling resources and threats to the planet from climate change caused by human activities. This provided a new arena for political discord, as scientists published conflicting information on the subjects and people debated the accuracy of the information they heard. In one camp, there were people who didn't believe in climate change, or believed in it, but did not think it was due to human activities. In another camp were firm believers, who were positive that human activities were to blame for the increase in extreme weather events all over the globe.

140

With each new weather disaster that unfolded, more and more people came to accept that the climate was changing, although the cause was still up for debate for many. Those who still questioned the cause of the extreme changes that were becoming so evident objected to government efforts to address the issues in a way that cost taxpayers money. Many believed that the government's promotion of anthropogenic climate change was just another excuse to reach into their pockets.

For their part, the activists who were so certain about what lay behind the change in climate placed the blame on large corporations which, they believed, were motivated by greed to continue with business practices that threatened the planet and human health. They protested against "big business" and its efforts to squelch their concerns. Those who took their protests to the extreme—crossing the line from civil disobedience to criminal behavior—were included under the watchful eye of the FBI, which was now on the lookout for both international and domestic terrorists.

The debate also inspired a movement of people focused on careful use of their own—and the Earth's—resources and on ways to become more self-sufficient, through activities such as growing their own food and practicing ways to become less reliant on modern technology, including electricity. People came to realize that sustainable living was an integral part of preparedness. The mantras of an earlier time became significant for many:

"Use it up, wear it out, make it do, or do without."

"Waste not, want not."

When Terror Attacks

On October 12, 2000, suicide bombers brought their brand of terror to an unsuspecting U.S. Navy vessel, the billion-dollar destroyer USS *Cole*, which was in the process of being refueled in the Yemen tanker port of Aden. Shortly after the refueling got under way, a small craft approached and headed directly for the ship and, laden with explosives, blasted a 40-by-40-foot hole in the hull of the vessel. Seventeen people were killed; thirty-nine were injured.

141

One hundred agents from the FBI's Counter Terrorism Division immediately went to Yemen to work with the Yemeni government and the U.S. Navy on an investigation of the incident.[407] According to a January 2001 report by the Congressional Research Service, the investigation turned up evidence that the attack was likely carried out by Islamic militants, who may have had connections to a terrorist network known to be led by Osama bin Laden.[408]

The attack proved to be a harbinger for the horrific attack of September 11, 2001, when four domestic airliners, hijacked by terrorists, were used in murderous suicide attacks against key targets in the United States. Two of the planes were flown into New York City's Twin Towers; one was flown into the Pentagon. The fourth crash-landed in a field in Pennsylvania, after passengers launched an attack on the hijackers and distracted them from whatever their fourth target was, a target many believed to have been the White House. Altogether, nearly 3,000 people were killed in the attacks, including the hijackers.

Not knowing how many more terrorists might already be in the air, the government ordered all planes out of U.S. airspace, with the exception of military and police flights. Air traffic controllers were challenged with directing nearly 5,000 flights to the nearest available airport.[409] For the first time in the history of aviation, skies over the U.S. became completely empty. Most planes were grounded for two days.

With the country still reeling from the September 11 attacks, another attack unfolded, more quietly, and this one involved bioterrorism, by way of anthrax-infected letters that were sent to the offices of several news media outlets and two U.S. senators. Five people died from contact with the letters, and seventeen were sickened, in what the FBI called "the worst biological attacks in U.S. history."[410] Although many people were quick to blame whoever had carried out the September 11 attacks, no direct link could be found. The FBI subsequently launched one of its longest and most complex investigations ever, and was about to file charges in 2008 against Bruce E. Ivins, a biodefense researcher for the U.S Army, when Ivins committed suicide.[411] The agency closed the case in February 2010, releasing a 92-page report that concluded Ivins was the sole perpetrator in the anthrax case.

War Powers

Immediately following the September 11 attacks, the FBI launched the most massive investigation in its history.[412] They quickly learned the identity of the hijackers who died in the attacks, though not the person who had given them their orders. After all of them were found to be of Middle Eastern descent, suspicion quickly fell on Al Qaeda as the organization behind the attacks.

With the Twin Towers still smoldering, two weeks after the attacks, President George W. Bush declared a "War on Terror," a struggle against an abstract concept that could theoretically be found almost anywhere in the world. As political theorist Richard Jackson later wrote in his 2005 book, *Writing the War on Terrorism*, the language around the conceptual "War on Terror" seemed, to many, to be rhetoric that was deliberately used to take advantage of public anxiety about terrorist threats to win support for military — and sometimes other — action.[413]

A month after the attacks, riding a wave of nationalism, Congress quickly passed, and President Bush signed, the USA PATRIOT Act of 2001, whose acronym stands for: Uniting (and) Strengthening America (by) Providing Appropriate Tools Required (to) Intercept (and) Obstruct Terrorism.[414] The Act became the tool the government used to prosecute the nebulous war, a way to rationalize the detention of people who were "suspected" of being terrorists without charging them with a crime, and for holding them indefinitely.

Armed with the blessing of the PATRIOT Act, the FBI began seeking out and arresting people they thought might be connected with the terrorists who had carried out the September 11 attacks, which often meant they targeted people who appeared to be, or were of Middle Eastern descent, and they arrested any who were found to be in this country illegally. During the weeks and months following the attacks, the FBI detained 762 illegal immigrants whom they labeled as "unlawful combatants," and sent them to a detention camp established at the Guantanamo Bay Naval Base in Cuba in January 2002.

According to a 2003 report in the *New York Times*, an investigation by the Justice Department's Inspector General concluded that many people with no connection to terrorism had endured imprisonment in "unduly harsh conditions" at the Guantanamo Bay facility. The IG's report alleged that the FBI had made "little attempt to distinguish between immigrants who had possible ties to terrorism and those swept up by chance in the investigation." [415]

In the name of fighting terrorism, the PATRIOT Act was also used to expand government's reach into the private lives of its citizens. It allowed the government to look at records on a person's activity being held by third parties, such as Internet providers and credit card companies, and expanded the government's ability to search private property without notifying the owner. It also expanded exceptions to the Fourth Amendment that facilitated the collection of foreign intelligence information and allowed the collection of routing information in electronic communications along with the content. [416] With the PATRIOT Act in place, the government no longer had to demonstrate that anyone it was investigating was an "agent of a foreign power," or that there was "probable cause" to suspect criminal activity, as the Constitution requires. The Act all but eliminated judicial oversight of the expanded governmental powers.[417]

The PATRIOT Act became a flashpoint that lit up a debate over how much power the government should be accorded to scrutinize the lives of the American people. For many of the American people, it was another reason not to trust that government.

The terrorist attacks of September 2001 — including the anthrax attack — had caused the U.S. government to reevaluate its newly declared enemy, terrorism, and to include under that umbrella "domestic terrorists."[418] This increased the concerns from many quarters about the implications of the PATRIOT Act for American civil liberties, and some lawmakers looked for every opportunity to protect further erosion of Americans' rights.

Ten years later, lawmakers were still arguing about threats to civil liberties posed by the PATRIOT Act and related legislation. In November 2011, Kentucky Senator Rand Paul summed up the concerns of many when he spoke before the Senate in opposition to an amendment to the National Defense Authorization Act for Fiscal 2012 (S.1867) that would have allowed indefinite detention of Americans suspected of terror-related crimes or associations. He said that the amendment would put "every single American citizen at risk." He told lawmakers:

"There are laws on the books now that characterize who might be a terrorist. Someone missing fingers on their hands is a suspect, according to the Department of Justice. Someone who has guns, someone who has ammunition that is weatherproofed, someone who has more than seven days of food in their house can be considered a potential terrorist." [419]

Paul said that the amendment was of great concern especially because "we are engaged in a war that appears to have no end." He pointed out that there had been no benchmarks established to mark the end of the "War on Terror" — a war that encompassed conflict with al-Qaeda and any other foreign terrorist group deemed to be a threat to the U.S. He asserted:

"The detainee provisions of the defense authorization bill do another grave harm to freedom: they imply perpetual war for the first time in the history of the United States.[420]

Paul reminded lawmakers of the warning offered by one of the country's Founding Fathers, Ben Franklin:

"We should not attempt to trade liberty for security; if we do we may end up with neither."

The amendment was ultimately defeated, but the framework provided by the PATRIOT Act for intrusion into the lives of Americans remained.

Systemic Schizophrenia

The terrorist attacks of September 11, 2001, prompted an unprecedented focus on civil defense and national security in the U.S., yet at the same time created a sort of governmental "split personality": the benevolent benefactor which, in the name of encouraging and helping its citizens become more prepared for disasters, offered advice on food storage, water storage, "bug-out" bags and more; and a seemingly more sinister entity that viewed some of the people who might engage in these activities as potential terrorists, as pointed out by Senator Paul in his 2011 address to the Senate.

The Rise of DHS

After the terrorist attacks, the government undertook a major reassessment of civil defense and national security. Officials recognized that the two were inexorably linked, and that the more appropriate approach was consideration of overall "homeland security." Subsequently, the Office of Homeland Security was created by executive order in October 2001, and was charged with developing an all-encompassing strategy to protect the country from terrorist attacks, whether foreign or domestic, as well as natural and manmade disasters. President Bush named Pennsylvania Governor Tom Ridge to head the office.

Part of the strategy included more citizen involvement, and the USA Freedom Corps initiative was developed to "promote a culture of service, citizenship, and responsibility in America."[421] Under this initiative, the Citizen Corps program was developed to engage citizen volunteers in helping their communities become better prepared to "prevent, protect, respond to, and recover from all hazards." Education and training were made available through a number of community-level programs, including the Community Emergency Response Teams (CERT), Fire Corps, Neighborhood Watch, Medical Reserve Corps, and Volunteers in Police Service.

The national security strategy envisioned by the Bush administration was eventually published in a report released by the Office of Homeland Security. The report, "National Strategy for Homeland Security" (NSHS), recommended the creation of a Department of Homeland Security (DHS), which would serve as "the primary federal point of contact" for homeland security-related initiatives at the state, local, and private levels. With bipartisan support in the Senate and House of Representatives and the support of the president, the Homeland Security Act of 2002 was passed, creating the new cabinet-level department. Bush appointed Ridge as the first DHS Secretary in January 2003.

The broad responsibilities assigned to the new department forced a sweeping reorganization, in which the DHS inherited nearly 200,000 people from twenty-two federal agencies and was given a budget of $37 billion to make it all work.[422] A number of directives, goals, and plans set up the framework for its role, among them a presidential directive issued in December 2003 stating that preparedness would include readiness against "threatened or actual domestic terrorist attacks, major disasters, and other emergencies."[423] The directive also charged DHS with leading the effort to actively encourage the participation of private citizens in preparedness efforts.

In February 2005, Michael Chertoff succeeded Ridge as DHS Secretary, and initiated a "Second Stage Review" of the department. A six-point agenda for DHS emerged from the review:[424]

- Improve preparedness for catastrophic events
- Strengthen border security and enforcement of federal immigration laws
- Strengthen transportation security without diminishing mobility
- Improve the sharing of information between the U.S. government and the private sector
- Improve management of DHS financial and human resources as well as procurement and information technology
- Readjust alliances within DHS to enable the highest level of performance of its mission

To support this agenda, the department grew in size and power. Today, it consists of four major "directorates" employing more than 240,000 people and encompassing twenty-four agencies, among them FEMA, the U.S. Coast Guard, the Secret Service, the Transportation Safety Administration, U.S. Immigration Customs and Enforcement, U.S. Customs and Border Protection, and the Federal Bureau of Investigation (FBI).[425]

It is the FBI that is charged with investigating acts of terrorism. Since 2001, it has been occupied with investigating global acts of terrorism and has become increasingly concerned about domestic terrorism.[426] The agency considers the top domestic terror threats to be "Americans attacking Americans based on U.S.-based extremist ideologies." [427] In particular, the FBI is concerned about the so-called "lone wolf," someone who acts alone to undertake violent attacks.

In a free society committed to the protection of its civil liberties, identifying a "lone wolf" can be a difficult task that challenges law enforcement to predict when someone's expression of free speech could cross the line into acts of violence. The FBI says it is "not shy" about using all the means at its disposal to seek out domestic terrorists and prevent "homegrown terrorism." Those anti-terror tools, it says, include "time-tested investigative techniques such as the use of surveillance and informants as well as the new intelligence skills and information-sharing channels" it has cultivated since the September 2001 terror attacks.[428]

One of the ways the FBI has cultivated its information-sharing channels is through the use of "Communities Against Terrorism" flyers that were widely distributed sometime after 2007. [429] Although the flyers were not made public and are not posted on the FBI website, they were distributed to places like mass transportation entities, hotels and motels, home improvement and large retail stores, mail centers, and other retail establishments.[430] The flyers caution individuals working at these locations to be suspicious of—and possibly report to authorities—people engaged in what the FBI considers to be suspicious activity. Among those considered to be "suspect" are people who:

- Request specific room assignments or locations at hotels
- Refuse cleaning service at hotels or motels
- Use cash for large transactions
- Park vehicles in isolated areas
- Purchase large amounts of ammunition or model aircraft fuel
- Have missing fingers or burns on their bodies
- Seem overly concerned about privacy at Internet cafés (e.g., using encryption software)
- Purchase night vision equipment and camouflage apparel

Another way the FBI has cultivated its information-sharing channels has been through a partnership with the Department of Defense's National Security Agency (NSA). According to documents leaked to the public in 2013 by former NSA contractor Edward Snowden, the NSA routinely spies on the communications and online activity of millions of Americans—whether or not there is cause to suspect them of anything—by collecting what the agency calls "metadata" about those communications—transactional information that could include the origin and destination of phone calls and emails, and high-level information about online activity.[431] However, according to technology experts, "metadata" is hardly benign, and could easily lead to significant intrusions into the privacy of Americans—such as tracking their whereabouts and their activities.[432]

Responding to the leaks, government officials said the NSA surveillance was authorized by Section 215 of the PATRIOT Act and by the Foreign Intelligence Surveillance Act of 1978. However some officials claimed they were unaware of the scope of the surveillance, and promised a review.[433]

Guidance for Citizens

One of the first projects undertaken by the DHS in February 2003 was the creation of a citizen-oriented website to help promote individual preparedness. The website, www.ready.gov, falls under the auspices of FEMA and can be accessed directly or via a link from FEMA's main website, www.FEMA.gov. Ready.gov offers advice on how people can assess their risks for disasters and detailed instructions on how they can prepare. It even provides a list of calamities for people to consider in their preparations:[434]

- Natural disasters, such as earthquakes, floods, drought, extreme heat, hurricanes, landslides, wildfires, tornadoes, volcanoes, wildfires, extreme winter weather, and even "space weather," such as solar flares that could damage the power grid
- Pandemics
- House fires
- Technological and accidental hazards
- Terrorist attacks

The site lists steps people can take to become more prepared:

- Build and maintain disaster supplies kits, and store them for easy access
- Develop an emergency plan that takes into account the number and ages of people in the family, and pets
- Create an emergency plan that considers the potential hazards in travel destinations and in locations frequented by family members
- Plan for a possible "bugout"—what to do if evacuation is needed; how to assemble family and supplies; where to go, under what circumstances

149

The site advises people to store water — at least one gallon per day, per person, for at least three days. It offers detailed preparedness-planning information for anyone seeking to build an emergency plan, for just about any eventuality. And it advises people to store "at least" three days' worth of food. (Although, according to Senator Paul, FBI eyebrows might be raised if they store more than a week's worth.)

Dangers Declassified

One of the hallmarks of a free society is the availability of information to its citizens. While international diplomacy, foreign relations, and domestic and international security might dictate that access to certain information be restricted, in the U.S. there are laws that limit, in most cases, the amount of time that information can remain classified. On the low end, the threshold is 25 years, but some documents can be kept classified for 50 years, and with rare exception, as long as 75 years.

The Freedom of Information Act (FOIA), passed in 1966, allows that any citizen has a legally enforceable right to access federal records that are no longer classified. With the advent of the Internet, the federal government began making some of this information available online, although without any fanfare that would alert people to its presence on the Web.

The National Security Agency, the organization charged with reviewing classified records before their release to the National Archives and Records Administration (NARA), ultimately posts many declassified documents to its website. The site contains an index to entries consisting of millions of pages of information. Nearly 5,000 of them contain more than a million pages of information dating from before World War I through World War II alone.[435]

The site is a treasure trove for journalists and researchers seeking insights into past governmental actions. In some cases, their findings have turned up some startling discoveries about our distant and not-so-distant past.

Americans as Guinea Pigs

Documents declassified by the Pentagon in 2002 revealed that, while the attention of the country during the Cold War was ostensibly focused on the containment of Communism, the threat from nuclear weapons, and protecting the nation against a nuclear attack, the U.S. government was secretly conducting experiments in chemical and biological warfare, in direct violation of the United Nations Geneva Protocol it had ratified in 1925.[436],[437] The documents disclosed testing that had been conducted as far back as 1942 and continued throughout the Cold War. Some tests involved exposing unknowing military personnel to chemical and biological agents; others involved releasing diluted bacteria or "simulants" into the open air, to determine dispersal patterns.

A 2007 documentary produced by the Public Broadcasting Station (PBS), "The Living Weapon," recounts the details of the testing program.[438] It states that President Roosevelt authorized the program in 1942, motivated by "a fear of powerful enemies," a fear that "took the United States down a path to develop a new weapon of mass destruction."

The experimental program started at Maryland's Camp Detrick and involved a handful of virologists and bacteriologists whose work was as closely guarded and as closely scrutinized as the Manhattan Project. Although some government officials questioned the need for the project after the world witnessed the power and devastation wrought by the Hiroshima bomb, work on it only intensified as the Cold War unfolded, driven by fear of the enemy and a need to not be outmatched by enemy weapons.

The PBS report describes two decades of testing that included the release of diluted chemical and bacteriological agents in ventilation systems at the Pentagon and Washington International Airport as well as in New York's subway system, public areas in St. Louis and San Francisco, and in the deserts of Utah. The report states that the "most conclusive" test took place on Johnston Atoll in the Pacific in 1964. Former chief of product development at Camp Detrick, Bill Patrick, told interviewers for the PBS documentary that researchers had found animals as far as 70 kilometers downwind from the point of spray that had been infected.

According to an October 2002 Associated Press report published on the website of the UCLA School of Public Health's Department of Epidemiology, the nerve-gas tests in the Utah desert had killed 6,400 sheep. The report also states that the Defense Department finally admitted in early 2002 that some of the tests conducted in the 1960s used real chemical and biological weapons, not just "simulants."[439]

Part of the government testing program included Project 112, known as "SHAD"—Shipboard Hazard and Defense—which conducted testing on ships at sea in order to identify the vulnerability of warships to chemical and biological attacks and to develop procedures to react to such attacks without jeopardizing the ships' ability to wage war. Inquiries from the Veterans Administration spurred the Pentagon's 2002 declassification of documents, as the VA sought information for reference in response to veterans' claims of health issues resulting from the SHAD tests.[440] More documents were later declassified as the VA continued to make inquiries on behalf of affected veterans.

In 2008 California Representative Michael Thompson and Montana Representative Denny Rehberg introduced H.R. 5954 to ensure compensation for veterans experiencing health issues related to the SHAD testing.[441] Speaking before the House Committee on Veterans' Affairs on June 12, 2008, Thompson said that the bill was being introduced "to allow veterans who were unknowingly used as guinea pigs in chemical and biological tests by their own government to seek medical care and compensation for their resulting illnesses."[442] He said the test had exposed "at least 6,000 service members without their knowledge to extremely harmful chemical and biological weapons." He added that there could be many others who didn't yet know they had been exposed.

Thompson told the committee that he had questioned the Department of Defense (DOD) about SHAD in 1999 and was told that it didn't exist. Then, he said, he was told that "the tests existed, but only simulants were used." He continued in his statement to reveal a pattern of deceit and denial by both the DOD and the VA:

> *"Finally, after three years of investigating, the DOD finally revealed that these tests involved live agents, in some cases Vx and Sarin nerve gases and E. Coli, along with a whole host of other substances known to cause extreme illness in humans. But despite these shocking revelations, the DOD has without reason stopped looking for records of Project 112 service personnel and notifying the veterans subjected to these tests. The VA still does not recognize any long-term health consequences from exposure to these agents. As [former tug boat commander] Jack Alderson will testify today, members of his crew and*

152

other affected service members have since developed abnormal cancers and acute respiratory issues but are routinely rejected by the VA."

Thompson's bill, which became part of the 2008 Defense Authorization Act, prompted a clinical study by the Institute of Medicine (IOM) that was not yet completed as of June 2013.

Pandemic Possibilities

Although the United States in 1969 rejected all forms of biological and chemical warfare, it reserved the right to continue biological research for the purposes of defense as well as immunization and safety.[443] Since 2001 alone the government has spent more than $50 billion on research into biological weapons for defensive purposes, including research into deadly strains of anthrax to test against current vaccines.[444]

One of the biological agents still being researched by the Pentagon is a virus that the U.S. had "weaponized" before ending its chemical and biological weapons program in 1969.[445] The airborne illness, known as "Q fever," is considered a "class B bioterrorism agent" by the Centers for Disease Control and Prevention. According to the CDC, the "class B" ranking indicates the second-highest level of priority, and is assigned to biological agents that are:

- Easily disseminated or transmitted from person to person
- Result in high mortality rates and have the potential for major public health impact
- Might cause public panic and social disruption
- Require special action for public health preparedness[446]

Q fever primarily afflicts goats and sheep, but was contracted by U.S troops who served in the Iraq war, raising the suspicion that the regime of Saddam Hussein may have developed a Q fever-based biological weapon. Although most cases of Q fever are not fatal, the virus can be debilitating, and scientists worry that, unlike many other viruses, this one can survive high temperatures and could be difficult to detect.

Although the government's big fear is that biological agents like Q fever could fall into the hands of rogue regimes and terrorist groups, who would surely use them without compunction, there is also the danger that the very existence of these organisms in a testing lab could pose a threat to the population by way of accidents or sabotage.

Nukes Over North Carolina

While conducting research for his 2013 book, *Command and Control: Nuclear Weapons, the Damascus Accident, and the Illusion of Safety,* investigative journalist Eric Schlosser gained access to documents that had been declassified, but were *not* posted online and were still being held "close to the vest" by the U.S. government. The documents, obtained by Schlosser through a Freedom of Information Act request, revealed a near nuclear accident in 1961 that would have wiped out much of the Eastern seaboard.[447],[448]

On Jan. 24, 1961, a B-52 bomber out of Seymour Johnson Air Force Base in Goldsboro, North Carolina — carrying two four-megaton hydrogen bombs that were 250 times more powerful than the bomb that devastated Hiroshima, Japan, in 1945 — broke up in mid-flight and dropped its payload on farmland in Goldsboro. According to the declassified report, one of the bombs broke apart upon impact, but the other opened its parachute and engaged trigger mechanisms, as if it were being armed and fired. A single low-voltage switch integral to the detonation process failed, and was the only thing that kept the tragic accident — which killed three of the eight crew members — from becoming a nuclear catastrophe.

Nuclear War Games

While unsuspecting Americans were enjoying their first-ever taste of McNuggets in 1983 and clamoring for everything J. Crew, celebrating Sally Ride's trip on the *Challenger* space shuttle, and filling theaters to see *Return of the Jedi,* the United States came closer to nuclear war than at any other time in its history — according to documents only recently declassified, between 2010 and 2013. A document released in January 2011 — a 1999 report by the National Security Agency — calls the 1983 incident "the most dangerous Soviet-American confrontation since the Cuban Missile Crisis." [449]

154

In November 1983, amid a climate of growing tension between the U.S. and the U.S.S.R., the United States and its Western European NATO allies engaged in routine military maneuvers dubbed "Autumn Forge." The maneuvers, involving about 40,000 NATO troops positioned in Europe around NATO's central military command headquarters in Belgium, included operation "Able Archer 83." This ten-day exercise, which coincidentally followed closely on the heels of the U.S. deployment of Pershing missiles in West Germany, was designed to fully simulate a nuclear attack. Conditions were ripe for what historians say was a "high risk of an accidental nuclear war.[450,451]

Two years earlier, the Soviets had launched operation RYAN, an acronym derived from the Russian words for "nuclear missile attack." The operation, which reports say was prompted by Soviet paranoia and fears of an impending missile strike by the U.S., was a massive intelligence-gathering exercise whose objective was to seek out signs that the U.S. was preparing for an attack.

As Able Archer got under way, RYAN operatives mistook signs, signals, and procedures for the real thing, and notified Soviet leaders that an attack was imminent. The Soviet government readied its own nuclear resources in response — from nuclear bombers parked on the tarmac of military airfields with engines running to loaded-and-ready missile silos — and braced themselves for the next steps. Some Soviet officials lobbied for a preemptive strike, but leaders chose to wait it out, with their "finger on the trigger."

At the conclusion of the Able Archer exercises, as the active signs that had pointed to an attack disappeared, the Soviets finally ordered their forces to stand down. And those enjoying *Star Wars* on the big screen were none the wiser.

But nuclear nations continue to practice for the "real thing," keeping ever present fears of accidental nuclear war.[452,453]

Crumbling Economy?

Ever since the Great Depression, there have been predictions of another U.S. economic collapse, and the economic events of recent years have continued to fuel those predictions. One of the longest economic downturns since the Great Depression started in 2007 and continued through 2008.[454] Although economists debate the details and nuances of what caused it, most attribute it to a precipitous decline in the housing market, accompanied by questionable mortgage lending practices by major banks. The National Bureau of Economic Research declared what came to be known as the "Great Recession" officially over in June 2009, however, many experts did not agree with that conclusion; Americans were reported to be "still struggling" as of the last half of 2013.[455],[456]

Economist Robert Wiedemer was one of those who accurately predicted the 2008 recession and is a believer that there are more financial rough waters ahead. In a book he co-wrote in 2011 with his brother, David Wiedemer, and Cindy S. Spitzer, he offered advice on how people could prepare financially for the "coming crash." *Aftershock: Protect Yourself and Profit in the Next Global Financial Meltdown* offered a "definitive look" at what was in store for 2012 and beyond.

Financial analysts concerned that a collapse is still in the offing point to burgeoning U.S. debt, which, at more than $17 trillion (as of the end of 2013), is seen as being completely out of control—an economic bombshell waiting to explode. The national debt first reached $1 trillion during the presidency of Ronald Reagan, and despite declarations from both the Republicans and the Democrats that "enough is enough," and promises to reign in spending, the debt has continued to multiply at a frightening pace under every president since Reagan.[457]

Life in the Dark

Survivalist author and blogger James Wesley Rawles has called electricity the "linchpin" of modern society—the one thing that holds it all together. Advances in technology have made modern society—particularly here in the United States—more dependent than ever on electrical energy. The electronics, information networks, telecommunications, transportation systems, and financial systems that drive life in the U.S. are not only dependent on electricity, but are also largely dependent upon each other, often in intricate ways, making our country more vulnerable than ever to events that could disrupt this intertwined web.

Americans' expectations that there will always be an uninterrupted supply of electricity to power their automated world of household appliances, computers, cell phones, traffic lights, elevators, furnaces, and air conditioners, fuel panic when that power is interrupted. And power outages do happen, caused by everything from extreme weather to high consumer demand to squirrels in transformers and equipment failures on an aging electric grid. The American economy loses billions of dollars per year to power failures.[458]

The biggest power blackout in North American history occurred on August 14, 2003, and left an estimated 50 million people in the dark in parts of the U.S. and Canada for up to two days.[459] The widespread blackout was triggered by trees brushing against high voltage lines in Ohio and was compounded by a computer error that sparked a chain reaction, overloading circuits and tripping breakers at power stations across eight states and into Canada.[460]

Thousands of commuters in New York were stranded in subway tunnels and on commuter trains. In office buildings, people were stuck in elevators; those who weren't, streamed outside as they faced stifling mid-August heat without the benefit of air conditioning. The outage rendered automatic teller machines useless, and people used to paying for things electronically found they couldn't buy batteries or flashlights unless they had cash. Police in New York reported several incidents of looting and break-ins at darkened stores.

The power failure triggered the automatic shutdown of seven nuclear power plants in New York and New Jersey and two in the Midwest. Air travel was seriously impacted in the states directly affected by the blackout, resulting in delays and cancellations that affected travelers as far away as San Francisco. The massive blackout prompted government officials to launch a long-overdue review of the country's timeworn power grid.

In the ensuing years, as technology has expanded by leaps and bounds, it has become apparent that the grid is vulnerable to more than the frailties of outdated equipment and the assaults of extreme weather events. The modern era has ushered in threats that were unknown at the end of World War II, but have since become increasingly apparent.

157

Threats from Cyberspace

The advent of the Internet has enabled computerized connections that tie together businesses and industries as well as individuals, groups, and governments. From banking to shopping, to the management of power stations and water supplies, access to just about everything is controlled electronically. Enter hackers—people who have sufficient knowledge of computers and computer programs to gain online entry to systems in order to steal information or money, cause disruption—or even gain control of the systems that are part of the country's critical infrastructure. Hackers have become ubiquitous in the virtual world of cyberspace, giving businesses and governments increasing cause for alarm. And some governments—including the United States—have used hacker methods for their own purposes.

In 2010, it was discovered that the United States and Israel had collaborated on the creation of a computer "worm," or virus, to use in sabotaging Iran's nuclear program. Called "Stuxnet," the computer program was one developed to target industrial control systems, such as those used to manage facilities such as power plants, waste processing systems and dams—without the operators of these facilities knowing.[461] According to the *New York Times*, President Obama secretly authorized "increasingly sophisticated attacks on the computer systems that run Iran's main nuclear enrichment facilities," thereby "significantly expanding America's first sustained use of cyberweapons..."[462]

America has also been on the receiving end of cyber attacks. In September 2013, U.S. agents uncovered a two-year-long cyber warfare campaign waged by Chinese hackers trying to steal the secrets behind American drone technology.[463] And in November 2013, there were reports of two serious hacking incidents:

- The newly launched "Obamacare" website, for those seeking health insurance under the Affordable Care Act, was reported to have been hacked at least sixteen times (considered a "small number" in comparison to the hundreds of cyber assaults launched on federal government websites each day).[464]
- The FBI discovered that government computers in several different agencies had been hacked, and sensitive information was stolen, in a yearlong hacking campaign waged by an unknown assailant.[465]

No industry or system is immune from attack — even the electric grid.

Nature's Worst Redefined

Just when Americans thought they had seen the worst nature had to offer, a series of natural disasters unleashed their fury all over the world between 2004 and 2013, giving new meaning to "the worst," and giving people new reasons to think about preparedness.

Super Quakes

The first such disaster took place in Southeast Asia on the day after Christmas in 2004, when a massive earthquake — with an estimated magnitude of 9.1 to 9.3 on the Richter scale — struck off the coast of Sumatra, Indonesia.[466] The quake spawned a giant tsunami, a tidal wave that engulfed coastal communities across fourteen countries in the region, leaving nearly 230,000 people dead and close to 1.7 million homeless. Remnants of the waves reached as far away as Nova Scotia and Peru.[467] It was one of the worst natural disasters in human history.

Less than a year later, the biggest earthquake to strike Pakistan in 100 years killed more than 80,000 people and left at least 4 million homeless. Damage from the 7.6-magnitude quake was also reported in parts of Afghanistan and India.[468]

In January 2010, a catastrophic quake struck the impoverished island nation of Haiti. Registering 7.0 on the Richter scale, the quake was the largest to hit the country in 200 years. It devastated the capital, Port-au-Prince, and surrounding communities, reducing buildings and infrastructure to rubble. More than 200,000 people were killed, 300,000 were injured, and an estimated 1.3 million were left homeless.[469] Over the ensuing days, the country endured at least 42 aftershocks.[470] The disaster sparked an outpouring of aid from all over the world, but three years later, the ravaged infrastructure remained in disrepair. An estimated one-fifth of the people who had been left homeless still lived in tent camps, without adequate sanitation or power.[471]

The fourth most powerful earthquake ever recorded struck Honshu, the largest and most highly populated island in Japan, on March 11,

159

2011. The US Geological Survey puts the magnitude of the quake at 9.0 on the Richter scale, making it the largest earthquake to strike Japan in 130 years.[472] It spawned tsunami waves that struck the east coast of Japan and even touched the United States, reaching as far away as the Hawaiian Islands. The massive quake was followed by more than 50 aftershocks, many with a magnitude of 6.0 or greater.[473] In its aftermath, the quake and its aftershocks left more than 10,000 people dead, left thousands homeless, and left millions without water, adequate sanitation, or power. [474] It also damaged three reactors at the Fukushima Daiichi nuclear power plant, creating a partial meltdown at least as bad as the 1986 Chernobyl disaster, with both classified as a 7.0 − "major accident" − on International Atomic Energy Agency's INES scale.[475] More than 170,000 people living within a 12-mile radius of the plant were evacuated, amid fears of radiation exposure.[476]

As of 2013, the Japanese government was still dealing with the after effects of the earthquake and the nuclear accident, a process expected to continue for decades.[477,478] Meanwhile, in the U.S., people began to fear exposure to radiation as debris from the Japanese quake began to wash ashore along the West Coast. While reports from Russia and China asserted that concentrated radiation from the Fukushima plant were being carried by ocean currents toward the shores of the U.S., scientists from the International Pacific Research Center in Hawaii offered assurances that the radiation would be so diluted by the time it reached the U.S., that it would pose no risks to human health.[479]

Super Storms

As some parts of the world were being devastated by earthquakes unlike any seen before, others − including the United States − were being ravaged by "super storms."

On August 29, 2005, a powerful Category 3 hurricane stormed in off the Gulf of Mexico and pounded coastal Louisiana, Alabama, and Mississippi. Hurricane Katrina gave its worst to New Orleans, with a raging ocean surf that breached levees and flooded more than 80 percent of the city − a city of nearly half a million people.[480,481]

The day before the storm hit, New Orleans Mayor Ray Nagin ordered mandatory evacuations, and designated the city's massive stadium, the

Super Dome, as a shelter for people who were unable to get out. Hundreds of thousands of people heeded the warning and fled to inland Louisiana and neighboring states. However, tens of thousands of people ignored the evacuation order and refused to leave their homes. Many later had to be rescued from their rooftops, after the flooding covered everything else.[482]

Many of those who couldn't evacuate took shelter in the Super Dome, which was not adequately supplied to take care of the thousands who showed up. People who sought refuge there later described deplorable, unsanitary conditions, crime, and long waits in line for food—which consisted largely of military meals-ready-to-eat (MREs).[483]

Looters all over the city took advantage of the chaos to help themselves to everything from groceries to medicines, clothing, jewelry, and anything else they could find.[484]

The federal government was slow to respond to the disaster. It took FEMA days to set up operations in New Orleans, and FEMA personnel arrived unprepared to deal with a disaster of that scale. Later, it was found that training for the National Response Plan, which was put in place to coordinate disaster response, had not been completed in all the government agencies responsible for disaster response, and had never been tested. President Bush demanded a review of the country's plans and procedures for responding to catastrophes like Katrina, assigning responsibility for the review to the DHS and Department of Transportation. The resulting report stated that the U.S. suffered from "a failure to account for the full scope of catastrophic events; outmoded planning processes, products, and tools; and inadequate attention to coordination." [485] However, the administration and DHS continued to emphasize that "state and local governments must be the first line of defense against disaster and attack."[486]

But, ominously, state and local officials actually gave some residents more cause for alarm, when they began confiscating legally registered firearms from citizens on September 8. According to a report in the *New York Times*, the New Orleans superintendent of police, P. Edwin Compass III gave the order for police to take away the weapons ahead of a "mass forced evacuation" of residents still living in the city.

"Only law enforcement are allowed to have weapons," Compass told reporters.

161

However, hundreds of security guards hired by companies like the Blackwater Security Agency were allowed to keep their weapons, which included assault rifles such as M-16s. Compass said he had no plans to make them surrender their weapons.

The *Times* reported that New Orleans had turned into an armed camp, patrolled by thousands of military personnel and law enforcement officers from federal, state, and local levels.[487]

In 2007, the National Rifle Association (NRA) filed suit against the city of New Orleans for violation of people's Second Amendment rights after Hurricane Katrina, claiming that city officials had illegally confiscated firearms and left people "at the mercy of roving gangs, home invaders, and other criminals." The NRA alleged that more than 1,000 guns had been taken.[488] The suit was settled in 2008, after city officials agreed to return hundreds of confiscated weapons to their owners.[489]

Hurricane Katrina left in its wake nearly 2,000 people dead and more than a million homeless.[490] Damage was estimated to be more than $100 billion, making it the most destructive storm in U.S. history.[491] Some of those who fled the city never returned; five years after Hurricane Katrina, the city had 29 percent fewer residents than before the disaster.[492] And the specter of an armed camp whose inhabitants were unable to defend themselves was indelibly etched in the minds of many, arguably being part of the tipping point that inspired renewed interest in the preparedness movement.

Hurricanes were not the only "super storms" to hit the U.S. Freak winter storms struck the Northeast in 2008 and 2011, leaving millions of people without power, some for more than a week and others, for nearly a month.

In December 2008, freezing rain blanketed New England and upstate New York, leaving a coating of ice on everything. The ice coating was strong enough to bring down trees and limbs in seven states, resulting in downed power lines, impassable roads, and debris strewn about everywhere. Many areas were left looking like war zones. People who were able, and needed to, evacuated their homes to local shelters—if there were any. Others sought refuge in nearby hotels, but often found that either others had beaten them to it and there was no vacancy, or that the hotels were also affected by the power outages. Some people in

Central Massachusetts had to go as far as Cape Cod to find hotels with vacancies. But many New Englanders in the hardest-hit rural areas, who were no strangers to severe winter storms, had alternative means of heating and lighting, and were able to stay in their homes until the power was restored.

In 2011, the day before Halloween, an unusual, massive northeaster brought heavy snow to a wide swath of the Northeast that stretched from Virginia to Canada. Trees, still covered with leaves, snapped, cracked, and fell under the weight of the snow, leaving behind damage reminiscent of the 2008 ice storm. More than 3 million people were left without power, some for at least a week.[493]

Almost exactly a year later, a monster storm dubbed "Superstorm Sandy" delivered more destruction to the beleaguered East Coast. Tropical Storm Sandy formed in the Caribbean on October 22, and was upgraded to a Category 3 hurricane two days later. After making landfall over Jamaica and Cuba, it lost some of its steam and left the Caribbean as a Category 1 storm. The storm passed through the Bahamas on October 27 and then churned out into the Atlantic on a path toward the East Coast of the U.S., picking up power along the way. By October 28, it was the largest tropical storm every recorded in the Atlantic.[494] On October 29 it took an unusual sharp left turn, instead of taking the northward track typical of most tropical storms, and came ashore northeast of Atlantic City, joining forces with a winter storm from the west and frigid air from the north to create a "super storm" like none seen before.[495]

The center of the storm slammed into coastal New Jersey and New York, while the swirling spirals that made up the body of the massive gale battered the Eastern seaboard from Florida to Maine. On the westward track it maintained after wreaking havoc on the coast, the storm brought its destruction across the Appalachian Mountains and as far inland as Michigan and Wisconsin.

The areas hardest hit by Superstorm Sandy were in New Jersey and New York, which were both devastated by high winds and flooding. In New York City, nearly 375,000 people were evacuated from low-lying parts of New York City; floodwaters filled subway tunnels and airport runways.[496] In New Jersey, the storm left the shoreline—and the famous Atlantic City boardwalk—in ruins.

Inland, the storm created blizzard conditions in Tennessee, North Carolina, and West Virginia, where it dumped an estimated three feet of snow, and brought high winds to Michigan and Wisconsin.

In all, the storm affected twenty-four states, destroying nearly 650,000 homes and leaving close to 9 million people without power.[497] At least 125 people were killed in the U.S. Estimated damage was in the neighborhood of $62 billion,[498] making it the costliest cyclone in the U.S. since 1900 — after Hurricane Katrina.[499]

Response by FEMA to the disaster was far more effective than its response to Hurricane Katrina, by most accounts. New Jersey Governor Chris Christie, in an interview on NBC's "Today Show," said that the response from FEMA had been "great."[500] However, some people who didn't personally see FEMA responders complained that the agency hadn't helped at all. Bill Carwile, head of disaster response operations at FEMA, responded to such accusations with frustration in an interview with *The Huffington Post*. He said:

> *"What is it that makes people think the federal government should take control of their lives?" FEMA, he said, had become "a generic name for 'nobody's solved our problem."*

After the storm, many people returning to their homes discovered they had been robbed. There were reports of gas being siphoned from cars and criminals posing as relief workers. Some opportunists picked through the rubble of the homes, taking whatever they could find.[501]

In 2013, a little more than a year after Superstorm Sandy struck the U.S., the most powerful cyclonic storm ever recorded *anywhere* devastated the Philippine Islands.[502] At this writing, the overall impact is still being assessed. However, this much is known:[503,504]

- Typhoon Haiyan was a maximum category-five storm with ground winds of up to 235 miles per hour
- The storm affected an estimated 4 million people; at least 5,000 people have been killed. Some believe the death toll could top 10,000.
- According to the United Nations, 2.5 million people are in need of food assistance.

According to a report in the *Wall Street Journal*, one of the cities hardest hit was Tacloban, a city of 220,000 people, which took a direct hit from the typhoon. Despite having days to prepare for the storm, city and national officials found that their preparations had been woefully inadequate for a storm of this magnitude. They failed to stock a sufficient amount of supplies and were unable to move many of the most exposed people out of the storm's path. For nearly 24 hours, officials had no means to even call for assistance.[505]

Monster Tornadoes

Some of the deadliest and most destructive tornadoes in this country's history took place between 2008 and 2013.

The National Climactic Data Center (NCDC) of the U.S. National Oceanic and Atmospheric Administration says that the U.S. experiences, on average, more than 1,000 tornadoes per year, more than any other country in the world.[506] Most are considered weak, as measured on the Fujita Scale. Data collected by the NCDC suggests that there has been an upward trend in the frequency of tornadoes since 1990, although the agency attributes some of that to "increased national Doppler radar coverage, increasing population, and greater attention to tornado reporting." And although the data indicates there has been only a slight increase in the incidence of *very* strong tornadoes in recent years, the seemingly minor uptick on the chart belies the devastation they have caused.

In 2007 the original Fujita Scale, used to represent a tornado's intensity and wind velocity based on damage observed after the event, was modified, to the Enhanced Fujita Scale. Rankings on the original Fujita Scale ranged from F0 to F5, with F5 being the most intense. The new scale, which rates tornadoes from EF0 to EF5, takes into account more specific information about structure damage and uses revised estimated wind speeds. Here, for example, are the lowest and highest rankings on each scale:

Fujita Scale (1971 – 2006)[507]	Enhanced Fujita Scale (2007)[508]
F0 = winds less than 73 mph; Light damage: chimneys, signs; broken branches, shallow-rooted	EF0 = winds 65 to 85 mph; Light damage: some barns, outbuildings, broken branches,

trees uprooted	damage to siding or gutters
F5 = winds 261 to 318 mph; Incredible damage: "Strong frame houses leveled off foundations and swept away; automobile-sized missiles fly through the air in excess of 100 meters (109 yds); trees debarked; incredible phenomena will occur."	EF5 = winds 200 to 234 mph; Incredible damage: Strong frame houses leveled off foundations and swept away; automobile-sized missiles fly through the air in excess of 100 meters (109 yds); trees debarked; incredible phenomena will occur."

According to both scales, tornadoes with winds in excess of 319 mph would be "inconceivable."

The NCDC says that about 95 percent of the tornadoes in the U.S. usually have an intensity of EF3 or less. Of those rated at EF3 or above, only a small fraction achieve category EF5 status—an estimated .1 percent of all tornadoes in the U.S. Given that about 1,000 hit the U.S. in a year, it is likely that twenty could be classified as "violent," and one might even achieve "incredible" status. [509]

According to a December 2008 report by NOAA's Storm Prediction Center, the number of reported tornadoes in 2008 was more than twice the 10-year average.[510] Of the 2,192 tornadoes reported, 36 were classified as strong to violent, with a rating of EF3-EF5. NOAA says that number equaled the average number of *all* such tornadoes reported in the fifty-eight years since tornado tracking began.

In January 2008, there were 54 tornadoes reported across the Midwest. In early February, a cluster of 87 tornadoes struck the southeastern part of the country. The month of May saw a record 460 tornadoes reported, and June followed suit with 289 confirmed tornadoes in two "outbreaks." Between January and May, 170 people were killed by tornadoes, making it the eighth deadliest five-month period since 1968.[511]

The year 2010 was the seventh most active year for tornadoes since record-keeping began in 1950, with 1,282 twisters reported on the ground.[512] Tornadoes were reported in all but four of the lower 48 states (Delaware, Massachusetts, Rhode Island, and Nevada) in 2010, and some of those states were hit unexpectedly hard. The 17 tornadoes reported in Arizona tied that state's record, which was set in 1972. The 48 reported in Minnesota broke the state's previous records, and the outbreak there included more EF-4 or stronger events than any since 1967. Four EF-4 tornadoes struck North Dakota, Iowa, and Wisconsin, an unusually strong outbreak for this part of the country. In December, a total of fifty-three tornadoes — which included three EF-3 tornadoes — were reported in Arkansas, Missouri, Illinois, Louisiana, and Mississippi, more than twice the average tornado count of twenty-three typically reported for that month.

One of the most deadly tornado seasons on record took place in 2011. According to NOAA, there were seven outbreaks of tornadoes and severe weather that each resulted in damage estimated at more than $1 billion. Damage from all outbreaks that year exceeded $28 billion. There were 551 fatalities from these twisters, the most since record-keeping began.[513]

Six of the twisters reported in 2011 were classified as EF-5, tying the record set in 1974. One of those — a monster estimated to be nearly a mile wide — happened in Joplin, Missouri — a city of more than 50,000 people — in May 2011. The Joplin tornado, one of the deadliest in U.S. history, had winds in excess of 200 mph. It killed 158 people and injured more than a thousand.[514] By some estimates, it crushed one-third of the city.[515] And as if the residents of Joplin hadn't suffered enough, looters moved in to take what they could find, even as people were trying to put the pieces of their lives back together.[516]

Although a post-storm assessment by the National Weather Service credits timely actions by the media, emergency management teams, local businesses, schools, and the general public with preventing more fatalities, it notes that most of Joplin's residents did not take immediate action upon hearing the tornado sirens. Instead, they chose to stay put and assess the threat for themselves. Based on their previous experience with severe weather, many did not take the threat seriously until they saw or heard the twister, or heard further confirmation of the threat in media reports. When they did act, the report says, most people followed the advice of severe-weather education campaigns, and took shelter in places like basements, interior rooms or hallways, or crawl spaces, which proved to be life-saving.

The Church of Jesus Christ of Latter-Day Saints reported that many of its members in Joplin were able to help neighbors by sharing their own stored food and emergency supplies. Not everyone's stores were spared by the tornado, but those that were, offered solace to people whose homes had been destroyed and whose lives were turned upside down.[517]

The 2013 tornado season will be remembered for at least two powerful tornado outbreaks that tore through the country's heartland:

In May 2013, a monstrous EF-5 tornado leveled Moore, Oklahoma—a city that had, unbelievably, already been devastated by an EF-5 twister in 1999. The funnel that struck in 2013 was estimated to be more than a mile wide and stayed on the ground for an estimated 14 miles.[518] It damaged thousands of homes and left 24 people dead; damage from the tornado was estimated to be more than $2 billion.[519] And as with other disasters, this one attracted looters of every stripe. Some came from as far away as New York and Virginia to search the rubble of ravaged homes in Moore for everything from appliances and electronics to copper wire and piping.[520]

An unusual late-season tornado outbreak in the Midwest on November 17, 2013, sent seven twisters across Illinois, Indiana, Michigan, and Wisconsin. [521,522] Illinois was hardest hit, with two EF-4 twisters destroying at least a thousand homes. Six people died; 200 were injured. Hundreds of thousands of people were left without power. Thirteen counties were declared disaster areas.[523]

Transitioning Towns

Author Richard Heinberg, who in 1995 raised the alarm about "killing the planet," issued a clarion call for attention to Earth's dwindling resources, particularly oil, in a series of books he released between 2003 and 2013 that were based in part on the earlier work of M. King Hubbert, gained worldwide attention.

The documentary *End of Suburbia*, released in 2004, underscored the concern about the predicted peak and subsequent decline in the world's oil supply, with a dozen experts, including Heinberg and oil-industry analyst Matthew Simmons, weighing in on the subject with supporting facts and figures. The topic of peak oil joined climate change as a flashpoint for discord among people who were believers and those who were not. But it also inspired a number of grassroots movements seeking to build resilience into communities in the face of dwindling oil supplies and perceived threats from a changing climate and faltering economies.

The most notable such movement started in the United Kingdom, where in 2005 activist Rob Hopkins led an effort, starting in Kinsale, Ireland, to help communities create "energy descent" plans as a way to transition from a culture dependent on fossil fuels to one able to sustain itself as independently as possible. The movement, branded "Transition Towns," quickly spread, with thousands of chapters popping up all over the world.[524] Hallmarks of the movement included building a strong local economy, building resilient food systems, and maintaining a hopeful vision for the future.

The concern about peak oil drew adherents in the prepping community, and while there may have been many people who were *not* on board with the motivating principles behind the transition town movement—the eventual peak and decline of the world's oil supply—the principles, techniques, and practices promoted by the Transition Town movement found their way into mainstream thinking and also onto the list of skills valued by preppers. Ideas such as permaculture, reducing energy use, and reducing dependence on long supply chains were embraced by people seeking to build resilience into their own lives and the lives of their communities. Resilience—"the ability of an individual or community to withstand societal or ecological shocks"[525]—was recognized as a foundational objective of being prepared. The lines between preppers, back-to-the-landers, and survivalists began to blur as it became evident that all were focused on sustainable living, a lifestyle defined as one that:

> "...creates and maintains the conditions under which humans and nature can exist in productive harmony, that permit fulfilling the social, economic and other requirements of present and future generations."[526]

Part Two:

A Look at Modern Preppers

"The concept of self-sufficiency has been undermined in value over a scant few generations. The vast majority of the population seems to look down their noses upon self-reliance as some quaint dusty relic, entertained only by the hyperparanoid or those hopelessly incapable of fitting into mainstream society."

— Cody Lundin, *When All Hell Breaks Loose: Stuff You Need to Survive When Disaster Strikes*

"There's no harm in hoping for the best as long as you're prepared for the worst."

— Stephen King, *Different Seasons*

"Private-sector preparedness is not a luxury; it is a cost of doing business in the post-9/11 world. It is ignored at a tremendous potential cost in lives, money and national security."

— The 9-11 Commission Report

Part Two:

A Look at Modern Preppers

Chapter Five: What is Modern Preparedness?

The disasters of the early 21st century served as a wake-up call to many people about being prepared. The catastrophes inspired an abundance of preparedness-related resources that included websites, books, and businesses.

It seems that Hurricane Katrina, specifically, provided the impetus for "prepper networks" that sprang up all over the country and for prepper websites that began to multiply across the Internet. James Wesley Rawles concurs. In a recent interview, he said, "Hurricane Katrina was a turning point, and Superstorm Sandy was just confirmation that people need to be prepared."

That sentiment is underscored by contributors to Rawles' SurvivalBlog website. One, "R.L.," reflected:

> *"Katrina and Sandy ... brought their local civilizations to a grinding halt. They [the affected citizens] had the benefit of being so localized that the rest of the nation was able to extricate them from their difficulties. What if the destruction were more nationwide?"*

Rawles, a former U.S. Army intelligence officer, said he started his website a couple of months before Hurricane Katrina hit, as a way to promote his book, *Patriots: Surviving the Coming Collapse*, which he first published in 1998 (and re-released in 2009). After Katrina, he noticed a surge in visits to the site.[527]

"It was downloaded by more than 70,000 people," he said.

Rawles said he thinks the events that have most influenced modern prepping, besides Hurricane Katrina and Superstorm Sandy, have been natural disasters like the 2004 tsunami in Southeast Asia and the 2011 earthquake that caused the nuclear accident at the Fukushima nuclear plant in Japan.

Rawles said that, although he doesn't think the September 11 attacks in 2001 were a "watershed event" for prepping, because together they were an "isolated incident," they had a huge psychological impact on Americans.

"It showed people how vulnerable the country is," he said.

Rawles posts to his blog daily, and currently has a huge following all over the world, as measured by the 320,000 unique visits his site gets each week; there have been close to 51 million unique visits to the site since its inception.

Rawles has also found there is a big demand for his books — which, in addition to *Patriots,* include: *How to Survive the End of the World as We Know It: Tactics, Techniques, and Technologies for Uncertain Times* (2010); *Survivors: A Novel of the Coming Collapse* (2011), *Founders: A Novel of the Coming Collapse* (2012); *Expatriates: A Novel of the Coming Global Collapse* (2013). All of his books are filled with practical information for would-be preppers, and the highlights and underlines in the Kindle versions attest that people have been taking notes.

In addition to his blog and his books, Rawles has found that his skills as a survivalist are also in demand. He spends 5 to 10 hours a month as a consultant, advising people about survival retreats.

For some people, the September 11 attacks *were* a watershed event. It was what prompted Jeff and Amy Davis to start their online business, The Ready Store (www.TheReadyStore.com). Brandon Garrett, a spokesperson for the company, said, "After September 11, there was a lot more talk about being self-sufficient and being able to depend on yourself instead of others or the government. People started to realize that they had to be ready at a moment's notice for the unexpected. Jeff Davis, our founder, started selling 72-hour kits online; people wanted a way that they could bug out easily if things hit the fan."

Preparedness teacher and consultant Kellene Bishop of PreparednessPro.com said in an interview for this book that the September 2011 attacks, along with Hurricane Katrina, were what influenced her to "step up her game" when it came to prepping.[528] In fact, she says it may have been Hurricane Katrina that helped turn prepping into an identifiable cultural phenomenon. "Then," she said, "the recession that started in late 2007 woke people up."

Bishop, who in 2012 was featured on National Geographic's "Doomsday Preppers" TV show, said that she started her information-packed website, PreparednessPro.com, in the year 2000, out of a commitment to teaching others about how — and why — to be prepared. Her initial inspiration came by way of a preparedness fair she attended. She became concerned about the information that was presented, she said, and decided, "If you can't join 'em, beat 'em!"

She started her blog in 2009, and in the spirit of "stepping up her game" she has since added to her suite of prepper resources a Facebook page, an online radio program, and a YouTube channel, where she posts videos offering information about storing food and cooking with ingredients from stored food.

"We need to educate people," she said. "That's why I did Doomsday Preppers."

Bishop also sells educational DVDs and, mindful of the looting and lawlessness that has followed nearly every disaster that has come along in recent years, she teaches self-defense classes for women. And she has more plans in store to provide resources to preppers. She said she is in the process of creating an "umbrella" site that will encompass other sites and blogs that focus on specialized prepping interests. She said the Preparedness Pro site will be for "beginning and intermediate" preppers, while some of the other sites in her plans will offer information for those who have moved to the next level.

Despite her involvement with an assorted number of prepping activities since 2000, Bishop says that she never heard the term "prepper" until she heard it on "Doomsday Preppers."

Tom Martin, of the American Preppers Network, agrees that natural disasters have prompted many people to begin prepping. He said in a 2013 interview that there was "a noticeable increase in interest" at the APN website after Hurricane Sandy struck the East Coast in the fall of 2012. He added:

> "People learned you can't rely on government to save you. Even FEMA, at its website Ready.gov, advises people to be prepared. They know they can't get to you immediately."

Ron Douglas, president of the Colorado-based Self-Reliance Expo, said Hurricane Katrina was one of the things that motivated him to start the Expo, which he did in 2010.[529] The other thing that influenced him was a major blizzard in Colorado. He said that the area where he lived was without power for a week. After three days, a neighbor came to his house and asked if he could use his truck to venture out to the store, because his family was completely out of food. Douglas invited him into his well-stocked basement to help himself to whatever food he needed.

"I was shocked to realize how totally unprepared some people were," he said.

Douglas said that the Self-Reliance Expo was the first of its kind and remains the largest among similar expos. He said that about 4,000 people attended the first Expo in 2010; attendance at subsequent Expos has been as high as 16,500.

The Movement Today

People often try to make distinctions among the iterations of preparedness lifestyles that have made an appearance in our culture over the years. Some blame the media for trying to put a label on lifestyles with which they are unfamiliar — labels that are quickly adopted by the public to stereotype and ridicule lifestyles they don't understand. For example:

- Back-to-the-landers used to be called "earthy-crunchy" — people who eat granola and buy organic products. (They have also been called tree-huggers and hippies stuck in the '60s, where the movement first gained its identity.)
- The term "survivalist" conjured up images of reclusive Rambos or Ted Kazinski types, living primitively off the land and nursing grudges against the Establishment.
- "Peak oiler" summoned pictures of left-wing radicals who think the world is soon going to run completely out of oil and actively campaign for everyone to use less of it.
- Thanks primarily to recent media accounts and reality shows like National Geographic's "Doomsday Preppers," the most

recent term, "prepper," calls to mind gun-toting paranoids obsessed with the end of the world.

Rawles says that today there's a "blurring of distinction" among survivalists, back-to-the-landers, homesteaders, the green building and sustainability movements, and local foods movements. He says, "They have the same basic goals."

At their core, all are concerned with surviving whatever life throws at them, and with sustaining their lifestyles — and those of their families — into the future, on their own terms. They may be motivated by different values or political beliefs, but in the end, they share many lifestyle characteristics. All are concerned with planning for unforeseen circumstances: they all understand the common sense behind preparing against blizzards and tornadoes. No matter where they are along the preparedness continuum, most seem to value things like independence and self-reliance, basic survival skills, knowing how to grow their own food (whether or not they have the means to do so), conserving energy, and understanding basic first aid.

It seems that "prepper" is just the latest label given to people who take preparedness very seriously, although not everyone who practices preparedness identifies themselves as a "prepper"; — many people have never even heard of the term. *Backwoods Home Magazine* editor Dave Duffy said he first heard the term "prepper" about five years ago, and wondered, "What's a prepper?" He thinks the expression "prepper movement" is "just a way to repackage something that's always been there." He said, "First it was the environmental movement, then the self-sufficiency movement, then the conspiracy movement, then the militia movement …."

Jack Spirko, host of the online radio show, The Survival Podcast, has been called "the face of the modern survivalist movement, a realist representing individuals relying on themselves rather than the government."[530] According to Spirko, the foundational principle of modern survivalism is, "doing things today to prepare for disaster that help you out if nothing goes wrong at all."

Spirko has told his listeners:

> *"As long as you worry about a label, you're missing the entire point. Preppers have been made just as radical by the media now as*

177

survivalists [used to be]. … What you call yourself doesn't matter — what you do, does." And, he says, *"It is only common sense to be prepared and to take responsibility for ourselves and our children."* [531]

In the end, modern preparedness is very much like the "old-fashioned" version — the Biblical ant storing up food during the summer, getting ready for winter; the Mormon prophet Joseph Smith, admonishing his followers to "prepare every needful thing."

Modern Prepping Lifestyles

A writer for CNNMoney, who visited the Life Changes, Be Ready! Expo in Lakeland, Florida, in November 2013, came away with a new appreciation for preppers. He said:

> *"Contrary to images of deluded or gun-obsessed 'lone wolves,' many preppers are average consumers reacting to concrete worries, and their way of thinking is spreading, fueling an emerging lifestyle trend."*[532]

At the risk of creating new labels, which is not the intent here at all, it might be instructive to look at preppers based on their "style" of prepping. Regardless of what motivates them, and regardless of the common threads that bind them together, people who prepare do seem to fall into three basic categories, based on the degree to which their lives are influenced by their focus on preparedness:

1. "Practical preppers"
2. "Whole Life preppers"
3. "Societal hardship preppers"

"Practical preppers" are those people whose preparedness efforts center around emergency planning, usually related to home emergencies, such as house fires, or extreme weather, such as hurricanes or blizzards — events have primarily local, short-term effects. They may not consider themselves "preppers"; like Duffy, they may never have heard the word. At the very least, they may have on hand a generator, extra batteries for their flashlights, and many of the emergency supplies recommended by the Federal Emergency Management Agency (FEMA), including three days' worth of food and water. Many are drawn to participate in local FEMA-supported CERT programs, where they are trained to assess the effects of disasters in assigned areas of their communities and to provide assistance to emergency first responders.

"Whole life" preppers are people whose lifestyles naturally foster and result in being reasonably prepared for the unexpected, whether the unexpected brings consequences of short- or long-term duration. For some, it is the way they have always lived. They value self-reliance and are often concerned about reducing their dependence on manmade systems. They pursue self-sufficiency and are apt to be people who grow and preserve their own food; they may have at least a year's worth put by. They focus on health and wellbeing as necessary elements of being prepared and may seek out ways to become less reliant on the medical establishment. They like to use alternate energy sources; some live off-grid. Today's "whole life" preppers are yesterday's homesteaders. However, "whole life" preppers can be found in every locale.

Like "practical preppers," "whole life preppers" may not consider themselves to be "preppers" and may never have heard the word. However, those who do identify as preppers are tuned in to—though not obsessed by—potential emergencies or disasters that could have a significant impact on their lifestyle, and are attentive to the ways in which they could sustain their lifestyle after such events. Their survival skills are as important to them as their homesteading skills.

Bearing in mind the civil disorder and looting that has often followed disasters in our recent history, "whole life" preppers are likely to include self-defense in their preparedness "bag of tricks"—which usually also includes the supplies recommended by FEMA (and maybe some FEMA never thought of). Finally, they value their community of friends and neighbors as important elements of preparedness and, like "practical preppers," may participate in their community's CERT program.

"Societal hardship" preppers are very focused on specific threats and events—locally, nationally, and even internationally—that have the potential to bring about serious civil disorder, and they gear many of their preparations toward mitigating the conditions those events could bring, whether for the short term or indefinitely. Their preparations are likely to include the trappings of wilderness survival as well as a strong emphasis on self-defense. They are apt to have secret "bug-out" locations, and may even have access to underground shelters, or bunkers. Like "whole life" and "practical" preppers, they value their network of friends and neighbors in promoting community preparedness.

Of course, like any categories of things, these are not absolute. Traits of each category can often be found in all three.

Kellene Bishop says that the fundamental premise of being prepared is eliminating vulnerabilities. Regardless of the category into which they seem to fall, today's preppers are concerned with the rule of redundancy: "Three is two, two is one, and one is none." In other words, if you have three sources for something and one source fails, you still have two. If you have two sources and one fails, you still have one. But if you have only one source and it fails, you have nothing.

The "rule" emphasizes having a backup plan and building redundancy into all critical life support systems. Spirko advises his listeners to assess their current situation and understand the things they're reliant upon—things that are "just assumed" to be there on a daily basis—and to start building a plan to address each one. Those areas likely include food, water, shelter, power, fuel, warmth, clothing, communications, and self-defense. The "rule" suggests that backup plans for these areas take into account needs for both short- and long-term emergencies.

As an example, people who store food recognize that it could eventually run out during a long-term emergency. Following the "rule of three," their challenge is to find other sources of food once that happens. For many, the answer is to grow and preserve it themselves; for others it is to hunt or forage for wild foods. Similarly, if something happens to interrupt the flow of water from the kitchen tap, alternate sources must be found, be it stored water, rain barrels, or nearby streams and lakes.

The degree to which people are able to practice preparedness is often dependent on where they live and other life circumstances. As of 2013, the U.S. population stood at more than 317 million; roughly 8 percent live in major cities that have populations of 1 million to more than 8 million people. [533] Activities such as growing food, as with other means of self-sufficiency, are difficult to pursue in areas where the population density is more than two thousand people per square mile. Urban preppers, it would seem, are limited to plans to sustain themselves in a disaster for the short term, until help arrives, or to leave the area—temporarily or for good. Their plans to "shelter in place" might include stored food and water, alternate means of lighting, and a bug-out bag complete with many of the items recommended by FEMA, including a tent and a sleeping bag. In addition, they might be developing skills in self-defense and survival.

For others, financial circumstances may limit the level to which they can be prepared. Not everyone can afford to have backups to all their critical life systems; not everyone can afford to move to the country or buy property to use as a bug-out location. However, the advice from just about all seasoned preppers is: do what you can, with what you have, where you are. And, to help with those financial circumstances, work toward becoming free of debt.

Spirko cautions his listeners that becoming debt-free is "the most important thing in the world right now." He says:

> *"The person that's debt-free — if they lose their job, it's a helluva lot less of an event for them than the person that's mired in debt and is one paycheck away from being thrown out of their house."* [534]

Evolution of a Prepper

The goal of Ron Douglas' Self-Reliance Expo is to raise awareness about preparedness and help people become better prepared for emergencies. As his website explains, "Whether you are new to the concept or have lived your whole like on a farm, we have something to help you improve your knowledge, build your skills, or equip you in times of need."[535] Douglas says that, for him, prepping has been a way of life since he was a kid. He recalls that, with his dad in the military, "We always had MREs on hand." He always knew that those meals-ready-to-eat were an option for food in an emergency. He also credits his penchant for being prepared to his background growing up as a Boy Scout. But not everyone is born into a family of preppers; some people make a conscious choice as adults to embark on the journey toward prepping. And it is often not as easy a journey as that sentence makes it sound.

People whose eyes are suddenly opened to reasons to be prepared—whether through witnessing natural disasters or through coming to an understanding about the potential consequences of world events — are challenged with overcoming "normalcy bias." Normalcy bias is a mental state where people assume that because something has never happened to them before, it never will. It influences them to adopt the most positive outlook possible in interpreting signs of danger in order to support their underlying belief that everything will always be OK. Once they have gotten past their normalcy bias, people often experience emotions similar to those in the Kübler-Ross five stages of grief. In the Kübler-Ross model, there are: [536]

1. Denial and isolation
2. Anger
3. Bargaining
4. Depression
5. Acceptance

For newly awakened preppers, there are:

1. Denial and isolation
2. Anger
3. Depression
4. Acceptance
5. Movement toward action

New preppers may continue to struggle with the idea that something bad *could* happen, regardless of the scale of the threat under consideration. They often feel isolated when those close to them, still enveloped in normalcy bias, refuse to discuss their concerns about what could happen, and become angry when those in their support network refuse to help them with preparedness plans. They can become depressed thinking about the possible outcomes of threatening situations, and feel daunted by the seemingly steep learning curve they face if they've made no emergency plans at all. But when they finally accept what could happen, they are apt to turn from "normalcy bias" to the Wall Street adage: "Past performance is no guarantee of future results." They become moved to act to protect themselves and their families, and they tend to seek out like-minded people for help.

That action can lead to a lifestyle change, a change which Rawles says can mean "giving up a lot." In pursuit of preparedness and self-sufficiency, he and his family live somewhere in what Rawles calls the "American Redoubt," in the mountain states of the Pacific Northwest, where they keep what he likes to call a "low profile," and are prepared to live totally off-grid, if need be. In addition to writing books, maintaining his blog, and offering advice on retreat locations, Rawles spends his time with his family, maintaining a large garden, hunting game, raising livestock, and keeping predators away from those livestock. He has on hand a supply of food to last nearly three years.

Becoming a prepper is more than stocking up on beans, bullets, and Band-Aids. It takes a commitment to planning; it can mean a change to a more frugal way of thinking, as finances become reallocated to support preparedness efforts. It can mean spending more time on self-education, not only about preparedness in general, but also in specific skills needed to become more self-sufficient.

Philosophies of Modern Prepping

People in the preparedness movement usually find themselves guided by certain underlying principles. Some leaders in the prepper community explicitly express their beliefs as a philosophy; others sprinkle them throughout the "getting started" information they offer to would-be preppers in their educational materials.

Bishop has developed what she calls the "Ten Principles of Preparedness©," which guide her own preparedness efforts and are reflected in what she writes and teaches.[537] In priority order, they are:

1. *Spiritual preparedness*
2. *Mental preparedness*
3. *Physical preparedness*
4. *Medical preparedness*
5. *Clothing/Shelter preparedness*
6. *Fuel preparedness*
7. *Water preparedness*
8. *Food preparedness*
9. *Financial preparedness*
10. *Communication preparedness*

The first four, which she considers to be most important, are often overlooked by people concerned only with beefing up their supplies of food, water, and ammunition. Bishop says that key to any life of preparedness is first being connected to one's core convictions. As she explains on her website:

> "No matter how physically prepared a person is with know-how, supplies, strategies and tactical maneuvers, there will ALWAYS be a challenge thrown at us that simply cannot be fixed with 'things.' Being tied in to one's core values and beliefs will often be the only thing that can get a person through tough times."

Second, she says, is mental preparedness, without which people may lack the know-how and "mental fortitude" to use what's in their preparedness tool kit. Similarly, without being physically prepared (#3), people may be unable to perform the tasks required of them in an emergency situation. Her Principle #4 emphasizes taking charge of one's health. She says:

> "We simply cannot be independent and free to act if we are completely at the mercy of economy, misinformation, etc., for our health."

Spirko has also organized his core philosophy into ten core values that are evident in the things he says and does:[538]

1. *Everything you do to prepare for emergencies, disasters or economic turmoil should be blended into your life in a way that improves your life even if nothing disastrous ever occurs.*
2. *Debt is financial cancer! Minimize it, pay it off early and stay away from credit cards.*
3. *Growing your own food is for everyone .... To produce ... as little as 10 percent of what you use reduces your dependence on "the system."*
4. *Tax is theft; the best way to combat it is to understand every legal deduction you can take or create. ... Every dollar you keep can be used to improve your self-sufficiency; every dollar taken from you can be used to make your dependence on the government stronger.*
5. *Food stored is an exceptional investment.*
6. *Plan for disaster in the following order of priority – Personal-Localized-Regional-State-National-Global. ...the most probable "disaster" for any individual is personal.*
7. *The best way to promote "green energy" is via economics – renewable energy is great if you do it in a way that saves you money.*
8. *Owning land is true wealth.*

184

9. *Use common-sense methods of hedging against "disaster." Pragmatic things like cash emergency funds, good insurance, and secondary income streams ... can make your life a lot less miserable when something goes wrong.*
10. *The biggest thing you can do is understand that you are in control of your life and that what you do matters.*

Rawles says he falls into the "guns-and-groceries" camp of survivalism. His prepping philosophy is simple: prepare for the basics. He says, "Even someone on a limited budget can start by stocking food and getting a means to filter water." His basics also include self-defense. He says, "I think it's naïve for people to think that they might not have to defend themselves. I look at firearms like any other tool — it's a device that has no volition of its own; it can be used for good or evil; its use is entirely up to its owner."

The American Preppers Network emphasizes "self-reliance through increased personal responsibility."[539] They advocate:

- *"It is up to you to provide for you and your family in difficult times."*
- *"First and foremost to being a prepper is a mental attitude – that of 'I am responsible for me'."*
- A prepper is *"an independent citizen capable of supporting themselves."*
- *"Preppers are 'ready for anything'."*

Just as personal responsibility is a common element in modern prepper philosophy, so is political awareness. Whether prepper political views lean left or right—and both are present in the prepper community—preppers all seem to be keenly aware of the geopolitical climate in the world at any given time, and how those could play out in terms of threats to the country, or even the U.S. Constitution.

Assessing what percentage of preppers are conservatives and what percentage are liberals may be as futile as counting grains of sand on the beach, since part of being responsibly prepared—and part of the unwritten prepper "code of behavior"—means keeping your preparations to yourself. It's unlikely that preppers will ever participate in a survey to help anyone determine how many of them there actually are, or what their views are on politics and the world. However, "chatter" on prepper websites and blogs makes it clear that, regardless of their political leanings, most preppers are strong supporters of the Second Amendment, which protects the rights of citizens to bear arms. This has undoubtedly been responsible for the tendency among those who are uninitiated to label all preppers as "right-wing survivalists." Among the general public, there is a lack of understanding about why gun rights are so significant to so many, beyond being free to hunt animals for survival. In a nutshell, there are three *other* reasons why the right to bear arms is so important to preppers:

- For self-defense
- To act in defense of the country in the event of an enemy attack
- Resistance to oppression by the government

The Influence of Technology

One important thing that has changed since back-to-the-landers first made their appearance in the '60s is the speed with which advances in technology have taken place and the scale of change that those advances have brought. Technology has become both a blessing and a curse. Besides the conveniences given to us by modern appliances and tools, and the ever-advancing communications capabilities that have made us increasingly aware of the goings-on in the world around us, technology has also created an interconnected world with vulnerabilities that never before existed, such as cyber warfare, espionage, and threats to our computer-controlled infrastructure.

Internet Communities

The interconnectedness afforded by the Internet has created a medium in which the modern prepper community has grown, thrived, and matured. Rawles said he's witnessed this phenomenon himself. "It wasn't until the advent of the worldwide Web that prepping caught on with great popularity," he said, noting that in 2005, when he started SurvivalBlog.com, there were "only a couple thousand blogs on preparedness in existence." That number seems to have increased exponentially.

People who identify themselves as preppers can seek out—and find—many like-minded individuals in online Internet forums, where they can discuss their concerns about what the future might hold and share ideas and plans.

Preppers today are hungry to educate themselves in basic skills that have been lost to modern living, and often turn to the Internet for help. They are also eager to help educate others about things they've learned; some use YouTube to share information on everything from food storage to building raised garden beds and getting started in prepping. In fact, many prepper websites are dedicated to educating people about being prepared. The American Preppers Network for example, has as its motto "Freedom Through Teaching Others Self-Reliance." The motto of Spirko's Survival Podcast is "To help you live a better life, if times get tough, or even if they don't." Bishop's Preparedness Pro website is "devoted to providing guidance and encouragement for peaceful preparedness."[540]

The advent of blogging — where anybody can set up an online presence and offer their own unique views of the world — has helped challenge traditional explanations about national and world events and has stirred online conversations about what they could mean. Most prepper websites have a blog component; most also offer lists of resources and information to help would-be preppers get started and to help seasoned preppers take things to the next level.

However, the ease with which websites and blogs can be set up allows people to present themselves as knowledgeable experts whether they really are or not. A contributor to Rawles' SurvivalBlog website, "Allen C.," lamented this in his essay "Why I Hate Preppers" in 2012:[541]

> *"If there is only one ill consequence of the prepper movement it is the avalanche of inexperienced people giving advice in user groups when their only qualification is that they read something similar elsewhere on the 'net."*

Some website hosts rely on the experts, rather than simply passing on information they've come across themselves. People tuning in to Spirko's Survival Podcast might find Spirko and his authoritative guests discussing such diverse topics as the economy, solar energy, small-scale farming, survival gardening, food storage, wilderness survival, personal liberty, homesteading, preparing for natural disasters, and understanding caliber and ballistics.[542]

The American Preppers Network contains an assortment of articles and blog posts about current events and reasons to be prepared, and offers a number of resources for not only getting started in prepping, but also for living sustainably (e.g., homesteading, food and health, energy); survival (bugging out, emergency medical, firearms, fishing, and foraging); and overall preparedness considerations (family, financial, and general).[543]

Rawles' website offers a wealth of information and commentary by many contributors about current events as they could bear on preparedness, along with an abundance of ideas and information for every level of prepper. A sampling of the subjects discussed on the site includes:[544]

- Disaster Preparedness
- Self-Sufficiency
- Contrarian Investing
- Survival Logistics
- Survival Tools and Firearms
- Hunting, Fishing, and Trapping
- Survival Retreat Locales
- Photovoltaic and Other Off-Grid Power
- Communications
- Bartering and the Alpha Strategy
- Restoration and Modification of Survival Vehicles
- Fuel Storage and Alternative Fuels
- Marksmanship
- Emerging Threats

Some blogs and websites concentrate more on discussing *why* people might want to prepare, rather than on the various aspects of prepping. They report on and discuss national and world events that could bring an end to life as we know it—*not* an apocalypse, but threats to our freedom, our finances, or our health. These sites often also include preparedness information for anyone moved to act after taking in the information they offer.

As an example, Alex Jones hosts a nationally syndicated talk show on his website, www.infowars.com. He offers his show as an "alternative news" source covering events that "mainstream news" outlets may not cover or may choose to "gloss over." He has been labeled a "conspiracy theorist" for presenting interpretations of world events that don't fit the descriptions presented by more traditional news broadcasts. One such report relates to the aftermath of the 2011 earthquake in Japan that resulted in a catastrophic failure at the Fukushima nuclear plant. In late 2013, as health officials in California tried to minimize to the media the potential impact of debris from the meltdown that was showing up on West Coast shores, Jones' reporting emphasized the extremely elevated levels of radiation showing up in that debris, and also highlighted a story that received little, if any, attention from major media outlets: that seventy-one U.S. sailors had been stricken with a number of different cancers very soon after helping with relief operations at the Fukushima plant.[545]

Some websites are dedicated to specific topics of concern. Author, lawyer, and financial expert Michael Snyder, for instance, hosts a website that covers all things related to a potential collapse of the U.S. economy, an event that has been predicted by many in the financial world—and the prepping community. His site offers in-depth information and analysis on what he considers to be signs of such a collapse, as well as links to sites offering supplies for anyone hoping to ride it out.[546] Author and legal expert Mark Levin hosts a podcast where he discusses and analyzes concerns about abuses of big government and the erosion of American liberties.[547]

On Steroids: Foresight and Hindsight

Besides connecting people via the Internet, technology has offered immeasurable improvements in the areas of meteorology, astronomy, and other branches of science, providing the ability to forecast significant natural events well in advance, and giving people more warning about them than ever before.

Weather forecasters can see blizzards coming days in advance, and can predict snowfall inches by area—and by hour. Using computer modeling, they can correlate ocean tides with oncoming tempests and can predict the resultant flooding—by location and scale.

Geologists can monitor activity deep beneath the surface of the earth and can predict earthquakes and volcanic eruptions, although not yet with the advance warning or precision they would like. However, with the pace at which technology changes, it seems that's only a matter of time. (Meanwhile, some of the things they are discovering are things that many people might not really want to know about—like the massive caldera percolating under Yellowstone National Park which, if it erupts, could truly bring an end to life as we know it.[548]) Lacking an accurate means of predicting exactly when volcanoes will erupt, all scientists can do is offer assurances based on what the history about past volcanic activity has told them.

Besides giving us advance warning about disasters, technology has brought us the means to communicate about them almost instantaneously after they happen. Within hours of catastrophes striking almost anywhere in the world, graphic accounts about them can be found on television and online; up-close, 'round-the-clock coverage puts us in touch with the horrors they bring.

Gadgets and Gear

Thanks to advances in technology, modern preppers have available to them tools that weren't available to back-to-the-landers, such as "smart" cell phones, laptop computers, global-positioning systems, surveillance systems, and sophisticated weapons for self-defense. Not all of these tools would be first in a bug-out bag designed for a short-term emergency, but many could be indispensable in long-term survival situations. Some of today's gadgets can keep electronics powered; there are also innovative non-electric tools that have been developed that could help in a disaster situation.

Advances in solar technology have led to the development of devices that would be useful in both short- and long-term disaster scenarios, among them:

- solar-powered/hand-crank emergency radios and flashlights
- solar-powered chargers for batteries and small electronics
- solar-powered water pump
- solar-powered generator

In the category of non-electronic preparedness aids are:

- Paracord bracelet—a popular bracelet made of up to 20 feet of woven, heavy-duty parachute cord, which can be unwound

190

and used in survival situations for things like securing equipment, making a temporary outdoor shelter, making snares to trap small animals, or primitive nets to catch fish

- Portable water filtration systems — including one in the form of a simple straw
- Folding firebox camp stove — as small as 5 inches square, it can be used as a stove and grill plate
- BioLite Camp Stove — not only helps cook dinner, but also turns heat from the flame into electricity that can be used to power small electronics by way of a USB port
- Rocket stove — a small type of cook stove that can be used for cooking and heating, featuring a high-temperature, high-efficiency combustion chamber fueled by small pieces of wood

However, seasoned preppers will usually tell you that skills trump gadgets.

Reskilling

Modern preppers are mindful that preparedness requires certain skills, whether they are planning for emergencies of short- or long-term duration. People forced out of their homes by natural disasters may need basic camping and survival skills if they have no shelter immediately available to them: setting up a tent or makeshift shelter, starting a fire, finding and purifying water. Even people "sheltering in" after a disaster must at least know how to find and purify water, should their stored supply run out.

Most preppers give self-education a high priority in their preparedness planning, turning not only to the Internet for information, but also to magazines, bookstores, and their local libraries. Many are drawn to the growing number of prepper-related conferences and expos in the country, such as Douglas' Self-Reliance Expo; the National Preppers & Survivalists Expo; the International Disaster Conference & Expo; the Life Changes, Be Ready Preparedness and Gun Expo; and the Berryville (Virginia) Gun and Prepper Expo, to name a few.

Some preppers seek out workshops or seminars devoted to specific skills they want to develop, such as those related to food production, self-defense, or basic survival. They may take advantage of local evening adult-ed programs on topics like electronics or welding, and enroll in local first-aid courses.

Realizing the demand for self-education, some prepper websites have taken to presenting online conferences, such as the "Survival Summit" conference offered in late January 2014, sponsored by the American Preppers Network. The Survival Summit featured a number of experts offering information on many diverse topics, including this sampling:[549]

- *How to Think Clearly in Life-or-Death Scenarios, by Travis Haley*
- *How to Grow Your Own Food, Without Irrigation, by Paul Wheaton*
- *Locating the Perfect Survival Retreat or Homestead, by Marjory Wildcraft*
- *Top 10 Off-the-Grid Cooking Solutions in a World Without Power, by Tess Pennington*
- *How to Survive A Nuclear Event & the Spreading Fallout, by Dr. James Hubbard*
- *How to Make Your Own Biodiesel When the Fuel Pumps Stop Working, by Graydon Blair*
- *Off-the-Grid Food Preservation Techniques, by Lisa Lynn*
- *Urban Foraging: How to Search a City for All the Food & Medicine You'd Ever Need, by Nicole Telkes*
- *Fortifying Your Home & Property Against Looters, by Jim Cobb*
- *Top 5 Bug-Out Mistakes Everyone Makes – and How NOT to Fall Victim to Them, by Jeff Anderson*
- *Trapping Strategies for Harvesting Creeks, Streams & Woodlands for All the Wild Game You Can Eat, by Bruce 'Buckshot' Hemming*
- *How to Treat Burns, Breaks, & Traumatic Injuries When the Paramedics Aren't Coming, by David Pruett*
- *47 Tips, Tricks, & Inventions for Developing an Off-Grid Water & Energy Plan, by Scott Hunt*

According to the organizers, more than 50,000 people tuned in.

Rediscovering Lost Arts

For many of those preparing to hunker down for the duration, it doesn't take long to realize that they are missing basic skills their great-grandparents had, skills that "back then" were basic to survival. And it becomes evident that maintaining good health and physical condition are key to even being able to perform some of the associated tasks, since they are heavily dependent on manual effort.

While "lost arts" can be a broad category, the lost arts sought out and valued by many preppers are those that could help them become less dependent on the trappings of modern society.

There was a time in our history when people did not have massive grocery stores to turn to when their food supplies were low. People once grew and preserved their own food; some fished and hunted for meat. There was a time when not everyone had cars to speed the trip out for supplies; most relied on horses, or their own two feet. There was a time when people built or made the things they needed. There was a time when people fixed things that broke themselves and made creative use of everything they owned. ("Use it up, wear it out, make it do, or do without.")

We all know the early history of our country, which started when a small group of Pilgrims braved an ocean voyage with only the clothes on their backs and few other possessions, and set up a primitive community on the shores of Plymouth Harbor. We're familiar with stories of the early Native Americans, who already knew something about living sustainably off the land and taught some of those skills to the newcomers. We know the history of pioneers who ventured west into the wilderness to explore and seek their fortunes, sustaining themselves with what they could find wherever they were. We know about the early cattlemen and sodbusters who made their living off the land in the Midwest.

Thinking through the details of what the day-to-day lives of our forebears must have been like begs the question: could *we* do that today if we had to? Today's preppers don't aspire to living lives of hardship, but follow the adage "Hope for the best; prepare for the worst." And with this in mind, many of them seek out opportunities to acquire some of the skills that were second nature to our ancestors, such as growing, preparing, and preserving food; in some cases, they even seek out antique tools to help.

While growing food may sound simple enough on the surface, a closer look reveals that gardening as our forebears did requires specific knowledge and tools to till, irrigate, fertilize, and harvest crops, using little or no electricity or machinery — skills that would be essential in a long-term "grid-down" scenario that is a concern for many. It means knowing how to save seeds from current crops to use in next year's planting, and knowing when and how to plant them. Keeping crops healthy means knowing something about things like pest management and companion planting.

Similarly, raising livestock requires skills that are not commonly practiced today — at least, by most of us. Raising livestock sustainably means being able to do it with little or no inputs from the outside, such as the feed store; raising poultry means knowing how to replenish the flock without relying on a hatchery. Growing feed for livestock means knowing how much is needed, what to grow, how to grow it, when and how to harvest it, and how to store it. Ultimately, raising livestock also means knowing how — and being willing — to slaughter animals, as well as knowing how to process and preserve the meat for the family dinner table.

Besides gardening and raising livestock, many of the so-called lost arts are, in fact, related to food and food production, such as:

- Sourcing food: hunting, trapping and fishing, and for those living in northern climates, maple sugaring
- Food preservation: canning, dehydrating, fermenting, smoking, root-cellaring
- Food preparation (e.g., bread-making, cheese-making, beer- and wine-making, grain-grinding)
- Bee-keeping

Those seeking to become self-reliant in maintaining their health may look to develop skills in the "lost art" of herbalism, which has now become a popular modality in the field of modern alternative medicine.

Skills in the fiber arts may be important for some people. For example, those who raise animals for meat and fiber may need to know about carding and spinning animal fibers, weaving, knitting, and crocheting. Some people may seek out skills in creating cording, rope, and even matting from plant material. Other "lost arts" might include the skills needed to manage a small wood lot — tree identification and growth habits, tree pruning, chainsaw (or manual saw) operation, and wood-splitting — or how to manage an orchard.

194

One important skill that some might consider a "lost art" is basic creative thinking. No one can prepare for absolutely every eventuality. It takes creative thinking to develop solutions for each unique situation — to do what you can, where you are, with what you have available.

Applying New Techniques and Learning from the Experts

The modern era has ushered in new techniques and equipment that offer improvements to homesteading-related practices, and experts have emerged to guide and lead the way.

On Beyond Agriculture

While the basic requirements of growing food haven't changed much since our forefathers did it, the modern era has ushered in new techniques and equipment that offer improvements to the process.

For example, permaculture, which first made an appearance in the 1970s, has now become a popular field of study, not only for practices designed to improve the sustainability of food production, but also for principles that can be broadly applied to help create permanent, sustainable communities:[550]

1. *Observe and interact*
2. *Catch and store energy*
3. *Obtain a yield*
4. *Apply self-regulation and accept feedback*
5. *Use and value renewable resources and services*
6. *Produce no waste*
7. *Design from patterns to details*
8. *Integrate rather than segregate*
9. *Use small and slow solutions*
10. *Use and value diversity*
11. *Use edges and value the marginal*
12. *Creatively use and respond to change*

Permaculture has become a popular topic on prepper websites and in prepper YouTube videos. Spirko himself has become an advocate and teacher of permaculture practices and principles, because he believes that "producing your own food and supporting local agriculture are critical to insuring ... personal independence."[551] He has used his three-acre homestead in Texas to showcase permaculture techniques such as using swales to help with irrigation and building hugelkultur garden beds, and has hosted a number of design workshops on his property, including one for designing urban gardens.

Spirko has created a number of educational DVDs and YouTube videos on the subject, and in 2013 was a guest speaker at the Permaculture Voices Conference in Temecula, California. According to his conference bio, one of Spirko's primary goals with respect to permaculture is to ensure that "it gains broader mainstream appeal and is adopted by many individuals who are not generally thought of as permaculture's target audience."[552]

Permaculture has had a prominent role among the discussion topics on Spirko's podcasts, which often feature guests who are experts in the field. Among his guests have been two well-respected permaculture authorities, Geoff Lawton and Paul Wheaton.

Lawton, who received a degree in Permaculture Design in 1995, is founder of the Australian Permaculture Research Institute.[553][554] He has taught and consulted with thousands of individuals and organizations all over the world and has implemented permaculture designs in seventeen countries. He was involved early on with the Transition Town movement in the UK, which came to rely heavily on permaculture principles. Now he is a popular figure in the prepper movement, a much-sought-after guest on programs like Spirko's. (He has consulted with Spirko on designing permaculture systems for his homestead.) His writings and videos are referenced on many prepper-related websites.

Wheaton, whose interest in gardening started in the early 1990s, took a master gardener class at the University of Montana in 1996, and quickly became one of the most knowledgeable people in the country about permaculture.[555] Lawton has called him the "Duke of Permaculture."[556] Wheaton has made a number of guest appearances on prepper-related radio programs and podcasts, on places such as the Prepper Broadcasting Network and Be Prepared Radio. According to Wheaton, permaculture promotes sustainability because it is all about creating symbiotic relationships with nature and letting nature do the

196

work, whether you're talking about vegetable gardening, raising livestock, or growing lawn.

Other techniques that have gained popularity in the prepping community, by way of the local foods movement, include hydroponics and vertical gardening, which offer food-growing options for people living in close quarters in urban areas—even apartment-dwellers.

Saving It for Later

In the world of food preservation, canning is another "old" skill that is coming back into vogue—not only in the prepper community, but also in the general population. University extension programs in at least a dozen states even offer "master food preserver" courses where people can learn everything they need to know to be successful at canning or otherwise preserving foods, using research-based methods approved by the USDA. For example, a program offered at the University of Maine features lectures on:[557]

- The latest information on food safety and food preservation
- Prevention of foodborne illness
- Food storage and safety
- Canning basics
- Canning acid foods
- Canning low-acid foods
- Pickled and fermented foods
- Preserving jams and jellies
- Freezing foods
- Drying food products

In Utah, home to the Mormon Church, which is a big advocate of "putting by" for the future, Utah State University offers a Master Food Preservers program that includes:[558]

- Economics and safety of preserved foods
- Canning fruits
- Canning tomatoes and tomato products
- Canning low-acid foods
- Canning meats
- Making jams and jellies

- Preserving foods through freezing
- Preserving foods through dehydration
- How to teach and demonstrate techniques

There are also food-preservation courses available online, such as the self-study program offered by the National Center for Home Food Preservation.[559]

For anyone, these skills offer a means to "eat local" all year long, and can be an economical way to stock the pantry with high-quality foods. For preppers, the additional appeal of skills such as canning, pickling, and drying is that these processes can keep foods in their preserved states for a very long time — even when the lights go out.

Food preservation and preparation have featured prominently in Bishop's work on the Preparedness Pro website and in her YouTube videos. She is a big proponent of canning — just about anything and everything — and offers myriad examples, all well researched, on how to do it. And equally important, she provides a wealth of information on how to cook with "shelf-stable" foods.

Backwoods Home Magazine writer Jackie Clay-Atkinson, popular in homesteading and prepping circles and known to some as a "canning goddess," writes frequently in the magazine and on her blog about food preservation — from canning to dehydrating, fermentation, and curing meat — and has published a number of books on the subject. Her cookbooks offer ideas on how to cook using home-preserved, shelf-stable foods from the pantry. A homesteader living in the remote reaches of Minnesota, Clay-Atkinson has been known to can everything from wild plums to moose meat.

There is an abundance of food preservation instruction available on the Internet, including many videos on YouTube, although it bears repeating that just because someone posts something on the Internet, it doesn't mean they're an expert. It pays to understand the basic USDA food-preservation safety guidelines, in order to know which videos or online articles are offering valid information and which are not.

Some of the instructional videos on YouTube and prepper websites provide information on how to use food preservation/preparation tools that were unavailable to our great-grandparents, including:

- pressure cookers with safety valves
- electric dehydrators
- solar kettles and ovens
- reusable canning lids ("Tattler" brand)
- steam juicers
- Vacuum-sealing appliances (e.g. "FoodSaver")

Preppers seeking to build a stock of food supplies must learn to follow the adage, "eat what you store, store what you eat," which requires certain skills in planning and inventorying, including FIFO — "first in, first out." Some prepper-oriented businesses offer food storage systems designed to make food rotation easy.

Thanks to some of today's innovations, anyone seeking to preserve their own food and set aside stores of food for their family's security can come to the tasks armed with everything they need for success.

Who ARE These People?

Contrary to the idea that preppers are "fringe extremists," preppers today come from all walks of life and every sector of society. Myriad news outlets have picked up the story of the rising prepper phenomenon and confirm, along with information found in online prepper forums, that the prepper community is made up of people from diverse backgrounds that include military veterans, suburban housewives, business professionals, writers, doctors, lawyers, corporate executives, and anyone anywhere who has lived through a disaster. Rawles says that a lot of the clients he consults for about survival retreats are mostly wealthy people like doctors and lawyers — those who can afford his $100 per hour consulting fee. And, he says, his consulting work has been "steady."

Roman Zrazhevskiy, cofounder of ReadyToGoSurvival.com, confirms that there are moneyed people in the prepping community, noting that a number of his customers are "big Wall Street brokers with brownstones on Park Avenue" — people who can afford the $400 to $700 price tags on his company's custom bug-out bags.

Assessing the makeup of the prepper population, Rawles says there is no "typical prepper," but he does see that the average population has changed. He says that, ten to fifteen years ago, the average reader of his blog was a white, conservative, Christian male. Now, however, he says the movement has "broadened considerably." However, he believes that most Americans who have ever worked in Emergency Services Management are preppers. In fact, he says, "EMS personnel are part of the core of the prepper movement"—along with military veterans, who, he says, "have witnessed destroyed infrastructure in places like Afghanistan, and recognize how vulnerable our society is."

Rawles says prepping crosses all lines—"socially, economically, politically, and religiously." Prepping has even drawn adherents from the political community itself. Former Republican Congressman Roscoe Bartlett of Maryland who, during his time on Capitol Hill became acutely aware of the vulnerability of the country's electric grid, literally headed for the hills after his retirement, settling into an off-grid, self-sufficient lifestyle in the mountains of West Virginia.[560] [561]

Rawles notes that there are "a few radical racists and yahoos out there" in the preparedness community, but adds, "What I love about prepping is people setting aside their differences to share information."

Ron Douglas, of the Self-Reliance Expo, says, "Preppers come in all shapes and sizes, with different reasons for prepping and different mindsets. There's no 'common political mindset.'" He says that customers of his Expos have included "hippies with dreadlocks, guys all camo'd out, and mothers pushing strollers"—all taking in the same Expo presentations.

Douglas says there is a wide spectrum of preppers, and that "average" preppers are those who "have a little food stored, and maybe a gun." More advanced preppers, he says, might have a year's supply of food stored. And, he says, "Extreme preppers won't show up at an Expo because they're afraid someone from the government's there taking pictures of them."

Tom Martin, of the American Preppers Network, says that people are being drawn to the preparedness movement "for varied reasons," and bring with them a broad spectrum of philosophies. "We've got people on the left, on the right, and everything in the middle," he says. "We've got people preparing for things as simple as a job loss to people preparing for natural disasters and economic disasters. ... Anything and everything."

Part Two:

A Look at Modern Preppers

Chapter Six: What Are People Preparing For?

Given the number of people that have become converts to preparedness in recent years and the preponderance of websites and books on the subject, one has to wonder: what are they preparing *for?*

Many people are simply looking to mitigate disruptions to their lives in the face of *any* likely disaster — "the end of the world as we know it" (TEOTWAWKI). And that could mean different things to different people. For example, the end of one person's world-as-they-know-it could be a job loss; for someone else, it could be dealing with inflation while living on a fixed income. As Self-Reliance Expo's Ron Douglas says, "Everybody has their own personal doomsday."

Asked what he thinks people are most concerned about today, Brandon Garrett, of Ready to Go Survival, said, "Sometimes that depends on where they live — what threats are imminent." He added, "While different threats are more common in particular parts of the country, there are some things that affect us all — things like economic downturns, droughts, and more."

Mike Peters, owner of The Ultimate Bunker, said he thinks people are preparing for a grid-down situation, civil unrest, and collapse of the government.

Roman Zrazhevskiy of Ready to go Survival said the biggest concern his customers seem to have are financial collapse and perpetual war. "Financial experts agree it's time to prep," he said.

The most obvious things most people prepare for are the hazards FEMA warns people about — "instant disasters" that could force people out of their homes, such as:

- Extreme storms—hurricanes, blizzards, tornadoes
- Natural disasters—landslides, earthquakes, volcanoes, tsunamis
- Fire
- Flooding
- Hazardous waste spills
- Nuclear accidents

Add to those, disasters that are more insidious and intense, which FEMA also cautions about:

- Pandemics
- "Space weather"—solar storms that could disrupt critical infrastructure on Earth
- Terrorist attacks—explosions, biological or chemical attacks, cyber attacks against critical systems, "dirty bomb" attacks, assaults on the U.S. power grid, or an EMP attack

Then there are perils FEMA does not warn about, which are, nevertheless, concerns for many:

- Partial or complete collapse of the U.S. economy
- Food shortages
- Fuel shortages
- Disruptions to the food supply chain
- Civil disorder
- Gradual breakdown of the nation's infrastructure—roads, dams, bridges, etc.
- "Black Swan" events—things that are random, completely unexpected and unpredictable, that have a significant impact
- Global warfare
- A tyrannical government

In reviewing the long list of possible threats, it becomes apparent that no one can prepare for *everything*. So preppers have to apply some risk-management thinking to determine which things on the list are most likely to affect *them*, in their own personal circumstances, and develop their preparedness plans accordingly.

However, there are threats on this list that may not be specific to a particular location and may be entirely unpredictable, making them more frightening than a powerful massive hurricane. This can result in some people being more focused than one might expect on particular disaster scenarios, a focus that many people view with disdain. It is this singularity of focus—which is featured on programs like National Geographic's "Doomsday Preppers"—that causes some people to roll their eyes when they hear the word 'prepper' and offer up a typical reply: "Oh, I choose not to live my life like *that*!"

Kellene Bishop says, "The idea of a 'potential threat' is laughable. I don't do things out of fear of what could happen."

Zrazhevskiy noted that his company isn't focused on a specific disaster scenario. "We offer a common-sense approach to prepping," he said, "to offer things to help people get through storms."

Ron Douglas is quick to point out that his Self-Reliance Expo doesn't promote "fear-based thinking." "We promote a lifestyle," he says. "We don't worry about doomsday."

That actually seems to be the predominant way of the thinking in the prepper community. A common motto found on prepper websites is: "Prepared, not scared."

Nevertheless, while most preppers seem focused on preparedness as a way of life rather than as protection against some specific hazard, there *are* certain events that consistently appear on prepper websites, in prepper forums, and in prepper fiction as things worthy of being prepared for.

Collapse of the Grid

The topic that seems to be of greatest concern to many is the collapse of the country's power grid. James Wesley Rawles, who sees electricity as the "lynchpin" of society, says that the biggest threats today are "anything that causes the grid to go down, such as solar flares, economic collapse, or global war." He adds, "For most Americans, if the power went out, they wouldn't know how to go back to primitive living, because they've never experienced it." In his view, the U.S. and Canada are "not as prepared as Third World countries; they're not used to regular privation."

Events in recent news reports have heightened fears about a grid-down possibility. In February 2014, the *Wall Street Journal* reported about an attack on a California power station that had taken place in April of 2013. According to the report, intruders cut telephone cables in an underground vault and subsequently opened fire on the facility, knocking out seventeen transformers during the 19-minute small arms attack, and causing $16 million in damage.[562] The plant was shut down for two months while repairs were made. According to the article, former chairman of the Federal Energy Regulatory Commission, Jon Wellinghoff, called the attack "the most significant incident of domestic terrorism involving the U.S. power grid that has ever occurred," although the FBI said it doesn't believe the incident was a terrorist attack. No one has been charged or arrested for the attack, leading Wellinghoff and others to fear that this was a test attack, and that plans for a larger attack could be in the making.

But a direct assault on power plants is not the only method by which terrorists could cause the grid to go dark. Other possibilities include attacks from cyber space and outer space.

Space-Age Stalkers

GlobalSecurity.org, a website dedicated to reporting news in the fields of "defense, space, intelligence, WMD, and homeland security,"[563] said in an October 2013 report that "electric companies are witnessing an unprecedented rise in cyber-attacks against their industrial control systems (ICS) and supervisory control and acquisition systems (SCADA) that monitor and regulate power grids."

Amid growing concerns about the vulnerability of the U.S. power grid, industry and federal agencies conducted a simulated cyber attack on the grid in November 2013. In an account by *The New York Times*, a team of experts battled an "unseen 'enemy' who tried to turn out the lights across America."[564] As the "dry run" for the real thing progressed, participants learned where the grid's weaknesses lay, as they watched the simulation of tens of millions of Americans being plunged into darkness. Hundreds of transmission lines and transformers were declared "damaged or destroyed"; there were 150 "casualties." The *Times* report said that the drill also included simulated "denial of service" attacks, in which the Internet was brought down by being overloaded with a flood of messages. According to the report, these are attacks that have actually been experienced by banks and other companies in the U.S.

However, concerns about the susceptibility of the power grid to attack were being discussed at the federal government level as far back as 2001, when the U.S. Congress, keenly aware of the potential effects of an EMP attack on grid, authorized the Department of Defense to commission a study of the EMP threat.

The EMP Commission was made up of a bipartisan panel of experts and was chaired by Dr. William R. Graham, the foremost EMP expert in the United States. It included members with expertise in nuclear weapons, technology, and military defense.[565] They, in turn, drew on the further expertise of leaders in industry and the scientific and intelligence communities.[566]

Surprising those who believed that nuclear weapons of this caliber were out of reach for terrorists and small countries who didn't have the money or technical expertise to pursue them, the commission concluded, among other things, that:

- "A determined adversary can achieve an EMP attack capability without having a high level of sophistication."[567]
- "An EMP attack is one way for a terrorist activity to use a small amount of nuclear weaponry … in an effort to produce a catastrophic impact on our society."[568]

The commission warned that certain types of relatively low-yield nuclear weapons could be used to generate "potentially catastrophic EMP effects over wide geographic areas," and claimed that "designs for variants of such weapons" had likely been trafficked illegally for at least twenty-five years.[569]

In its detailed, 181-page report, "Report of the Commission to Assess the Threat to the United States from Electromagnetic Pulse (EMP) Attack," the commission included many recommendations, among them:

- Operators of critical infrastructure systems should be trained to determine that an EMP attack has taken place.[570]
- An EMP event notification system should be developed.[571]

- Preventative measures should be taken to protect critical systems.

However, the report was released the same day as the report from the 9/11 Commission, and with the country still reeling from the horrific attacks of 9/11 and hungry to know how those attacks could have happened, the report about the threat from EMPs gained little attention from the public or Congress.[572] It did not go entirely unnoticed, though, and found its way into online discussion forums on prepper websites and into popular literature.

One of the most notable books on the subject is the novel *One Second After*, by William R. Forstchen, published in 2009. Forstchen's book about a man and his family in North Carolina struggling to survive after an EMP attack quickly made the *New York Times* best-seller list and remains among the top-selling books on Amazon.com. Before it was even released, it was cited on the floor of Congress as a book "all Americans should read."[573]

Former Speaker of the House Newt Gingrich, who has worked to educate people about the EMP threat since the release of the commission's report, wrote the forward to Forstchen's book. In it, he says:

> *"Few have talked about, let alone heard about, the terrible, in fact overwhelming, threat of EMP…Few in our government and in the public sector have openly confronted the threat offered by the use of but one nuclear weapon, in the hands of a determined enemy, who calibrates it to trigger a massive EMP burst. Such an event would destroy our complex, delicate high-tech society in an instant and throw all of our lives back to an existence equal to that of the Middle Ages."*[574]

In August 2010, EMP Commissioner Michael Frankel testified before Congress that, although the Commission had provided 75 unclassified recommendations, most aimed at the Department of Homeland Security, there had been no response out of DHS. He said, "The Commission's recommendations seem to have simply languished."[575]

Writing in the Afterword of *One Second After*, U.S. Navy Captain William D. Sanders says:

206

"One second after an EMP attack, it will be too late to ask two simple questions: what should we have done to prevent the attack, and why didn't we do it?"

Is the concern about a manmade EMP overstated? R. James Woolsey, former head of the Central Intelligence Agency under President Bill Clinton, wrote in a May 2013 *Wall Street Journal* article about the growing threat of an EMP attack from North Korea, and even suggested that the United States preemptively strike the country's nuclear facilities.[576] In November 2013, the National Intelligence Service in South Korea confirmed that North Korea was developing EMP weapons—aided by Russian technology that had been developed for that specific purpose.[577]

It was concern about the grid's vulnerability to an EMP attack that drove former Senator Roscoe Bartlett (R-Maryland) to retreat off-grid to a compound in the mountains of West Virginia after his retirement in 2013. Bartlett, a former research scientist and engineer whose resume includes work for NASA and the military, testified before Congress in 2009 about the vulnerability of the country's power grid to an electromagnetic pulse attack. He told those gathered about a conversation he'd had years earlier with members of Russia's legislative assembly, in which one of them bragged about how Russia could bring the U.S. to its knees, saying:

"We'd detonate a nuclear weapon high above your country, and shut down your power grid — and your communications — for six months or so."[578]

According to Bartlett, one of the other members present chimed in:

"If one weapon wouldn't do it, we have some spares. Like about 10,000."

While many preppers are focused on violent events—manmade or natural—that could bring down the power grid, some are aware of more subtle circumstances that could shut out the lights. Kellene Bishop notes, "Financial collapse would cause a massive power outage throughout the U.S. Power companies are living paycheck to paycheck. They're heavily leveraged in power purchase agreements. If those PPAs stopped on the open market, the companies would have no operating cash." And one by one, power companies would stop functioning.

207

Threats from Outer Space

Some experts believe a devastating solar storm is a more likely threat to the power grid than an EMP attack, and some say we're overdue for one. According to the authorities who pay attention to space weather, a significant solar storm can be expected to affect Earth about once every hundred years,[579] bringing with it the same effects as a manmade EMP. The last one was the 1859 Carrington Event. Scientists studying ice core samples have determined that the Carrington Event was the biggest solar storm in the last 500 years, more than twice the size of any other known storm of its kind. Experts say that if a Carrington-like event occurred today, it would "devastate the modern world."[580]

However, large-magnitude solar storms are not the only ones that can affect the Earth, and recognizing this, the U.S. government established the National Space Weather Program in 1994 (NSWP).[581] Since 2009, the NSWP has been convening forums of government officials and scientists to discuss space weather, its potential impact on our planet, and what measures can be taken to prevent or minimize its damage. The topics of discussion at the forum often include big solar events like the Carrington Event—and more recent solar storms, such as:[582]

- The March 1989 solar storm responsible for a power outage in Quebec that left 6 million people without power for nine hours
- Solar storms of Halloween 2003 that disabled instruments on Earth-orbiting satellites, causing permanent damage on some

But more conversation at the forum centers around smaller events which, according to the NSWP, happen all the time:

"The gaps between big events are not empty times of quiet. They are filled with lesser storms that can pose a threat to our increasingly high-tech society."[583]

Though not on the scale of an EMP-like event, smaller solar storms can wreak their own brand of havoc. Despite a low level of solar activity in 2012, many airlines were impacted by scheduling delays and increased fuel usage as the result of having to redirect air traffic out of the paths of solar bursts.

Speaking at the 2013 Space Weather Forum, NASA official Lika Guhathakurta said:

"Who needs an X-flare? …Small flares are powerful, too. They explode with as much energy as a billion atomic bombs dozens to hundreds of times every year. We feel their effects even when they don't make the news." [584]

Guhathakurta said that as our society becomes more reliant on high-tech devices, it is

"… increasingly vulnerable to solar storms, great and small."

While some states, such as Maine, have directed their public utilities to investigate measures to mitigate the effects of EMP attacks and space weather,[585] proposed federal legislation relating to protection of the entire national grid has languished in Congress and the Senate. The recently revealed April 2013 attack on the California power station has provoked renewed interest in taking action.

Collapse of the Economy

Running almost neck and neck with a grid outage as a concern for many preppers is a collapse of the U.S. economy, despite the optimistic outlook held by government officials. By 2013, the Great Recession was in the rear-view mirror, and key economic indicators seemed to support a positive view of the economy — unemployment was gradually declining, and the stock market continued to make impressive gains. But financiers and others paying close attention to the economy believed that the indicators masked what was really going on. One, billionaire Donald Trump, said in a December 2013 interview with *Money News* online that Americans should "prepare for financial ruin."[586] Trump said the then-official unemployment rate of 8.2 percent "isn't a real number," and asserted that the actual number was at least 15 percent and could be as high as 21 percent. He predicted that the national debt could soar above $21 trillion which, he said, was sure to lead to a downgrade in the U.S. credit rating.

Economist Robert Wiedemer takes an even dimmer view. He predicts "50 percent unemployment, a 90-percent stock market drop, and 100 percent annual inflation."[587] Goldman Sachs trader Terence Burnham, a professional money manager and former faculty member at the Harvard Business School, shares the view that another crash is "likely."[588] Burnham predicts an increase in interest rates, lower

209

spending, and more layoffs, and urges people to start saving at least 50 percent of their income.

The growing U.S. debt has sparked an increasing amount of conflict in Congress, with Republicans using what some would consider drastic measures to force the government to curb spending—including precipitating a two-week government shutdown in October 2013 and resisting pressure from Democrats to raise the debt ceiling.

Concerns about the ability of the U.S. government to pay its debts have prompted worries about a downgrade in the country's credit rating, which could have a ripple effect throughout the world and lead to the devaluation of the U.S. dollar.

Meanwhile, a top financial-threat advisor at the Pentagon, James Rickards, has warned that an "economic Pearl Harbor" is fast approaching the country.[589] Rickard warns that the U.S. economic system is vulnerable to "economic weapons of mass destruction," by countries "weaponizing complex investments such as derivatives and currencies, as well as commodities like oil and gold." He says America could see the collapse of its financial markets as well as "the end of the dollar's status as a reserve currency, and investments such as gold quickly surge to $7,000 an ounce as hostilities escalate."

Kellene Bishop says, "I think a financial collapse is likely; I'm surprised it hasn't hit yet. Each of us can understand the fact that we have nothing backing up the dollar."

What It Could Look Like

While some people might have difficulty envisioning how an economic collapse might manifest itself, others point to signs of serious economic troubles already being seen across the country, and fear that a collapse of the economy could lead to a gradual disintegration of civilized society. And what might that look like?

Economic troubles could force cities and states to make budget cuts and financial choices that lead to an increase in crime. As an example, the state of California—in response to a May 2011 ruling by the U.S. Supreme Court asserting that the state's prison system constituted "cruel and unusual punishment"—made the decision to release 30,000 prison inmates rather than build more prisons as the court suggested, because the costs of paying prison guards was so high.[590]

There are municipalities that have faced — and continue to face — tough budget choices because of growing gaps between what they owe in public pensions and the money they actually have. Author Michael Lewis says in his 2011 book *Boomerang* that the city of San Jose, California, "… owes so much more money than it can afford to pay its employees that it could cut its debts in half and still wind up broke."[591] The city — with a population of nearly a million people — cut back its staffing levels in 2011 to those of 1988, when it had 250,000 fewer residents to service.[592] Among those let go were firefighters and police officers.

San Jose continues to struggle to keep its head above water. A report in the *New York Times* in September 2013 says that San Jose spends 20 percent of its $1.1 billion general fund on pensions and retiree health care, an amount expected to grow.[593]

In December 2013, reports surfaced that the city of Chicago was facing a financial crisis because of a massive public pension shortfall. According to one report, the city has "the worst-funded public pension system of any major U.S. city." [594] It says that if the city doesn't find a way to deal with its pension problem, it could be in store for soaring property taxes and job cuts for teachers, police, firefighters, and other city workers.

Other cities that have started to show signs of economic collapse include: [595]

- San Vallejo, California — declared bankruptcy in 2008
- Mammoth Lakes, California — filed for bankruptcy in 2010, but filing was dismissed
- Harrisburg, Pennsylvania — filed for bankruptcy in 2010, but filing was dismissed
- Boise County, Idaho — filed for bankruptcy in 2010, but filing was dismissed
- Central Falls, Rhode Island — filed for bankruptcy in August 2011
- Jefferson County, Alabama — filed for bankruptcy in November 2011
- San Bernardino, California — filed for bankruptcy in 2012
- Stockton, California — filed for bankruptcy in 2012
- Detroit, Michigan — filed for bankruptcy in 2013

Discussion threads on prepper-focused websites advise people to prepare for a collapse by stocking up on food and useful hard assets that inflation may eventually put out of reach. Many sites urge people to get their money out of the stock market and put it into gold and silver, assets that will retain value no matter what happens to the U.S. dollar. They also offer information on where people can enroll in weapons training programs, to help protect themselves if lawlessness ensues.

Resource Shortages

Concern about possible resource shortages is something that drives many preppers to stock up on food, water, medicines, and fuel. A good number have as a goal to set aside at least a year's worth of food and medicines, several months' worth of fuel, and gallons of water, along with having backup sources for each.

Droughts in the western part of the country have seriously compromised the water supply in some western states. In hardest-hit California, the state at the end of January 2014 stopped water deliveries from a major source that had supplied water to five major regions, forcing them to turn to reservoirs that were already at below-average levels.[596]

Historic reduced flows in the Colorado River, on which 30 million people depend, prompted officials from the Bureau of Reclamation to warn in January 2014 that a persistent reduced flow in the river could lead to water rationing in Arizona, California, and parts of Nevada.[597]

And seemingly healthy water supplies can be compromised by things like chemical spills, as was seen in early 2014 after a chemical leak from a storage tank owned by coal producer Freedom Industries contaminated the water supply that served nine counties in the Kanawha Valley in West Virginia.[598] That disaster was compounded when a second spill of more than 100,000 gallons of "coal slurry" leaked from the Patriot Coal processing plant into a creek and eventually made its way into the Kanawha River. Officials at the Kanawha Valley Water Treatment Plant offered assurances that the second spill would not affect the public water supply. However, a month after the initial spill, residents were still receiving conflicting information about the safety of their water.[599]

The drought in California is expected to take its toll on the rest of the country in the form of higher prices for the fruits and vegetables grown there. With California producing nearly half of the US-grown vegetables, fruits, and nuts, a potential price increase that some analysts put at 10 percent or more could have a significant impact on the economy — and on individuals' grocery bills.[600,601]

In early 2014 extreme winter weather prompted concerns about potential heating fuel shortages and skyrocketing prices for those fuels. For many preppers, advance planning can help mitigate the economic impact of price increases, either because they planned for heating fuel alternatives, or because preparations in other areas can allow them to allocate more funds to the purchase of fuel. The price and availability of energy is a big concern for many preppers, who are acutely aware of how an energy shortage could impact transportation, and ultimately, the food supply.

Civil Disorder

One element of modern prepping that has gained much media attention is the focus of some preppers on self-defense, particularly with firearms. Media reports seem biased toward questioning the need for that level of self-defense, and the possession of firearms has been a flashpoint in this country's political discourse about rights granted by the Second Amendment to the Constitution.

But a look at some of the disasters in our recent history reveals that these events are increasingly accompanied by crimes that threaten disaster victims and their possessions, a phenomenon that has not gone unnoticed by preppers. The looting that has followed disasters like Super Storm Sandy or Hurricane Katrina is a stark reminder of how little it takes for people's behavior to devolve into lawlessness.

A more recent example of people out of control — not even related to a disaster — occurred in October 2013, when a problem with the electronic benefits cards in the country's SNAP program (Supplemental Nutrition Assistance Program) made the benefits temporarily unavailable to

213

recipients in seventeen states. Because of the glitch, retailers couldn't confirm that they would be paid, so most declined the purchases until the problem was fixed several hours later. However, panic ensued, as people feared being unable to buy groceries, and when a Walmart in Louisiana elected to allow shoppers to use the cards, even without knowing what limits they actually had, chaos erupted as people emptied shelves at the store—not only of food, but of anything they could fit in their shopping carts. When the problem was fixed, many people abandoned their full-to-overflowing shopping carts and fled the store.[602]

Government Out of Order

Dave Duffy of *Backwoods Home Magazine* says he hears from a lot of people who consider themselves part of the prepper movement, and says that their number-one concern seems to be "fear of an overbearing government; fears that freedoms are being taken away." He believes this has driven what he sees as a "surge of Libertarianism" in the last few years, along with growth in the prepper movement.

Scandals emerging from the Obama administration in late 2013 and early 2014 have fueled these concerns, particularly the National Security Agency spying scandal revealed by former NSA contractor Edward Snowden in June 2013. Details disclosed that the NSA surveillance program reached into details of Americans' lives to an extent never before imagined—even by George Orwell in the classic novel *1984*. The government claimed that its extensive information-gathering was necessary to protect the homeland from terrorists, but the public remained unconvinced.

As Obama's signature Affordable Care Act—commonly known as Obamacare—was rolled out in October 2013, people became aware that promises made by the president as he was trying to secure support for the law were untrue. His oft-repeated statement, "If you like your health-care plan, you can keep it," was dubbed "Lie of the Year" by PolitiFact.com.[603] Americans who had expected to keep their health insurance found it being canceled because it did not meet "minimum requirements" set by Obamacare, and as a result found themselves compelled to buy insurance they didn't want or need (such as maternity coverage for a 62-year-old male). As details of the plan became apparent, many people viewed it as a scheme to "redistribute wealth."[604]

With Americans becoming increasingly distrustful of the federal government under the Obama administration, the president himself fueled those sentiments by stating his intention to work around what he considered to be an uncooperative Congress by enacting laws through Executive Orders. Legislators in Congress expressed growing alarm by what they saw as presidential overreach; some accused him of outright lawlessness and of violating the Constitution.[605]

This followed on the heals of a scandal revealed in early 2013, where the Internal Revenue Service had apparently been targeting conservative groups applying for tax-exempt status and subjecting them to a level of scrutiny that was not applied to other groups. Many of those conservative applications were denied; some remained in limbo while the IRS awaited answers to questions that the groups found particularly intrusive and unnecessary.

Meanwhile, there were already growing fears among conservatives and Libertarians that they were being targeted for some reason, and that something more sinister was going on. People pointed to a study released in mid-2012 by the Department of Homeland Security that appeared to characterize people who were "reverent of individual liberty" as "extreme right-wing" terrorists. The topic gained much attention on Internet discussion boards. The report, "Hot spots of Terrorism and Other Crimes in the United States, 1970 to 2008," was amended with a disclaimer in July 2012, saying:

> "To be clear, the National Consortium for the Study of Terrorism and Responses to Terrorism (START) does not classify individuals as terrorists or extremists based on ideological perspectives. START and the Global Terrorism Database on which the Report is based, defines terrorism and terrorist attacks as 'the threatened or actual use of illegal force and violence by a non-state actor to attain a political, economic, religious, or social goal through fear, coercion, or intimidation.' The report is based on the key premise that the groups and individuals analyzed have actually carried out or attempted to carry out violent attacks in the United States for any political, social, religious, or economic goal. This is what qualifies them as terrorists, not their ideological orientation."[606]

In 2013, it was discovered that DHS had begun making bulk purchases of ammunition, which continued into early 2014, when it ordered more than 140,000 rounds of ammunition.[607]

And fanning the flames of suspicion about conservatives being targeted was a February 2014 report about a mock disaster conducted by the Ohio National Guard in January 2013, in which supporters of the Second Amendment, with "anti-government" views, were characterized as domestic terrorists.[608]

Even more ominous than the potential targeting by the government is what many believe to be a government agenda to completely disarm the American people, by using a number of mass shootings that have taken place in this country as justification for implementing gun control laws. Gun control advocates continue to assert that these incidents would not happen if people didn't have guns — or only certain people had them for certain purposes ("hunting is OK"), while people concerned with vigorously defending the Second Amendment right to bear arms make the argument that guns don't kill people — people do. Preppers are among those focused on protecting that right — not only for hunting in a TEOTWAWKI scenario, but also to defend themselves against looters and criminals and, if necessary, against a government bent on oppression.

Part Two:

A Look at Modern Preppers

Chapter Seven: How Do Preppers Prep?

People come to the idea of prepping at different times and from different perspectives, and how they prepare is influenced by their views on the importance of preparedness, their family situation, and the specific risks associated with where they live.

As we previously noted, for some people, preparedness is a familiar way of life, rather than a separate activity deserving of specific focus. For others, prepping is merely a way to be ready for a brief power outage during a hurricane or a blizzard — something that isn't given much thought until hurricane season, or winter.

For a large number of people — those who have swelled the ranks of preppers in the last ten years or so — prepping is a way to mitigate the long-term effects of a number of disaster scenarios. People in this group, when considering natural disasters like hurricanes or blizzards, are apt to apply more "what-if" thinking to imagine how they could be affected if the outcome were different from what might normally be expected — if a power outage went on for days or weeks, rather than hours, for example. And advice about emergency preparedness in books and magazines reinforces the importance of thinking for the long haul. Author Gary F. Arnet, in his article "Preparing for Disaster" in the *Emergency Preparedness and Survival Guide* published by *Backwoods Home Magazine*, says:

> *"It is not unreasonable to expect to have to take care of yourself for several weeks or longer. Some scenarios in which the economy or infrastructure is damaged by biological or nuclear terrorism suggest the need to care for your own needs for a year or longer."*[609]

Some people come to prepping after witnessing actual disasters and realizing that they are just as vulnerable as anyone else. Others are inspired by what they find at the library — popular science fiction and post-apocalyptic novels, by acquaintances who are involved in prepping, or even by television programs and movies. Once they start to realize all the things that could happen, they begin to assess all of the vulnerabilities in their lives, and may conclude that they are woefully unprepared—especially if they encounter other preppers who seem to "have it all together." So, where and how do they begin?

Planning

As people get involved in prepping, they quickly learn the value of the mantra "plan, prepare, and practice." They spend a good deal of time on self-education, starting with understanding the preparedness lifestyle and learning how to put together solid plans for dealing with the unexpected.

As Kellene Bishop counsels in the Ten Principles of Preparedness on her PreparednessPro website, the basic foundation of living a life of preparedness starts with the right spiritual and mental attitude— connectedness to core beliefs and values, and an understanding of what might be required of a person during an emergency. Similarly, the American Preppers Network offers guidance in "Five Principles of Preparedness" to help people "walk the path of the prepper."[610] Those include:

- *Principle One*: Practice thrift and frugality
- *Principle Two*: Seek to be Independent
- *Principle Three*: Become Industrious
- *Principle Four*: Strive Towards Self Reliance
- *Principle Five*: Aspire to have a year's supply of every needful thing

"Walking the path of the prepper" is envisioned as a lifestyle that emphasizes self-reliance through self-education, continually learning and mastering new skills, learning from mentors, becoming a mentor, and studying and practicing with others.

People eager to skip the foundational thinking and jump right into storing beans, bullets, and BAND-AIDs® run the risk of getting lost in the "hobby" aspect some find in prepping, and may eventually start to wonder, "What if nothing ever happens that I need my stored items for?" Wisdom from experienced preppers is that the goal is not to cower in fear of a disaster that may never happen, but to build resilience into one's lifestyle, so that if something unforeseen does happen, the impact is little more than a "bump in the road."

Advice from all corners—from FEMA to popular prepper websites—about building emergency readiness into one's life, is to start with a basic plan. When planning for emergencies, preppers are encouraged to first assess specific risks near their homes. How has the area been impacted in the past, and by what? Are there particular hazards nearby? For example, is there an active rail line in the vicinity that transports hazardous materials? Is there a highway in close proximity that could pose the threat of a hazardous spill or disastrous accident that could shut down the road? Does the community have an emergency plan in place? Does it have warning systems and procedures?

Because emergencies can happen when people are away from home—such as on business trips or vacations, or are separated from family members, such as when children are at school and parents are at work—sound preparedness planning applies the same risk-assessment thinking to these places. And going one step further, a good plan takes into account the emergency preparedness procedures that are in place in each of these locations.

Once risks have been identified, preppers must consider options for either "sheltering in place" at home—or wherever they happen to be—or evacuating. One important consideration for preppers is identifying what kinds of events would prompt them to evacuate their homes—as well as who will make that call, how, and when. And, equally important is determining where they will go, how they will get there, what they will take with them, and how long they will stay at their "go-to" location.

Finally, key to most emergency preparedness plans are the arrangements for keeping family members safe wherever they are, for reuniting them, and for getting everyone safely back home.

Some people advise that preppers document all of their emergency plans, and keep copies available for all family members.

Beyond basic plans for reacting to emergencies, many preppers work on plans to build resilience into their lives simply as a way of living. They work to fulfill the "rule of three" we mentioned earlier ("three is two; two is one; one is none"), which calls for multiple backups to critical systems and supplies, including food, water, and energy.

These are the people that have generated an increasing amount of interest in learning basic homesteading skills and techniques in the areas of growing and preserving food, raising livestock, and herbal medicine. These are the people who have begun to recognize the importance of community when it comes to being prepared, and who work to forge connections among like-minded people.

Preparing

In developing plans for either disaster scenario—sheltering in place or evacuating—people consider the specific needs of all the people—and animals—in the family for enduring short- and long-term disruptions in their lives, with a focus on fulfilling basic needs, such as food and water. And they position themselves to activate their emergency plans on a moment's notice.

The Bug-out Bag

A seemingly simple task beginning preppers check off their "to-do" list is creating an emergency kit (known to preppers as a "bug-out bag," or BOB) for each person in the household, in the event that some "instant disaster"—such as a house fire—forces an evacuation from home. FEMA advises on Ready.gov, that this basic kit contain:

- One gallon of water per person per day for at least three days, for drinking and sanitation
- At least a three-day supply of non-perishable food
- Battery-powered or hand-crank radio and a NOAA Weather Radio with tone alert and extra batteries for both
- Flashlight and extra batteries
- First aid kit
- Whistle to signal for help

- Dust mask
- Moist towelettes, garbage bags and plastic ties for personal sanitation
- Manual can opener for food
- Local maps
- Cell phone with chargers, inverter or solar charger
- Cash for purchases, in the event that a power outage makes debit and credit cards unusable

However, this task can become more complicated when preppers start thinking about all the contingencies they might face and expand this list to include things that, taken together, might even be difficult to carry in a single bag. A contributor to Rawles' SurvivalBlog website, "Talon," says that in his view, the minimum requirements for a standard bug-out bag include all of the above, as well as:[611]

- Water and food

  o Water bottle with filter
  o Coffee filters to strain sediment from water
  o Dehydrated food for at least seven days, entrées only
  o Heavy-duty fork and spoon
  o A means of cooking food, such as a multi-fuel camp stove or MRE cook pouch.
  o P-38 can opener

- Clothing

  o One set of camouflage-style clothing appropriate for your location
  o One pair of combat-style boots that are well broken in to your feet
  o Camo rain gear or winter gear as needed
  o Hat
  o Sun glasses
  o Tactical belt for pants
  o Dry socks

- Tactical Equipment:

  o Flint and steel with magnesium bar for starting fires
  o Sealed plastic bagful of dryer lint, for fire starter

- o LED keychain flashlight with green lens (to read maps)
- o Compass
- o GPS
- o Camel-back style hydration system with inline filter
- o Multi-purpose tool
- o Small tactical-type flashlight
- o Six spare batteries for lights, flashlights, GPS, etc.
- o One spare flashlight bulb for each style of light
- o Small binoculars
- o Two-way radios with pouches and headsets
- o Wristwatch with covered dial/face
- o Knee pads
- o Ruggedized cell phone with spare battery
- o Cell-phone charger for 12 volt and 110 volt
- o Topographical maps
- o Heavy-duty zip-style plastic bags to keep things dry

- Shelter

  - o Thermal-insulated sleeping pad
  - o Good quality, large-size mylar blanket or rainfly tarp

- Weapons and Ammunition

  - o Semiauto handgun with a holster and four loaded magazines
  - o An additional 50 rounds of ammunition for the handgun
  - o A fixed-blade combat knife
  - o A folding tactical knife
  - o A tomahawk with sheath
  - o A compact weapons-cleaning kit

- Other

  - o Spare prescription glasses or contact lenses
  - o Toilet paper (and know about natural alternatives in the area)
  - o Toothbrush
  - o Ten 6-inch black zip ties (to repair equipment in the field)
  - o Ten heavy-duty 12-inch black zip ties

- One roll black electric tape (UL listed)
- Partial roll of camouflage heavy-duty duct tape
- 100 feet of para cord
- Potassium iodide tablets (to protect against the effects of radioactive iodine)
- Several 1-gallon size zip-style plastic bags (spares)
- Two leaf/yard-size trash bags
- Two small roles of picture hanging wire to use for snares etc.
- Hooks, flies, lures, line, sinkers, swivels, weighted treble snagging hook with steel leader
- One small plastic container of cayenne pepper
- Mosquito repellent
- Coagula XL, 2 ounces (a blood coagulant accelerator that used for open wounds and internal bleeding)
- Dysentery Stop, 2 ounces (an anti-diarrheal remedy)

While the FEMA-recommended emergency kit is designed to get someone through 72 hours without outside assistance, FEMA recommends that people consider also having on hand enough supplies for sheltering *as long as two weeks*.[612]

The expanded version of the bug-out bag, including the recommendations from Rawles' SurvivalBlog, is intended to help in a long-term emergency that might include a period of wilderness survival.

Part of evacuation planning is locating the emergency kit where it is readily accessible. FEMA actually recommends having multiple versions of the emergency kit — one for home, one for work, and one in the car, where there may be other stored items for a road emergency, such as :

- Jumper cables
- Flares or reflective triangles
- Folding shovel
- Walking shoes and shoelaces
- Work gloves
- Disposable camera
- Emergency phone numbers on a laminated card
- Items for maintaining "sanity" during an emergency, such as a deck of cards, books, or a small journal and pen or pencil

Some people have emergency bags containing only the bare essentials, which they carry with them most of the time (sometimes called "get-home bags").

The Bug-out Location

A critical part of an emergency plan is identifying a place to go in the event that evacuation is necessary, as well as how to get there. For "instant" emergencies, people often turn to nearby friends, neighbors, or family members to provide shelter for the short term. For longer-term situations, some people have a "survival retreat" within one gas tank's drive from home, such as a vacation home (known to preppers as a "bug-out location," or BOL).

Spirko advises, "If someone comes to your door and tells you you've gotta go now — because of a weather event or any other type of event — know where you're going to go. Have three places to go and three ways to get there. Have the maps printed out and contact information for all your family. Keep it all in a packet in your car."[613]

Plans to reach the go-to location need to include not only an identified route that is unlikely to be impeded by other traffic evacuating the area, but also the transportation that will be used to get there. For many people, that is simply the primary vehicle they own, but for others it could be a camper or other vehicle specifically designated for use in an evacuation scenario (also known as a "bug-out vehicle," or BOV).

Security

Whether preppers' emergency plans for a long-term disaster situation include evacuating to a bug-out location or making do at home, one of the major concerns is that thousands of unprepared people will turn to looting, stealing, and other forms of violence in order to survive. With this in mind, most preppers include in their plans ways to prevent intruders from gaining access to their shelter, and the means to protect themselves in the event that they do.

Kellene Bishop says, "You have to be realistic about people coming looking for food." She says she understands that, and in a crisis plans on helping her community. But, she says, "It will be on *my* terms." Her suggestion is that people looking for food during an emergency be asked to work for it. "It's not government welfare," she says. "If you give your stuff away, people no longer need you around, and they can be emboldened to take anything you have."

Survival

An integral part of preparing for emergencies, whether for events of short- or long-term duration, is cultivating certain helpful skills, and many preppers devote some of their preparedness efforts to just that. Those skills might include:

- Basic survival skills — knowing:

    o At least two ways to start a fire
    o How to build a simple shelter
    o How to find and purify water
    o How to find food, through foraging and hunting
    o Basic first-aid
    o How to make creative use of whatever is available

- Self-defense skills — hand combat and weapons

- Skills to maintain physical conditioning for survival and self-defense

- Skills around maintaining heightened "situational awareness" — being observant about what's going on around you, and being cognizant of places to avoid. (For example, locations considered among the worst places to be in an emergency include grocery stores, gas stations, hospitals, and banks.)

- Skills to address medical emergencies

Preppers looking to build these skills often seek out specialized training to help.

Food Storage and Supplies

Storing food and other supplies is high on the prepper "to-do" list, whether planning for emergency situations or working toward self-reliance.

Besides having emergency bug-out bags for all family members, preppers also have a store of supplies in their homes and at their designated go-to locations, if they have one. This could include several months' worth of food, fuel, medicines, first-aid supplies, hygiene items, cleaning supplies, cooking utensils, tools, and weapons.

Many preppers have a goal of storing at least a year's supply of food and have plans to grow as much of their own as possible to replenish their stock as it is used up. (Resources such as the website of the Church of Latter-Day Saints offer guidance in calculating how much food to store per person, per three-month period, as well as recommendations on what foods to store.[614]) However, people who live in small dwellings, such as apartments, have the added challenge of identifying *where* they will store supplies, how much they can reasonably expect to store, and what, if anything, they might be able to grow.

In planning for a long-term emergency situation, people are challenged with finding ways to preserve food, since conventional methods, such as freezing, are not likely to be available. Many preppers spend time learning food-preservation techniques they can use on a regular basis, whether there is an emergency or not. These include dehydrating, fermenting, pickling, smoking, and canning.

It is important to note that preppers do not consider their food storage to be a static thing. They live by the rule, "Store what you eat; eat what you store." This calls for developing plans in how food will be rotated out of storage, as well as menu planning to use the foods that have been stored.

Water

Having a steady supply of water is even more important than having stored and renewable sources for food. Preppers know that people can survive as long as three weeks without food, but can survive only three days without water. And besides having water for drinking, people also need water for cooking and washing. Some experts advise having available at least one gallon of water per day per person, but when *all* the needs for water are taken into account, a better figure for planning may be at least two gallons per person, per day.

In preparing for adequate water availability, preppers first seek out backups to their primary water supply, such as streams, ponds, or even rain barrels or cisterns. Then they look for ways to purify water from less-than-pristine sources, such as boiling, filtration, chemical purification, or a combination of all three. There are companies that make filters in all shapes and sizes for this, and those filters are highly sought after by preppers. There are well-known techniques to purify water using bleach, iodine, or water purification tablets, although these are considered techniques of last resort.

Energy

In our energy-driven world, being without power for any length of time is disconcerting, and the idea of being without it for days or weeks can be alarming. One piece of equipment that most preppers consider a necessity — especially if they live in areas that have experienced power outages as a result of extreme weather — is a generator, to help power appliances and lights. And there are all shapes and sizes to be had. But realizing that generators require some type of fuel, which could become scarce in a long-term emergency situation, many preppers turn to solar technology to help solve their energy challenges. This requires cultivating yet another skill set: knowing a little something about electricity and how solar power works.

Besides having an energy source to power equipment and appliances, another important requirement is having energy for heat in cold weather as well as for cooking. Some people are able to solve this challenge through the use of a wood stove for both heating and cooking during cold weather, and an outdoor grill for cooking in warmer weather.

One solution that intrigues preppers is a "rocket stove" — a compact, high-efficiency cooking stove designed to use small-diameter wood for fuel—and its cousin, the "rocket mass heater," which uses the same principles for room heating.

Another option for cooking is a solar oven, which has proven very effective—when the sun's out.

Communications

In any emergency, whether of short- or long-term duration, preppers see it as critical to stay connected with the outside world to understand the situation and current conditions, which makes communications an important part of any emergency plan. FEMA advises people to have, at the very least, a battery-powered or hand-cranked radio connected to the National Oceanic and Atmospheric Administration (NOAA) National Weather Service radio network, along with extra batteries. (The NOAA National Weather Radio network is an all-hazards broadcasting network that reports on weather forecasts, warnings, watches, and other hazards 24 hours a day, seven days a week.)

Many people take their communications preparations one or two steps further, investing in walkie talkies, CB (Citizen's Band) radio equipment, or ham radios. All of these options involve a certain level of training; using a ham radio also requires a license.

Finances

The degree to which people are able to build and implement their emergency plans, including their store of supplies, is frequently dependent on their financial resources, which means prioritizing the plans that will be implemented, when, and how.

As we've discussed, becoming financially independent is considered a part of being prepared. In fact, advice from the prepping community is that, given what is seen as an uncertain financial future ahead for the country, putting money into "hard assets" like gold and silver—and even food and supplies—is a wiser choice than building up a big bank account. It doesn't take a lot of money to start prepping; people can begin gradually and add to what they need over time. And although

228

many preppers may aspire to having a secure go-to site in an isolated setting, that may be out of reach for some.

As Rawles says, "Not everyone can live in the boonies away from people. For those who can't, even setting aside a one-year food supply and a means to filter water will increase their chances of survival in an emergency tremendously."

Some preppers with limited resources build bartering into their overall plans, as a way to trade for things they might need.

While people with limited means may work toward a lifestyle of preparedness where they are, with what they have available, people with ample financial resources have been known to seek out survival retreats on hundreds of acres of land in remote locations, protected by sophisticated surveillance systems and intruder deterrents. Some engage consultants, such as Rawles, to help with the selection of an appropriate retreat. Others have invested in underground bunkers to protect against just about any hazard.

Practice Makes Perfect

It could be said that, unless a person periodically takes a "dry run" through his/her preparedness plan, it's just so much theory. That's why many preppers build repeated practice into their plans.

Until they've driven to their bug-out location, preppers won't know if they've selected the best route to get there. Until they've practiced loading the gear they plan to take with them if they have to bug out, they won't know if it's feasible, or if they can do it in a short amount of time, under pressure. Unless they've practiced some of those survival skills, they won't know how effective they'll be in an emergency situation.

Testing the basics is equally—if not more—important, since "instant emergencies" such as house fires are apt to happen more often than a large-scale disaster. Preppers are advised to lead family drills that simulate a household emergency. Do family members know where their bug-out bag is? Do they have time to grab it? Do they know the escape routes from the house? Do they know where to meet when they leave?

Some people practice their emergency plans by turning off the electricity for a day or so to see what life would be like without it. Will their plans for cooking work? Will their plans for backup power work? How will they fare psychologically when there is no power for electronics (like TV) and only candles or kerosene lamps for light?

Part Two:

A Look at Modern Preppers

Chapter Eight: The Business of Prepping

As modern preparedness has grown, so have the businesses that support it. And by all accounts, the preparedness market is a multi-billion dollar industry, encompassing everything from bug-out bags to bunkers, survival gear, long-term food storage, and more. Besides inspiring businesses that cater specifically to preppers, prepping has helped swell demand for things not associated exclusively with prepping, like camping equipment, guns and knives, generators, gardening supplies, water filters, extension cords, flashlights, batteries, and duct tape. With millions of people prepping in one way or another, even sales from "small potatoes" items add up to big money. Following is a sampling of what's out there for preppers.

Bug-out Bags

As we've discussed, people just getting started in emergency preparedness are advised to have on hand, at the very least, an emergency kit to help them get through 72 hours without outside help, if they have to evacuate their homes. People can build their own kits piece by piece, but there are dozens of suppliers prepared to assist, offering a variety of ready-to-go emergency kits.

Warehouse stores such as Costco and BJ's Wholesale Club offer ready-made bug-out bags ranging in price from about $75 to $180. Costco's $75 backpack kit, designed to hold two people over for 72 hours, comes with two pouches of drink mix, nine pouches with ready-to-heat dishes, a portable cook stove, a cook pot, fire starter, waterproof matches, a water filtration bottle, utensils and cups, two emergency blankets, and a first-aid kit. Their higher-end $180 kit, designed for two people for seven days, includes a laundry list of emergency essentials which, besides food, water, and an assortment of handy tools, also

231

incorporates things like flashlights, ponchos, a radio, light sticks, a tarp, and even a deck of playing cards.[615] BJ's offers a $99 kit designed to sustain four people for three days. The "Ready America Grab 'n Go 3-Day Deluxe 4-Person Emergency Survival Kit" includes not only food and water, but also four emergency blankets, a first-aid kit, an emergency power station, 10 yards of duct tape, and a multifunction pocket tool with pliers.[616]

But some people pay hundreds, even thousands of dollars for their ideal ready-made bug-out bags. Roman Zrazhevskiy, who, with his business partner Fabian Illanes founded Ready to Go Survival after Hurricane Sandy devastated parts of the East Coast in 2012, said that the two decided right away to make bug-out bags the primary focus of their business. Zrazhevskiy said that he and his partner, who both have experience as first responders, have comprehensive bug-out bags of their own, which they created over time through trial and error. He said they discovered that "sometimes you buy certain things you never use." They decided to use their own expertise and experience putting together their own emergency kits to create customized "Survival Systems" designed to serve as all-in-one emergency kits. Creating customized Survival Systems has been lucrative for the pair. Zrazhevskiy said that in their first year of business they sold at least one thousand Survival Systems—for $400 to $700 each.

Water

Sourcing a steady supply of drinkable water is a prime concern for preppers and, as with bug-out bags, there are many companies available to help with that. Some emergency preparedness suppliers sell cans and pouches of water to store for the long haul. But, as with food, stored water will last only so long, and finding another source is essential. Solutions for rendering "found water" drinkable can range from low-end, low-cost chemical additives, to higher-end water filtration systems.

Some people, keeping in mind the possibility of an emergency turning into a wilderness survival situation, take this into account when building their emergency plans. One option people turn to in putting together their bug-out bags is chemical water purification products, which are sold by several emergency preparedness stores and websites.

They include iodine-based and chlorine dioxide-based tablets such as those manufactured by Potable Aqua, which are frequently used by the military and relief organizations. The Potable Aqua iodine-based tablets, intended only for short-term situations where the available water is of uncertain bacteriological quality, can be purchased in bottles of 50, to treat 25 quarts of water, for about $6 each. The company's chlorine dioxide tablets, available in bottles of 20 or 30, are for situations where the microbiological quality of available water is questionable. One tablet is required for each quart of water being treated. Bottles of 20 tablets can be purchased starting at around $10 each.

While there are many different manufacturers of whole-house water filtration systems out there, there is a segment of the industry that caters specifically to the emergency preparedness market, offering solutions that are portable and easy to use. Here are three:

1. Vestergaard Company offers three highly portable versions of its LifeStraw filtration systems. The smallest—and easiest to slip into a bug-out bag—is the LifeStraw personal water filter, which TIME Magazine named "the Best Invention of 2005." Weighing only 2 ounces, and small enough to carry in a pocket or hang on a string around the neck, the LifeStraw personal filter is capable of filtering at least 264 gallons of water, removing up to 99.9 percent of waterborne bacteria and protozoan cysts. [617] It is used just like a drinking straw and can be purchased for about $20. The company also offers the LifeStraw personal filter in a sports bottle—the "Go Water Bottle" for around $60. Vestergaard also makes a larger filtration unit, LifeStraw Family 1.0, designed to filter up to 18,000 liters of water, enough to supply a family of five with clean drinking water for as long as three years.[618] Lightweight and portable, the unit is suitable for camping and emergency situations, and is available for about $80.

2. Katadyn Products is another company that makes a number of portable water filtration units that are intended for use by campers, backpackers, or even business travelers, and are designed to hold up under extreme conditions. The filtration systems, which remove particulate, bacteria, and protozoa such as giardia and cryptosporidia,[619] are designed to meet the water

filtration needs of one to four people, and range in price from $70 to $370.

3. Berkey Filters, like its competitors, offers several compact filtration systems. The systems are sized to serve different-sized groups of people, from small families to large groups of up to 150 people,[620] and are designed to take into account not only the water requirements for drinking, but also for hygiene and sanitation. They are all small enough to be portable—the biggest one, the "Crown Berkey," measuring just 11 inches deep by 30 inches high. The units range in price from about $228 to $625.

Food

Most advice for beginning preppers is to work toward building up at least a year's supply of food. The typical suggestion is to start gradually, by buying a few extra of the needed items with each trip to the grocery store. And whether at the grocery store or online, there are many businesses that are eager to help new preppers get started with food storage and to help experienced preppers continue on their prepping journey. Those businesses include not only the suppliers selling the storage foods, but also the companies that process and package the food, companies that manufacture and sell food-storage buckets and openers, and companies that manufacture and sell special food-storage shelving, built to make first-in-first-out food rotation easier.

For people looking to forego the process of a gradual increase in their pantry storage, preferring instead to secure an immediate supply, there are a number of stores and websites that specialize in selling pre-assembled kits—consisting primarily of dehydrated and freeze-dried foods and meals-ready-to-eat (MREs)—for periods ranging from one month to a year. People can expect to pay around $70 for a three-month, one-person kit, and more than $1,000 for a one-year, one-person kit. A deluxe one-year, one-person kit can cost as much as $9,800.

Some warehouse grocery stores also sell pre-assembled kits in their stores and online. For example, Sam's Club offers a 30-day kit for one person for $69.98 in its online store, as well as one-year supplies for one person, ranging in price from $798 to $1,498.[621] Costco offers a one-month emergency food supply in its online store for $99[622]. BJ's Wholesale Club sells emergency food storage kits that range in price from $78 for a one-person, one-month supply, to a one-year, two-person supply for $1,599.[623]

There are scores of online shops where preppers can not only purchase foods for long-term storage, but can also get advice on what they should buy. The Utah-based Church of Jesus Christ of Latter-day Saints offers an online calculator to help set goals for certain foods based on the number of people in the family, and based on government nutrition guidelines.[624] With goals set, users of the calculator can purchase what they need from the online store. The Latter-day Saints store sells a $31 "starter kit" to help get people acquainted with storage foods by providing one can each of flour, red wheat, white wheat, rice, pinto beans, and oats, along with recipes and pamphlets that offer guidance in building a food-storage plan.[625] The site also offers, by the case, foods that have a shelf life of 30 years or more, such as wheat, rice, corn, sugar, rolled oats, and apple slices, ranging in price from about $24 to $44, for 20 to 35 pounds of food.

Emergency Essentials, in Orem, Utah, has been in business since 1987, when it started selling powdered milk. It has since expanded its product line to include a wide variety of storage foods, including freeze-dried and dehydrated foods, as well as cooking supplies, camping equipment, emergency kits, communications and lighting solutions, garden seeds, tools, and many other items. The company's website offers a free food storage analyzer[626], which, like the LDS calculator, helps people analyze how many days of food storage they have in their pantry and its nutritional content. The analyzer has a convenient shopping list function that can create an order based on foods the company sells. Among those foods are grains, vegetables, beans, legumes, cereals, pasta, powdered dairy products, soup mixes, broths, baking mixes, desserts and dessert mixes, drink mixes, a wide variety of freeze-dried fruits and vegetables, and MREs. All items can be purchased in single containers, but some are conveniently packaged in one-year-supply combinations, which range in price from $1,450 to $4,800. Some of the one-year kits are so popular that, as of February 2014, the were back-ordered, including the Premium 2000 One Year Food Supply, listed at $3,867.69, but on sale for $2,699.95[627], and the Gourmet Plus Supply, listed for $6,879.99, but on sale for $4,799.95. That kit also includes an emergency kit, first-aid kit, a water filter and water storage kit, a small, portable cookstove, and a drink-mixing pitcher. To help its customers save money, Emergency Essentials offers a money-saving group purchase program, which allows people to combine their purchases into bulk orders.[628]

Another Utah-based business that offers long-term food storage and related supplies is The Ready Store. The company got its start selling bug-out bags in 2001 after the September 11 terrorist attacks but, according to spokesperson Brandon Garrett, "quickly evolved," adding to its product line freeze-dried foods, outdoor equipment, knives, survival gear, and more. Garrett said, "The Ready Store has helped over 3 million people get prepared." The company offers foods that can be purchased in individual units or in combination supplies designed to last from one month to one year. Like Emergency Essentials, the Ready Store also offers a group-buy program, where participants can realize savings of 10 to 30 percent.[629]

Wise Company, also based in Utah, specializes in selling food kits, but also offers survival kits, containers of emergency fuel, low-end water filtration solutions, and garden seeds. The company's website has a food supply calculator that will present suggested food storage options from its product line based on the number of adults and children for whom long-term storage is needed. A family of four, including two children under the age of 10, can expect to pay around $4,000 for a one-year supply of food.[630] The company's food products, which include freeze-dried meats, fruits, and vegetables, as well as "grab 'n go" food kits, have been widely advertised on National Geographic's "Doomsday Preppers" TV show and touted by the company's official spokesperson, Marie Osmond, as well as by nationally-known radio talk-show hosts like Laura Ingram, George Noory, and Michael Savage.

Preppers interested more in building their own long-term food supply instead of buying it ready-made turn not only to a gradual increase by way of extra purchases at the grocery store, but also to bulk buys of fruits and vegetables that they can preserve themselves. They also turn to growing and preserving their own food, which has created a demand for the equipment and supplies needed to do that:

- Garden supplies, tools, and seeds
- Water-bath canners
- Pressure canners
- Canning jars and lids

236

- Dehydrators
- Food vacuum sealers

Many preppers thinking beyond the food they have stored, to how they're going to replenish their supply when it runs out, turn their attention to homesteading and all that entails, including raising livestock, making feed stores and poultry hatcheries among the other businesses that have benefited from the preparedness movement.

Shelter

After food, water, and basic emergency kits and plans, a prime consideration for preppers is having a safe haven to go to in an emergency. Some people plan to weather out most emergency situations in their own homes, because often there is no other choice, and they build their preparedness plans accordingly. A number of people make plans to bunk with relatives if they're forced to leave their homes. But many others, especially those living in urban areas, make seeking out a remote hideaway — a "bug-out location" — a priority.

Some people enlist the services of consultants, such as James Wesley Rawles, to help. This interest has spawned other consulting businesses, such as Survival Retreat Consulting, owned by Todd Savage, who was inspired by Rawles. Savage employs a team of professionals to counsel clients in retreat selection and related prepping considerations, such as survival farming and food storage.[631] Consultants not only help preppers seek out properties that meet their requirements for a survival retreat, but also help analyze the suitability of those properties based on the potential for food production, energy creation, and availability of water, as well as options for retreat defense.

The interest in survival retreats has also opened new opportunities in the real estate market, where realtors can promote specific types of properties to the prepper community, and in addition can offer their own consulting services to help preppers find the retreat that's right for them. In some cases, the remote locations being marketed to preppers are those that, years ago, might have languished with "for sale" signs for years, *because* they are so isolated.

Survival retreat consultants generally tend to favor locations in what's known as the "American Redoubt," a term coined by Rawles, who designated five states in the northwestern U.S. as the safest locations for survival retreats. Rawles and others don't consider the eastern states as advantageous locations for retreats because they are highly populated and are generally in close proximity to nuclear power plants.

Keeping in mind the chaos they believe will follow a major crisis in this country, for some preppers, a survival retreat is more than just a remote location—it must be secure. This has opened up opportunities for manufacturers of home security systems—as long as they can create warning systems that will operate if the grid goes down.

For still other preppers, an alarm-protected home in a remote location is not enough; for them, only an underground bunker will do. And that has created an expanded market for manufacturers of storm shelters as well as new opportunities for companies looking to create customized survival shelters.

Needless to say, a bunker is not an inexpensive proposition. Some preppers, looking for a low-cost solution, have turned to using metal shipping containers as bunkers. There is disagreement in the prepper community as to whether or not this is a wise choice, since shipping containers aren't built to withstand being buried underground. However, others say that, with the proper reinforcement and retrofitting, this could work. The containers cost upwards of $1,000, but customizing them to work as an underground bunker could cost considerably more.

People looking for customized, turnkey bunkers will find suppliers willing to help. Ultimate Bunker, located in Utah, offers bunkers in half a dozen sizes as well as safe rooms designed to fit inside an existing home. The company says that all of its bunkers are built according to FEMA guidelines for safe-room construction as well as specifications and guidelines from the National Storm Shelter Association.[632] The bunkers come with not only solid construction, lighting, and connections for water and sewer, but also with the protections you'd expect to have in a survival bunker—a security system and an air filtration system designed to filter out nuclear, biological, and chemical contaminants. They also come with some of the comforts of home, including:

238

- A small kitchen with an electric cook top, a microwave oven, and a table and chairs
- A bathroom with a shower and toilet
- Carpet and painted walls
- A flat-screen TV
- A solar panel with a power inverter and battery backup

The bunkers come in sizes that range from 10 by 20 feet to 40 by 50 feet, and range in price from $54,000 to $450,000 — uninstalled. The company's owner, Mike Peters, said they can cost twice as much installed. And he said that business has been steady.

The demand for bunkers has also created a market for properties containing abandoned missile silos, which some enterprising people, like developer Larry Hall, see as ideal structures to transform into survival bunkers. Years ago Hall purchased two vacant silos, extending underground 174 feet in an undisclosed location in Kansas, and proceeded to work toward his vision of turning them into luxury survival condos. For those who might think that the people who would be attracted to missile-silo bunkers are "fringe survival nuts," Hall says that his clients are "successful, educated and well-to-do individuals who simply want peace of mind in the event of a natural or manmade disaster."[633]

The silos contain fourteen levels, four of which are reserved for operations equipment and facilities. The remaining ten are divided into half- and full-floor units between 900 and 1,820 square feet in size, which altogether can accommodate up to seventy people. They come with price tags of between $1.5 million and $3 million.[634] They also come with the amenities one might expect in a luxury survival condo, among them:

- Fully furnished, professionally decorated rooms
- A full kitchen with high-end stainless steel appliances
- A washer and dryer
- A Jacuzzi tub in the master bath
- A 50-inch LED TV and home automation system
- A five-year food supply per person

In addition, there are common areas designed to alleviate the stress of hunkering down during a disaster, including:

- An indoor pool and spa
- A complete workout facility
- A theater
- A game arcade
- A bar and lounge
- A library and classroom
- An indoor shooting range
- A dog park
- A general store

Hall seems to have thought of everything: the silos also have a medical center and a means for organic hydroponic and aquaculture food production, and he has developed three contingency plans to help clients reach the facility in an emergency.

Hall finished the build-out of silo number one in December 2012 — and they sold out immediately. He has a waiting list for the units in the remaining bunker.

The List Goes On

Thinking through all the things a person might need in order to be prepared for emergencies, disasters, and a wholesale shift to sustainable living, it becomes apparent that there are many industries that have experienced the effects of people's march toward preparedness. Take education and training, for example. With preppers seeking out and soaking up new information like sponges and looking to acquire new skills — it isn't surprising that they have created a demand for in-person training, both group and individual, as well as demand for resources like magazines, books, and DVDs that offer "how-to" information in the areas of:

- Self-defense
- Fitness
- Survival skills
- Tactical training
- First aid and emergency medicine
- Firearms and shooting
- Electrical skills for building backup power systems (e.g., solar solutions)

- Gardening techniques
- Homesteading
- Food preservation and storage

This thirst for knowledge has helped grow the "prepper expo" industry. In the first half of 2014 alone, there were sixteen prepper expos and shows scheduled across thirteen different states. All offered educational seminars and featured countless exhibitors showcasing ideas, systems, tools, and wares to help people on their path to preparedness.

In addition, retail establishments popular with preppers have profited from the interest in preparedness. Camping and military surplus stores are considered go-to destinations for people looking for survival gear. Think tents, sleeping bags, camp stoves, backpacks, canteens, goggles, and gas masks. Even the local hardware store has something to offer preppers, including things as common and mundane as gasoline cans and stabilizer, rope, matches, and an assortment of handy tools.

When one considers the assortment and number of businesses that have benefited from the preparedness movement, it would seem that prepping has been good for the economy.

Part Two:

A Look at Modern Preppers

Chapter Nine: The Future of Prepping

Preparedness is all about thinking of the future. So what might the future hold for prepping itself? James Wesley Rawles thinks the prepping phenomenon will continue to grow. He said, "Because of the free flow of information today, especially via the Internet, it's inevitable that people will realize we have a fragile, interdependence which will increase as time goes on. The vulnerability of our society is only going to increase."

With each new disaster that has struck somewhere in the world, the prepping movement has gained believers. Hurricane Sandy was a wake-up call for many — including the federal government.

In 2013, the Department of Homeland Security gave U.S. disaster preparedness high priority. According to the National Strategy Recommendations published by DHS in its Fiscal Year 2013 Report to Congress, the United States led the world in losses from disasters in 2012. The report cites floods, wildfires, and droughts among those disasters, and specifically calls out Hurricane Sandy for "wreaking havoc" and causing blackouts along the East Coast.[635] The storm is reported to be the second-costliest in U.S. history[636], which has helped raise the stakes for the country in bringing preparedness into focus. The DHS report says that North America incurred $1.06 trillion in weather-related losses between 1980 and 2011, and cites a 2010 report from the National Bureau of Economic Research that predicts future losses of $1.2 to $7.1 trillion due to disasters over the next seventy-five years.[637] DHS also points out that, costs aside, the country's ability to recover from disasters has a direct bearing on national security.

The government's increased attention on preparedness driven by Hurricane Sandy added to the clarion call issued by way of Presidential Policy Directive PPD-8 on National Preparedness in March 2011. The directive states that its purpose is "aimed at strengthening the security and resilience of the United States through systematic preparation for the threats that pose the greatest risk to the security of the Nation." [638] It goes on to list among those threats not only "catastrophic natural disasters," but also acts of terrorism, cyber attacks, and pandemics — all things that have been, and continue to be, of concern to preppers.

Further, the directive acknowledges the role individuals play in responding to emergencies:

> "Our national preparedness is the shared responsibility of all levels of government, the private and nonprofit sectors, and individual citizens."

In fact, individual responsibility is emphasized throughout the documents DHS has published to guide national preparedness efforts. The "National Mitigation Framework" it published in May 2013 recognizes that people at every level of society have historically taken at least some responsibility for preparedness — including "the family that creates a sheltering plan in case of a tornado."[639]

DHS suggests that, through the Mitigation Framework, people at all levels can work together to develop a preparedness mindset, to create a "risk-conscious culture" that anticipates threats and hazards. It concedes that "individuals, families, neighborhoods, communities, and the private sector will play an increasingly active role in helping to meet future emergency management needs."[640]

While the federal government emphasizes individual responsibility in being prepared for emergencies and disasters, the Mitigation Framework and DHS recommendations on the topic suggest that the government still sees itself playing the lead role in that endeavor. Preppers — many of whom have come to question government motives about most things, would likely disagree, arguing that no one cares as much about the safety and security of your family as *you*.

And there are some threats of concern to many preppers that don't appear in the Mitigation Framework: economic collapse, societal collapse, and governmental tyranny. Although there are people who would argue that, of all the hazards and threats that are "out there," these may not be the most imminent, others would say that these

244

situations could surface as the byproduct of some unexpected event—and point to the looting that took place following Hurricane Sandy.

The more that people understand how they could be impacted by any one of a number of disaster scenarios, the more likely they are to make preparations to alleviate the effects of unexpected events. Many of those who have been involved in prepping for some time believe there is a pressing need for people to become prepared.

Preparedness Pro Kellene Bishop said, "I believe things are coming—it's in the Lord's care. There are more people coming on board that will get this. But many will run out of time. It's about more than food. A lot of preppers won't make it because they lack the spiritual and mental fortitude. They like the hobby aspect of it."

Like Bishop, Ultimate Bunker owner Mike Peters thinks the window of opportunity to become prepared is closing. He thinks "something" will happen soon. He said it could be a number of things that would act "like dominoes" and lead to a major disaster. He said, "For people who have made no preparations, it will be too late."

Our past has been filled with wars and wild weather and will likely continue to be. We still have fires, floods, droughts, and pestilence. The Yellowstone caldera is still bubbling underground, and the San Andreas Fault continues to squeak and groan, but still keeps us waiting for "the big one."

Storms still happen on the sun; the Carrington Event happened once—experts say it could happen again. Asteroids still careen through the universe; meteorites sometimes strike the Earth. Plagues have happened, and despite modern advances in medicine, experts believe they could happen again. Governments and politicians still pursue selfish ambitions; people still lie, cheat, steal, murder, and make bad decisions.

The wheels of technology continue to churn out marvels to make our lives easier; and the more we rely on them, the more vulnerable we become, as those marvels become the targets of terrorists and accidents waiting to happen.

It would seem that prepping as a phenomenon will continue to grow, as the proliferation of information on the Internet increases people's awareness about the dangers of modern life—and the consequences those dangers bring to those who are unprepared.

The more people make electronic connections with each other, the more they will share information about how to protect against the threats in today's world. Who knows? People who are now among the uninitiated may even come to think of preparedness as "disaster insurance"—rather than as just a fringe activity.

REFERENCES

Introduction

[1] Found at www.tvbythenumbers.com; Nielsen source was confirmed by Sara Bibel and Bill Gorman, spokespersons for the site.
[2] More information at http://en.wikipedia.org/wiki/Ted_Kaczynski.
[3] According to the U.S. Geological Survey's website (http://volcanoes.usgs.gov/volcanoes/yellowstone/yellowstone_sub_page_49.html) the Yellowstone caldera was identified through observations made by scientist Bob Christiansen in the 1960s and 1970s
[4] From Wikipedia: TV Guide Names the Top Cult Shows Ever – Today's News: Our Take TV Guide: June 29, 2007
[5] "NBC hopes absence makes 'Revolution' fans grow fonder," by Robert Bianco, USA Today, January 6, 2013, online at www.usatoday.com/story/life/tv/2013/01/06/nbc-revolution-winter-press-tour-bianco/1812135/, accessed May 15, 2013
[6] National Severe Weather Workshop 2008, online at www.norman.noaa.gov/NSWW2008/, accessed May 15, 2013
[7] Telephone interview with Tom Martin, Feb. 5, 2013

Chapter One

[8] Good News Bible: Today's English Version, 1976.
[9] "Ten Notable Apocalypses That (Obviously) Didn't Happen," by Mark Strauss, November 12, 2009, Smithsonian Magazine online at www.smithsonianmag.com/history-archaeology/Ten-Notable-Apocalypses-That-Obviously-Didnt-Happen.html#ixzz2KWGO9a9q, accessed August 13, 2013
[10] Matthew Restall and Amara Solari, 2012 and the End of the World (Rowman & Littlefield Publishers, Inc., 2011,) pp.7–12.
[11] Matthew Restall and Amara Solari, 2012 and the End of the World (Rowman & Littlefield Publishers, Inc., 2011,) pp. 27–29
[12] Genesis 6:9 to 9:28
[13] Pocket Guide to the Apocalypse: The Official Field Manual for the End of the World, by Jason Boyett, (2005), Relevant Media Group, ISBN 978-0-9760357-1-8
[14] Ibid.
[15] Christopher Columbus A Latter-Day Saint Perspective, by Arnold K. Garr, pp. 63–69 (Provo, Utah: Religious Studies Center, Brigham Young University, 1992)
[16] Historical Origins of Food Preservation, Brian A. Nummer, PhD., May 2002
[17] History of the National Weather Service, online at www.nws.noaa.gov/pa/history/index.php, accessed August 13, 2013

[18] From NOAA Technical Memorandum NWS NHC-6, online at www.nhc.noaa.gov/pdf/nws-nhc-6.pdf, accessed August 13, 2013
[19] Galveston Hurricane 1900, online at www.nhc.noaa.gov/outreach/history/#galveston
[20] Reported on the National Weather Service website, www.crh.noaa.gov
[21] *Restless Skies*, by Douglas, Paul, pp. 12–13 Barnes & Noble Publishing, Inc. (2004) ISBN 0-7607-6113-2.
[22] From the online almanac of the "Mass. Moments" project, initiated by the Massachusetts Foundation for the Humanities (Mass Humanities), online at http://massmoments.org/index.cfm?mid=77, accessed August 13, 2013 .
[23] National Weather Service online at www1.ncdc.noaa.gov/pub/data/blizzard/blizz.txt, accessed August 13, 2013
[24] From an online report by Jordan Weissmann for The Atlantic on the Great Blizzard of 1888, at www.theatlantic.com/business/archive/2012/10/the-great-blizzard-of-1888-the-last-storm-to-knock-out-wall-street/264299/, accessed august 13, 2013
[25] From "A Brief History of the Storm Prediction Center," by Stephen Corfidi, online at www.spc.noaa.gov/history/early.html, acccessed August 13, 2013
[26] "Tornado Alley, USA," by Sid Perkins, May 11, 2002, Science News. pp. 296–298.
[27] Tri-State Tornado website at www.crh.noaa.gov, accessed August 13, 2013
[28] "The Great 1906 San Francisco Earthquake," on the U.S. Geological Survey website at http://earthquake.usgs.gov/regional/nca/1906/18april/index.php, accessed July 17, 2013
[29] "Casualties and damage after the 1906 Earthquake," on the U.S. Geological Survey website at http://earthquake.usgs.gov/regional/nca/1906/18april/casualties.php, accessed July 17, 2013
[30] From a paper on "The Economics of World War I," by Carlos Lozada, for the National Bureau of Economic Research, online at www.nber.org, accessed July 17, 2013
[31] From "The Plattsburg Movement and its Legacy," by Donald M. Kington, for the Relevance Journal of the Great War Society, posted online at www.worldwar1.com
[32] Civil Defense and Homeland Security: A Short History of National Preparedness Efforts, published by the Department of Homeland Security, September 2006
[33] "World War One – Weapons," at www.historyonthenet.com, accessed July 17, 2013
[34] *The Day of Battle*, by Rick Atkinson (2007), Henry Holt and Company, p. 272
[35] "Civil Defense and Homeland Security: A Short History of National Preparedness Efforts," published by the Department of Homeland Security, September 2006.
[36] Records of the Council of National Defense, online at www.archives.gov
[37] "President Names Defense Advisers," New York Times, October 12, 1916

[38] "Black Tom Explosion," from Jersey City Past and Present at the website of New Jersey City University, www.ncju.edu/programs/jchistory

[39] "Liberty State Park: Black Tom Explosion," New Jersey Department of Environmental Protection, at www.state.nj.us/dep/parksandforests/parks/liberty_state_park

[40] "Past Imperfect," Smithsonian Magazine online November 1, 2011, at http://blogs.smithsonianmag.com/history/2011/11/sabotage-in-new-york, accessed July 17, 2013

[41] "Wartime Acts of Sabotage," PBS History Detectives, at www.pbs.org/opb/historydetectives/feature/wartime-acts-of-sabotage

[42] From government archives at www.archives.gov/research/foreign-policy/related-records/rg-63.html

[43] Archived *New York Times* article, "Hoover Decrees 'Victory Bread' and Cut Rations," published Jan. 27, 1918

[44] From The United States Statutes at Large, V. 40. (April 1917-March 1919), Sedition Act of 1918, section 3

[45] From *Savage Peace: Hope and Fear in America, 1919*, by Ann Hagedorn (2007), p. 25

[46] *New Brunswick, New Jersey, in the World War 1917–1918*, by John T. Wall; S.M. Christie Press (1921), pp. 70-75

[47] National Archives identifier number 295921; reference online at http://research.archives.gov

[48] From *Savage Peace: Hope and Fear in America, 1919*, by Ann Hagedorn (2007), p. 25

[49] From *Savage Peace: Hope and Fear in America, 1919*, by Ann Hagedorn (2007), p. 27

[50] Letter from the American Protective League to Samuel Pond, U.S. Food Administration; archived on the website of *Slate Magazine*, at www.slate.com/articles/news_and_politics

[51] From *A Secret Gift*, by Ted Gup (Penguin Books, 2010), p. 6

[52] *The Worst Hard Time*, by Timothy Egan (Houghton Mifflin Co. 2006), p.74

[53] From *A Secret Gift*, by Ted Gup (Penguin Books, 2010), p. 50

[54] *Regions in Transition*, by Rolland Dewing (Landham, Maryland: University Press of America, 2006), p. 5.

[55] PBS documentary by filmmaker Ken Burns; aired November 2012, online at www.pbs.org/about/news/archive/2012/dust-bowl-airdate/

[56] *The Worst Hard Time*, by Timothy Egan (Houghton Mifflin Co. 2006), p. 7

[57] *The Worst Hard Time*, by Timothy Egan (Houghton Mifflin Co. 2006), p.8

[58] *A History of Us: War, Peace and all that Jazz*, by Joy Hakim (New York: Oxford University Press, 1995)

[59] PBS interview with James Gregory, Associate Professor of History at the University of Washington, online at www.pbs.org/fmc/interviews/gregory.htm

[60] *The Worst Hard Time*, by Timothy Egan (Houghton Mifflin Co. 2006)

[61] *Cincinnati Enquirer*, "Infamous Floods," http://enquirer.com/flood_of_97/history5.html

[62] From U.S. Coast Guard historical account at
www.uscg.mil/history/articles/1937MissFloodHavern2011.pdf

[63] From *A Secret Gift*, by Ted Gup (Penguin Books, 2010), p. 154

[64] "Making Ends Meet in the Great Depression," by Joyce Wadler, April 2, 2009,
New York Times online at
www.nytimes.com/2009/04/02/garden/02depression.html

[65] From *A Secret Gift*, by Ted Gup (Penguin Books, 2010), p. 155

[66] *The Complete Illustrated History of the First and Second World Wars*, by
Donald Sommerville and Ian Westwell, Lorenz Books (2010), p. 263

[67] *The Complete Illustrated History of the First and Second World Wars*, by
Donald Sommerville and Ian Westwell, Lorenz Books (2010), p. 9

[68] *The Complete Illustrated History of the First and Second World Wars*, by
Donald Sommerville and Ian Westwell, Lorenz Books (2010), p. 326

[69] "Alien Total So Far Is Put at 4,741,971; Figure Is Far in Excess of Early
Estimate, Says Harrison," *The New York Times*, January 13, 1941, Section
BOOKS, Page 13, online archives at
http://query.nytimes.com/gst/abstract.html?res=F10716F9345D1B7B93C1A8178
AD85F458485F9

[70] "Only 2,971 Enemy Aliens Are Held; Rest of the 1,100,000 Being Watched
Here Are Unmolested," By Robert F. Whitney, January 04, 1942; from *New York
Times* online archives at
http://query.nytimes.com/gst/abstract.html?res=F40814FA3D58167B93C6A9178
AD85F468485F9

[71] *For the Duration*, by Lee Kennett (1985), p. 24

[72] *For the Duration*, by Lee Kennett (1985), p. 5

[73] *For the Duration*, by Lee Kennett (1985), p. 7

[74] *For the Duration*, by Lee Kennett (1985), p. 23

[75] *The Complete Illustrated History of the First and Second World Wars*, by
Donald Sommerville and Ian Westwell, Lorenz Books (2010), p. 326.

[76] *The Complete Illustrated History of the First and Second World Wars*, by
Donald Sommerville and Ian Westwell, Lorenz Books (2010), p. 327

[77] Franklin D. Roosevelt: "Fireside Chat.," December 9, 1941. Online by Gerhard
Peters and John T. Woolley, The American Presidency Project, at
www.presidency.ucsb.edu/ws/?pid=16056

[78] *The Complete Illustrated History of the First and Second World Wars*, by
Donald Sommerville and Ian Westwell, Lorenz Books (2010), p. 328

[79] *The Complete Illustrated History of the First and Second World Wars*, by
Donald Sommerville and Ian Westwell, Lorenz Books (2010), p. 352

[80] *For the Duration*, by Lee Kennett (1985), pp. 26 and 27

[81] *The Complete Illustrated History of the First and Second World Wars*, by
Donald Sommerville and Ian Westwell, Lorenz Books (2010), p. 342

[82] *The Complete Illustrated History of the First and Second World Wars*, by
Donald Sommerville and Ian Westwell, Lorenz Books (2010), p. 439

[83] *For the Duration*, by Lee Kennett (1985), p. 28

[84] *For the Duration*, by Lee Kennett (1985), p. 40

[85] *For the Duration*, by Lee Kennett (1985), p. 29

[86] Ibid.

[87] *For the Duration*, by Lee Kennett (1985), p. 33

[88] *For the Duration*, by Lee Kennett (1985), p. 30

[89] *For the Duration*, by Lee Kennett (1985), p. 38

[90] *For the Duration*, by Lee Kennett (1985), p. 35

[91] *For the Duration*, by Lee Kennett (1985), p. 44

[92] "The U.S. Home Front During World War II," article posted on the History Channel website, online at www.history.com/topics/us-home-front-during-world-war-ii

[93] "Brief History" of Rodale, Inc. online at www.rodaleinc.com/about-us/brief-history, accessed August 16, 2013

[94] *World War II in Mid-America*, by Robert C. Daniels (2012), AuthorHouse, p. 104

[95] *World War II in Mid-America*, by Robert C. Daniels (2012), AuthorHouse, p. 143

[96] Text of Executive Order 9066, online at www.ourdocuments.gov

[97] Densho Encyclopedia, online at http://encyclopedia.densho.org/Commission_on_Wartime_Relocation_and_Internment_of_Civilians/#Specific_Findings_and_Recommendations

[98] *Personal Justice Denied*, p. 459, National Archives online at www.archives.gov/research/japanese-americans/justice-denied/

[99] "Manhattan Project" at Encyclopedia Britannica online, www.britannica.com/print/topic/362098

[100] Ibid.

[101] "The Manhattan Project" at www.ushistory.org/us/51f.asp

[102] *Hiroshima: The World's Bomb*, by Andrew J. Rotter (2008) Oxford University Press, p. 156

[103] "Truman is Briefed on Manhattan Project," article online at http://www.history.com/this-day-in-history/truman-is-briefed-on-manhattan-project

[104] *Hiroshima: The World's Bomb*, by Andrew J. Rotter (2008) Oxford University Press, p. 131

[105] "The Atomic Bomb," article at PBS website, www.pbs.org/thewar/detail_5234.htm

[106] "The Costs of the Manhattan Project," Brookings Institute archives online at http://www.brookings.edu/about/projects/archive/nucweapons/manhattan

[107] *Hiroshima: The World's Bomb*, by Andrew J. Rotter (2008) Oxford University Press, p. 127

[108] "The Franck Report," June 11, 1945; I.S. National Archives, Washington, D.C., Record Group 77, Manhattan Engineer District Records, Harrison-Bundy File, folder #76; archived online at www.annen.com/decision/franck.html

[109] Downfall: the End of the Imperial Japanese Empire, by Richard B. Frank, (1999), p. 260; referenced at http://en.wikipedia.org/wiki/Franck_Report

[110] *Hiroshima: The World's Bomb*, by Andrew J. Rotter (2008) Oxford University Press, p. 160

[111] "Manhattan Project" at Encyclopedia Britannica online, www.britannica.com/print/topic/362098

[112] "The Decision to Drop the Bomb" at www.ushistory.org

[113] Text of the Potsdam Declaration, article 13, from the Pacific War Online Encyclopedia at http://pwencycl.kgbudge.com/P/o/Potsdam_Declaration.htm

[114] *The Complete Illustrated History of the First and Second World Wars*, by Donald Sommerville and Ian Westwell, Lorenz Books (2010), p. 490

[115] "The Decision to Drop the Bomb" at www.ushistory.org

[116] From *The Teachings of Spencer W. Kimball*, ed. Edward L. Kimball (1982), p. 372 at www.lds.org

Chapter Two

[117] "Why Did Japan Surrender?" by Gareth Cook, August 7, 2011, *The Boston Globe*; online at www.boston.com/bostonglobe/ideas/articles/2011/08/07/why_did_japan_surrender /, accessed April 30, 2013

[118] "Why Did We Drop the Bomb?" by Walter Isaacson, *TIME Magazine* April 18, 2005, online at www.time.com/time/magazine/article/0,9171,1050507,00.html, accessed May 23, 2013

[119] *The Complete Illustrated History of the First and Second World Wars*, by Donald Sommerville and Ian Westwell, Lorenz Books (2010), p.491

[120] *The Cold War: A New History*, by John Lewis Gaddis (2005), Penguin Press, pp. 18-19

[121] *The Cold War: A New History*, by John Lewis Gaddis (2005), Penguin Press, p. 25

[122] *The Cold War: A New History*, by John Lewis Gaddis (2005), Penguin Press, p. 26

[123] Ibid.

[124] "The Long Telegram," from website of George Washington University at www.gwu.edu/~nsarchiv/coldwar/documents/episode-1/kennan.htm (accessed 05-20-13)

[125] Winston S. Churchill "Iron Curtain Speech" (March 5, 1946), one at the Fordham University website, www.fordham.edu/halsall/mod/churchill-iron.asp, accessed May 20, 2013

[126] "The Novikov Telegram" (27 September 1946), Online at the website of City University of New York, http://academic.brooklyn.cuny.edu/history/johnson/novikov.htm, accessed May 27, 2013

[127] Harry S. Truman's "Special Message to the Congress on Greece and Turkey: The Truman Doctrine" (March 12, 1947), online at http://voicesofdemocracy.umd.edu/truman-special-message-speech-text/, accessed May 27, 2013

[128] *Civil Defense and Homeland Security: A Short History of National Preparedness Efforts*, 2006, p. 6, prepared by the Homeland Security National Preparedness Task Force; online at http://training.fema.gov/EMIWeb/edu/docs/DHS%20Civil%20Defense-HS%20-%20Short%20History.pdf, accessed May 27, 2013

[129] Ibid.

[130] Ibid.

[131] *Civil Defense and Homeland Security: A Short History of National Preparedness Efforts*, published by the Department of Homeland Security, September 2006, pp. 13-16

[132] "Hurricanes of 1955," by Gordon E. Dunn, Walter R. Davis, and Paul L. Moore, online at the website of the National Oceanic and Atmospheric Administration (NOAA), at http://docs.lib.noaa.gov/rescue/mwr/083/mwr-083-12-0315.pdf, accessed June 20, 2013

[133] *Civil Defense and Homeland Security: A Short History of National Preparedness Efforts*, published by the Department of Homeland Security, September 2006, p. 14

[134] "President Truman's Statement Announcing the First Soviet A-Bomb September 23, 1949," online at www.atomicarchive.com/Docs/Hydrogen/SovietAB.shtml, accessed May 31, 2013

[135] "Hydrogen Bomb Decision," online at PBS website www.pbs.org/wgbh/amex/bomb/peopleevents/pandeAMEX56.html, accessed May 31, 2013

[136] From Civil Defense Museum website at www.civildefensemuseum.com/history.html, accessed June 17, 2013

[137] *The Fifty-Year Wound*, by Derek Leebaert (2002), p. 124

[138] David Lilienthal Journals, vol. 2, pp. 24-25

[139] "Hydrogen Bomb Decision," online at PBS website www.pbs.org/wgbh/amex/bomb/peopleevents/pandeAMEX56.html, accessed May 31, 2013

[140] *The Cold War: A New History*, by John Lewis Gaddis (2005), Penguin Press, p.58

[141] "Truman announces development of H-bomb," History Channel online at www.history.com/this-day-in-history/truman-announces-development-of-h-bomb, accessed June 3, 2013

[142] "First Hydrogen Bomb Test," by The Learning Network, *New York Times* online at http://learning.blogs.nytimes.com/2011/11/01/nov-1-1952-first-hydrogen-bomb-test/, accessed June 3, 2013

[143] "Layer Cake Test," PBS online at www.pbs.org/wgbh/amex/bomb/peopleevents/pandeAMEX60.html, accessed June 24, 2013

[144] From Comprehensive Nuclear Test Ban Treaty Organization (CTBTO) website at www.ctbto.org/specials/infamous-anniversaries/1-march-1954-castle-bravo/, accessed June 11, 2013

[145] "Brave Test Fallout Pattern," online at www.atomicarchive.com/Maps/BravoMap.shtml, accessed June 11, 2013

[146] From the website of U.S. National Library of Medicine, National Institutes of Health, at www.ncbi.nlm.nih.gov/pmc/articles/PMC1446783/, accessed June 11, 2013

[147] From Comprehensive Nuclear Test Ban Treaty Organization (CTBTO) website at www.ctbto.org/specials/infamous-anniversaries/30-october-1961-the-tsar-bomba/, accessed June 11, 2013

[148] "Infamous Anniversaries," Preparatory Commission for the Comprehensive Nuclear-Test-Ban Treaty (CTBT), online at www.ctbto.org/specials/infamous-anniversaries/3-october-1952-first-british-nuclear-test/, accessed June 20, 2013

[149] "Infamous Anniversaries," Preparatory Commission for the Comprehensive Nuclear-Test-Ban Treaty (CTBT), online at www.ctbto.org/specials/infamous-anniversaries/13-february-1960-the-first-french-nuclear-test/, accessed June 20, 2013

[150] "China Joins A-bomb Club," History Channel online at www.history.com/this-day-in-history/china-joins-a-bomb-club, accessed June 20, 2013

[151] *Civil Defense and Homeland Security: A Short History of National Preparedness Efforts*, published by the Department of Homeland Security, September 2006, p. 7

[152] Ibid.

[153] The American Presidency Project, online at www.presidency.ucsb.edu/ws/?pid=13777, accessed June 7, 2013

[154] *Civil Defense and Homeland Security: A Short History of National Preparedness Efforts*, 2006, p. 8

[155] From the *Detroit News* online at http://blogs.detroitnews.com/history/1999/03/31/when-bomb-shelters-were-all-the-rage/

[156] *Civil Defense and Homeland Security: A Short History of National Preparedness Efforts*, 2006, pp.8-9

[157] *Civil Defense and Homeland Security: A Short History of National Preparedness Efforts*, 2006, p. 10

[158] *Civil Defense and Homeland Security: A Short History of National Preparedness Efforts*, 2006, p. 11

[159] "First nationwide civil defense drill held," the History Channel, online at www.history.com/this-day-in-history/first-nationwide-civil-defense-drill-held, accessed June 12, 2013

[160] "Deterrence and Survival in the Nuclear Age," by the Security Resources Panel of the president's Science Advisory Committee, online at George Washington University website, www.gwu.edu/~nsarchiv/NSAEBB/NSAEBB139/nitze02.pdf, accessed June 26, 2013

[161] *Civil Defense and Homeland Security: A Short History of National Preparedness Efforts*, 2006, p. 10

[162] *The Cold War: A New History*, by John Lewis Gaddis (2005), Penguin Press, p. 68

[163] *Civil Defense and Homeland Security: A Short History of National Preparedness Efforts*, 2006, p. 11

[164] *Civil Defense and Homeland Security: A Short History of National Preparedness Efforts*, 2006, p. 7

[165] New Jersey Statues online at the website of LawServer Online, Inc., www.lawserver.com/law/state/new-jersey/nj-laws/new_jersey_laws_54_4-3-48, accessed June 28, 2011

[166] "Code of Alabama - Title 40: Revenue and Taxation - Section 40-18-15," from Legal Research website at http://law.onecle.com/alabama/revenue-and-taxation/40-18-15.html, accessed June 28, 2013

[167] From the website of Crosscut Public Media http://crosscut.com/2010/04/13/mossback/19739/This-shelter-is-bomb/, accessed June 24, 2013

[168] *Civil Defense and Homeland Security: A Short History of National Preparedness Efforts*, 2006, p. 11

[169] *The Fifty-Year Wound*, by Derek Leebaert, (2002), p. 270

[170] *Civil Defense and Homeland Security: A Short History of National Preparedness Efforts*, 2006, p. 12

[171] Ibid.

[172] From the *Washington Times* online at www.washingtontimes.com/news/2011/jun/27/cold-war-bomb-shelters-a-garish-trip-back-in-tome/?page=all, accessed June 24, 2013

[173] "Mutual Assured Destruction," Nuclear Age Peace Foundation, online at http://www.nuclearfiles.org/menu/key-issues/nuclear-weapons/history/cold-war/strategy/strategy-mutual-assured-destruction.htm, accessed June 4, 2013

[174] "McCarthyism," by Arthur Miller, online at www.pbs.org/wnet/americanmasters/episodes/arthur-miller/mccarthyism/484/, accessed June 4, 2013

[175] "House Un-American Activities Committee," online at George Washington University website, www.gwu.edu/~erpapers/teachinger/glossary/huac.cfm, accessed June 4, 2013

[176] "Spies Who Spilled Atomic Bomb Secrets," Smithsonian Institute online at www.smithsonianmag.com/history-archaeology/Spies-Who-Spilled-Atomic-Bomb-Secrets.html, accessed June 4, 2013

[177] *The Cold War: A New History*, by John Lewis Gaddis (2005), Penguin Press, p. 40

[178] *The Cold War: A New History*, by John Lewis Gaddis (2005), Penguin Press, p.39

[179] "Enemies from Within": Senator Joseph R. McCarthy's Accusations of Disloyalty, from History Matters website, http://historymatters.gmu.edu/d/6456/, accessed June 4, 2013

[180] Arthur Miller: McCarthyism, August 23, 2006, at PBS online, www.pbs.org/wnet/americanmasters/episodes/arthur-miller/mccarthyism/484/, accessed June 7, 2013

[181] "Hollywood Ten," History Channel online at www.history.com/topics/hollywood-ten, accessed June 7, 2013

[182] *The Fifty-Year Wound*, by Derek Leebaert, (2002), p. 115

[183] *The Cold War: A New History*, by John Lewis Gaddis (2005), Penguin Press, p.41

[184] "Armistice ends the Korean War," History Channel online at www.history.com/this-day-in-history/armistice-ends-the-korean-war

[185] "Search for U.S. troops missing in Korean War set to resume in North Korea," by The Associated Press/New York Daily News, March 8, 2012, online at http://www.nydailynews.com/news/national/search-u-s-troops-missing-korean-war-set-resume-north-korea-article-1.1035410#ixzz2Wa5VSgHq, accessed June 18, 2013

[186] From "The Veterans Hour," www.veteranshour.com/nam.htm, accessed June 12, 2013

[187] *The Fifty-Year Wound*, by Derek Leebaert, (2002), pp. 13-14

[188] From "The Veterans Hour," Vietnam War statistics, online at www.veteranshour.com/vietnam_war_statistics.htm, accessed June 12, 2013

[189] "Nixon Announces Peace Settlement Reached in Paris," online at www.history.com/this-day-in-history/nixon-announces-peace-settlement-reached-in-paris, accessed June 12, 2013

[190] "Looking Back: The End of the Vietnam War," by Michael Ip, March 29, 2013, ABC News online at http://abcnews.go.com/blogs/headlines/2013/03/looking-back-the-end-of-the-vietnam-war/, accessed June 11, 2013

[191] *The Fifty-Year Wound*, by Derek Leebaert, (2002), p.425

[192] "U.S. Planes Bomb North Vietnam," The History Channel, online at www.history.com/this-day-in-history/us-planes-bomb-north-vietnam, accessed June 18, 2013

[193] "Agent Orange," The History channel, online at http://www.history.com/topics/agent-orange, accessed June 18, 2013

[194] "Agent Orange's Shameful Legacy," The Week magazine, online at http://theweek.com/article/index/232816/agent-oranges-shameful-legacy, accessed June 18, 013

[195] *The Day of Battle*, by Rick Atkinson (2007), Henry Holt and Company, p.271

[196] *The Day of Battle*, by Rick Atkinson (2007), Henry Holt and Company, p.277

[197] Ibid.

[198] Ibid.

[199] "Writers and Editors War Tax Protest," online archives of Hood University at http://jfk.hood.edu/Collection/Weisberg%20Subject%20Index%20Files/W%20Disk/Writers%20and%20Editors%20Protest/Item%2005.pdf, accessed July 1, 2013

[200] From the "Good Life Center at Forest Farm," online at http://goodlife.org/About/WhoWereHelenandScottNearing/tabid/94/Default.aspx, accessed July 1, 2013

[201] *The Cold War: A New History*, by John Lewis Gaddis (2005), Penguin Press, p. 70

[202] Geneva Summit," Encyclopedia Britannica online at www.britannica.com/EBchecked/topic/229068/Geneva-Summit, accessed July 5, 2013

[203] *The Cold War: A New History*, by John Lewis Gaddis (2005), Penguin Press, pp. 112 – 113

[204] "The Berlin Crisis, 1958-1961," U.S Department of State, Office of the Historian, online at http://history.state.gov/milestones/1953-1960/BerlinCrises, accessed July 8, 2013

[205] "The Berlin Crisis, 1958-1961," U.S. Department of State Office of the historian online at http://history.state.gov/milestones/1953-1960/BerlinCrises, accessed July 1, 2013

[206] "Batista forced out by Castro-led revolution," from the History Channel online at www.history.com/this-day-in-history/batista-forced-out-by-castro-led-revolution, accessed July 5, 2013

[207] "Fidel Castro," Encyclopedia Britannica online at www.britannica.com/EBchecked/topic/98822/Fidel-Castro#ref157340, accessed July 5, 2013

[208] "Fidel Castro: From Rebel to El Presidente," by Ben Brudevold-Newman, Nationa Public Radio online at www.npr.org/templates/story/story.php?storyId=5598311, accessed July 6, 2013

[209] "Bay of Pigs Invasion," from the History Channel online at www.history.com/topics/bay-of-pigs-invasion, accessed July 5, 2013

[210] "The Bay of Pigs," John F. Kennedy Presidential Library and Museum, online at http://www.jfklibrary.org/JFK/JFK-in-History/The-Bay-of-Pigs.aspx, accessed July 5, 2013

[211] "Cuban Missile Crisis" online at PBS.org, www.history.com/topics/cuban-missile-crisis accessed July 1, 2013

[212] "John F. Kennedy Assassinated," from the History Channel online at www.history.com/this-day-in-history/john-f-kennedy-assassinated, accessed July 3, 2013

[213] "Nation's Capital Still Recovering from 1968 Riots," CNN online at www.cnn.com/US/9804/04/mlk.dc.riots/, accessed July 6, 2013

[214] "Army Troops in Capital as Negroes Riot," by Ben A. Franklin, New York Times online at http://partners.nytimes.com/library/national/race/040668race-ra.html, accessed July 6, 2013

[215] "The Mobe," PBS online at www.pbs.org/independentlens/chicago10/mobe.html, accessed July 8, 2013

[216] Warren Commission Report, National Archives, online at www.archives.gov/research/jfk/warren-commission-report/, accessed July 3, 2013

[217] "Seeking answers on King's killer," by Vincent Dowd, British Broadcasting Corporation online at http://news.bbc.co.uk/2/hi/americas/7329763.stm, accessed July 8, 2013

[218] "Was James Earl Ray Martin Luther King's Killer? Doubts Remain," from the Huffington Post online at www.huffingtonpost.com/2008/04/04/was-james-earl-ray-martin_n_95030.html, accessed July 8, 2013

[219] From Council on Foreign Relations website at www.cfr.org/about/, accessed July 11, 2013

[220] M. King Hubbert website at www.hubbertpeak.com/hubbert/, accessed July 16, 2013

[221] "After the Oil Runs Out," by James Jordan and James R. Powell, *Washington Post*, June 6, 2004; online at www.washingtonpost.com/wp-dyn/articles/A17039-2004Jun4.html, accessed July 16, 2013

[222] "How 'Silent Spring' Ignited the Environmental Movement," by Eliza Griswold, *New York Times* online at www.nytimes.com/2012/09/23/magazine/how-silent-spring-ignited-the-environmental-movement.html?pagewanted=all&_r=0, accessed July 8, 2013

[223] "The Story of Silent Spring," Natural Resources Defense Council online at www.nrdc.org/health/pesticides/hcarson.asp, accessed July 8, 2013

[224] "From Calm Leadership, Lasting Change," by Nancy F. Koehn, *New York Times* online at www.nytimes.com/2012/10/28/business/rachel-carsons-lessons-50-years-after-silent-spring.html?pagewanted=all, accessed July 8, 2013

[225] "The San Andreas Fault," by Sandra S. Schulz and Robert E. Wallace, U.S. Geological Survey website at http://pubs.usgs.gov/gip/earthq3/safaultgip.html, acccessed July 17, 2013

[226] "The 1950s," History Channel online at www.history.com/topics/1950s, accessed July 11, 2013

[227] "Northeast Blackout of 1965," online at the Energy Library, www.theenergylibrary.com/node/13087, accessed July 23, 2013

[228] "The Great Northeast Blackout," The History Channel online at www.history.com/this-day-in-history/the-great-northeast-blackout, accessed July 23, 2013

[229] "Blackout History Project," George Mason University, VA; online at www.blackout.gmu.edu/archive/pdf/fpc_65.pdf, accessed July 23, 2013

[230] Letter from NERC president Michehl R. Gent to U.S. Committee on Energy and Commerce, August 29, 2003, online at www.nerc.com/docs/docs/testimony/NERC_answers_to_Tauzin_082903.pdf, accessed July 23, 2013

[231] National Bureau of Economics Research online at www.nber.org/cycles.html, accessed July 11, 2013

[232] Don Stephens autobiography online at www.facebook.com/pages/Don-Stephens/104041522966643#, accessed July 11, 2013

[233] Steve Jobs Stanford Commencement Speech June 2005 online at www.youtube.com/watch?v=D1R-jKKp3NA&t=12m45s, accessed July 16, 2013

258

Chapter Three

[234] *Civil Defense and Homeland Security: A Short History of National Preparedness Efforts*, 2006, p. 18

[235] "Demographic Trends in Rural and Small Town America," by Kenneth Johnson, University of New Hampshire, for the Carsey Institute, 2006, online at www.carseyinstitute.unh.edu/publications/Report_Demographics.pdf, accessed August 16, 2013

[236] Cover, *The Yankee Magazine Book of Forgotten Arts* (1978) compilation of the best of the best articles from that magazine

[237] *Making the Best of Basics*, summary online at www.amazon.com/Making-Best-Basics-Preparedness-Handbook/dp/1882723252, accessed July 25, 2013

[238] "The Only Book You'll Ever Really Need," by Maria Rodale, online at www.organicgardening.com/living/only-book-youll-ever-really-need, accessed July 24, 2013

[239] *Tappan on Survival*, (1981), in foreword by Jerry Pournelle

[240] "Best Sellers, June 22, 1981," *Time Magazine* online at www.time.com/time/magazine/article/0,9171,950566,00.html?promoid=googlep accessed July 19, 2013

[241] Telephone interview with Dave Duffy, August 8, 2013

[242] "OPEC Oil Embargo, 1973-1974," U. S. Dept. of State Office of the Historian, online at http://history.state.gov/milestones/1969-1976/OPEC, accessed August 3, 2013

[243] "OPEC states declare oil embargo," History Channel online at www.history.com/this-day-in-history/opec-states-declare-oil-embargo, accessed August 3, 2013

[244] "Amazing Pictures of the Oil Crisis Of 1973," Business Insider online at www.businessinsider.com/gas-signs-1970s-2011-8?op=1#ixzz2aurCcaDz, accessed August 3, 2013

[245] "Energy Crisis 1970s," History Channel online at www.history.com/topics/energy-crisis, accessed August 3, 2013

[246] "Iranian students storm U.S. embassy in Tehran, leading to oil embargo," History Channel online at www.history.com/this-day-in-history/iranian-students-storm-us-embassy-in-tehran-leading-to-oil-embargo, accessed August 5, 2013

[247] "The State of the Union Address Delivered Before a Joint Session of the Congress," The American Presidency Project of the University of California at Santa Barbara, online at www.presidency.ucsb.edu/ws/?pid=33079, accessed August 5, 2013

[248] "The Gulf: Read My Ships," by Michael Kramer, August 20, 1990, *Time Magazine*, online at www.time.com/time/magazine/article/0,9171,970924,00.html#ixzz2bxLR1SLH, accessed August 14, 2013

[249] "Timeline: 20 years of major oil spills," May 2010, Australia Broadcasting Commission online at www.abc.net.au/news/2010-05-03/timeline-20-years-of-major-oil-spills/419898, accessed August 14, 2013

[250] "Oil Spills Fast Facts," August 2013, CNN News online at www.cnn.com/2013/07/13/world/oil-spills-fast-facts, August 14, 2013

[251] "Persian Gulf War," History Channel online at www.history.com/topics/persian-gulf-war, accessed August 5, 2013

[252] "Kuwait Oil Fires," July 2012, NASA online at www.nasa.gov/mission_pages/landsat/news/40th-top10-kuwait.html, accessed August 14, 2013

[253] "Impact of the Gulf War," by Patrick Lee, January 1991, Los Angeles Times, online at http://articles.latimes.com/1991-01-18/business/fi-102_1_oil-prices, accessed August 14, 2013

[254] "Weekly U.S. Regular All Formulations Retail Gasoline Prices (Dollars per Gallon)," U.S. Energy Information Administration, online at www.eia.gov/dnav/pet/hist/LeafHandler.ashx?f=W&n=PET&s=EMM_EPMR_PTE_NUS_DPG, accessed August 14, 2013

[255] "Nuclear Power History: Timeline From Inception To Fukushima," from Reuters, via the *Huffington Post*, June 13, 2012, online at www.huffingtonpost.com/2012/06/13/timeline-nuclear-power-history-fukushima_n_1593278.html, accessed August 5, 2013

[256] "Nuclear Reactor Operational Status Tables," U.S. Energy Information Administration online at www.eia.gov/nuclear/reactors/stats_table3.html, accessed august 5, 2013

[257] "The History of Solar," U.S. Department of Energy online at www1.eere.energy.gov/solar/pdfs/solar_timeline.pdf, accessed August 5, 2013

[258] "The International Nuclear and Radiological Event Scale," International Atomic Energy Agency online at http://www-ns.iaea.org/tech-areas/emergency/ines.asp, accessed August 7, 2013

[259] "A Matter of Degree," International Atomic Energy Agency online at www.iaea.org/Publications/Magazines/Bulletin/Bull511/51102744649.html, accessed August 7, 2013

[260] "The Past Is Present at Three Mile Island Nuclear Power Plant," by Kasia Klimasinka Oct 20, 2012, *Bloomberg News* online at www.bloomberg.com/news/2012-10-20/the-past-is-present-at-three-mile-island-nuclear-power-plant.html, accessed August 7, 2013

[261] "Backgrounder on the Three Mile Island Accident," United States Nuclear Regulatory Commission report online at www.nrc.gov/reading-rm/doc-collections/fact-sheets/3mile-isle.html, accessed August 7, 2013

[262] "Three Mile Island Accident," World Nuclear Association, March 2001, online at www.world-nuclear.org/info/Safety-and-Security/Safety-of-Plants/Three-Mile-Island-accident/#.Ugus_axNwZA, accessed August 14, 2013

[263] "Backgrounder on Chernobyl Nuclear Power Plant Accident," United States Nuclear Regulatory Commission report online at www.nrc.gov/reading-rm/doc-collections/fact-sheets/chernobyl-bg.html, accessed August 8, 2013

[264] From Nuclear Age Peace Foundation online at www.wagingpeace.org/menu/action/urgent-actions/chernobyl/, accessed August 8, 2013

[265] "Chernobyl's Fallout Exceeded Hiroshima : Disaster's Output Termed 30 Times Heavier Than WWII Bombs" *Los Angeles Times*, August 17, 1986, online at http://articles.latimes.com/1986-08-17/news/mn-16573_1_hiroshima-atomic-bomb, accessed August 8, 2013

[266] "Backgrounder on Chernobyl Nuclear Power Plant Accident," United States Nuclear Regulatory Commission report online at www.nrc.gov/reading-rm/doc-collections/fact-sheets/chernobyl-bg.html, accessed August 8, 2013

[267] Ibid.

[268] Press Release IHA/630 of the U.N. Department of Humanitarian Affairs, November 24, 1997, online at www.un.org/ha/chernobyl/docs/iha639.htm, accessed August 8, 2013

[269] "In Focus: The Chernobyl Disaster: 25 Years Ago," by Alan Taylor, March 23, 2011, *The Atlantic Magazine* online at www.theatlantic.com/infocus/2011/03/the-chernobyl-disaster-25-years-ago/100033/, accessed August 8, 2013

[270] "Backgrounder on Chernobyl Nuclear Power Plant Accident," United States Nuclear Regulatory Commission report online at www.nrc.gov/reading-rm/doc-collections/fact-sheets/chernobyl-bg.html, accessed August 8, 2013

[271] "Factbox: Key facts on Chernobyl nuclear accident," March 15, 2011, Reuters News Agency, online at http://www.reuters.com/article/2011/03/15/uk-nuclear-chernobyl-facts-idUSTRE72E69R20110315, accessed August 9, 2013

[272] "Chernobyl's 25-year shadow," by Matthew Chance, April 21, 2011, CNN online at www.cnn.com/2011/WORLD/asiapcf/04/20/chernobyl.25.years/index.html, accessed August 9, 2013

[273] From Frontline: "Why Do Americans Fear Nuclear Power?" PBS online at www.pbs.org/wgbh/pages/frontline/shows/reaction/readings/chernobyl.html, accessed August 8, 2013

[274] "Factbox: Key facts on Chernobyl nuclear accident," March 15, 2011, Reuters News Agency, online at http://www.reuters.com/article/2011/03/15/uk-nuclear-chernobyl-facts-idUSTRE72E69R20110315, accessed August 9, 2013

[275] "Second arch section for Chernobyl cover," June 12, 2013, *World Nuclear News* online at www.world-nuclear-news.org/rs_second_arch_section_for_chernobyl_cover_1206131.html, accessed August 8, 2013

[276] "Global nuclear weapons inventories, 1945-2010," by Robert S. Norris and Hans M. Kristensen, Bulletin of the Atomic Scientists July 2010 vol. 66 no. 4 77-83, SAGE academic publishing, online at http://bos.sagepub.com/content/66/4/77.full, accessed July 18, 2013

[277] "Looking Back: The Nuclear Arms Control Legacy of Ronald Reagan," by Daryl G. Kimball, Arms Control Association online at www.armscontrol.org/act/2004_07-08/Reagan, accessed August 9, 2013

[278] "Global nuclear weapons inventories, 1945-2010," by Robert S. Norris and Hans M. Kristensen, Bulletin of the Atomic Scientists July 2010 vol. 66 no. 4 77-83, SAGE academic publishing, online at http://bos.sagepub.com/content/66/4/77.full, accessed July 18, 2013

[279] "Loose Nukes," January 2006, Council on Foreign Relations online at www.cfr.org/weapons-of-mass-destruction/loose-nukes/p9549, accessed August 13, 2013

[280] "What Happened to the Soviet Superpower's Nuclear Arsenal?" by Graham Allizon for the Harvard Kennedy School's Belfer Center for Science and International Affairs, March 2012, online at http://nuclearsummit.org/files/What_Happened_to_Soviet_Arsenals_3.14.12_final .pdf, accessed August 14, 2013

[281] "Nuclear Smuggling from the Former Soviet Union: Threats and Responses," by Rensselaer Lee, foreign Policy Institute, April 2001, published online by Boston University at www.bu.edu/globalbeat/nuclear/FPRI042701.html, accessed August 14, 2013

[282] "Trafficking in Nuclear and Radioactive Material in 2005," Staff Report, International Atomic Energy Agency, online at www.iaea.org/newscenter/news/2006/traffickingstats2005.html, accessed August 14, 2013

[283] "The Primitivist Critique of Civilization," by Richard Heinberg, 1995, online at www.primitivism.com/primitivist-critique.htm, accessed August 20, 2013

[284] "Love Canal: the Start of A movement," by Lois Marie Gibbs, 1983, online at Boston University's website at www.bu.edu/lovecanal/canal, accessed August 15, 2013

[285] "The Long History of a Toxic-Waste Nightmare," by Dennis Hevesi, 1988, New York Times; online at www.nytimes.com/1988/09/28/nyregion/the-long-history-of-a-toxic-waste-nightmare.html, accessed August 15, 2013

[286] "Evacuation of Kids Urged," by Mike Brown, Niagara Gazette, August 2, 1978, online at http://library.buffalo.edu/specialcollections/lovecanal/documents/clippings/8-2-781.html, accessed August 15, 2013

[287] "LOVE CANAL: Nearby neighborhood flourishing, despite lingering concerns," by Dan Miner, August 3, 2008, The Journal Register (Medina, NY), online at http://journal-register.com/local/x681317483/LOVE-CANAL-Nearby-neighborhood-flourishing-despite-lingering-concerns/print, accessed August 16, 2013

[288] "Love Canal Cleaned Up," by Lois Ember, for Chemical and Engineering News, online at http://pubs.acs.org/cen/today/8212lovecanal.html, accessed August 15, 2013

[289] "Love Canal Cleanup Called Finished," Associated Press report at NBC News online at www.nbcnews.com/id/4554426/ns/us_news-environment/t/love-canal-cleanup-called-finished/#.Ug0jfqxNwZA, accessed August 15, 2013

[290] "Ex-Love Canal residents meet with attorneys on health concerns," by Charlie Specht, November 16, 2012, The Buffalo News, online at

www.buffalonews.com/apps/pbcs.dll/article?AID=/20121116/CITYANDREGION
/121119412/1010, accessed August 16, 2013
[291] "Love Canal: the Start of A movement," by Lois Marie Gibbs, 1983, online at
Boston University's website at www.bu.edu/lovecanal/canal, accessed August 15,
2013
[292] "History of the Resource Conservation and Recovery Act," Environmental
Protection Agency online at www.epa.gov/osw/laws-regs/rcrahistory.htm,
accessed August 27, 2013
[293] "Underground Storage Tanks," Environmental Protection Agency online at
www.epa.gov/oust/ , accessed August 27, 2013
[294] Leaking Underground Storage Tanks (LUSTs), Environmental Protection
Agency website at
http://yosemite.epa.gov/r10/water.nsf/a90aa654320d57f88825666a0070acf6/712ef
3340f56f58e88256ce000036ba9, accessed August 30, 2013
[295] "Court orders administration to follow nuclear waste law," by George F. Will,
August 21, 2013, *Washington Post* online at
http://articles.washingtonpost.com/2013-08-21/opinions/41431930_1_nuclear-
waste-waste-repository-yucca-mountain, accessed August 27, 2013
[296] "Inventory of radioactive waste disposals at sea" August 1999, International
Atomic Energy Agency, online at www-
pub.iaea.org/MTCD/Publications/PDF/te_1105_prn.pdf, accessed August 27, 2013
[297] "Bush Lifts Drilling Moratorium," by Steven Lee Myers and Carl Hulse, July
2008, *New York Times*, online at
www.nytimes.com/2008/07/14/washington/14drillcnd.html?_r=0, accessed August
21, 2013
[298] "The 13 largest oil spills in history," by Laura Moss, July 16 2010, Mother
Nature Network online at www.mnn.com/earth-matters/wilderness-
resources/stories/the-13-largest-oil-spills-in-history, accessed August 16, 2013
[299] "Gulf War Disaster: A Brief History," online at
www.counterspill.org/article/gulf-war-oil-disaster-brief-history, accessed August
20, 2013
[300] Dr. Jacqueline Michel,geochemist and President of Research Planning, in a
May 2010 interview with Marco Werman on PRI's *The World* (a co-production of
WGBH/Boston, Public Radio International, and the BBC World Service), online at
www.theworld.org/2010/05/lessons-learned-from-gulf-war-oil-spill/, accessed
August 20, 2013
[301] From "The Wreck of the *Exxon Valdez*," final report of the Alaska Oil Spill
Commission, published February 1990 by the State of Alaska; online at the
website of the *Exxon Valdez* Oil Spill Trustee Council,
http://www.evostc.state.ak.us/facts/details.cfm, accessed August 20, 2013
[302] "Questions and Answers" online at the website of the
Exxon Valdez Oil Spill Trustee Council, www.evostc.state.ak.us/facts/qanda.cfm
accessed August 20, 2013
[303] "The *Exxon Valdez* Oil Spill: How Much Oil Remains?" Alaska Fisheries
Science Center, for the U.S. National Oceanic and Atmospheric Administration,

by Jeff Short, Stanley Rice, and Mandy Lindeberg, 2001, online at www.afsc.noaa.gov/Quarterly/jas2001/feature_jas01.htm, accessed August 20, 2013

[304] "Environmental Effects of *Exxon Valdez* Spill Still Being Felt," by Sarah Graham, December 19, 2003, *Scientific American*, online at www.scientificamerican.com/article.cfm?id=environmental-effects-of, accessed August 20, 2013

[305] "Incident News: Argo Merchant," the U.S. National Oceanic and Atmospheric Administration, online at http://incidentnews.noaa.gov/incident/6231, accessed August 20, 2013

[306] "Incident News: M/V Mega Borg," the U.S. National Oceanic and Atmospheric Administration, online at http://incidentnews.noaa.gov/incident/6748, accessed August 20, 2013

[307] "Incident News: Barge Bouchard 155," the U.S. National Oceanic and Atmospheric Administration, online at http://incidentnews.noaa.gov/incident/5141, accessed August 20, 2013

[308] "A 'Dead Zone' Grows in the Gulf of Mexico," by Carol Kaesuk Yoon, published by *The New York Times* in 1998, online at www.fishingnj.org/artdedzn.htm, accessed August 30, 2013

[309] "Fish-Free zone," by Pat Durkin, December 5, 2000, *National Geographic News*, online at http://news.nationalgeographic.com/news/2000/12/1204_fish.html, accessed August 30, 2013

[310] "Mercury poisoning of thousands confirmed," by Jonathan Watts, October 15, 2001, *The Guardian*, online at www.theguardian.com/world/2001/oct/16/japan.jonathanwatts, acccessed August 30, 2013

[311] "Mercury Poisoning Contaminates Food of Alaskan Natives," United Press International, April 26, 1972, published in the *The Bulletin* (Bend, Oregon), online at http://news.google.com/newspapers?nid=1243&dat=19720426&id=9CQVAAAAI BAJ&sjid=v_cDAAAAIBAJ&pg=4694,106013, accessed August 30, 2013

[312] "Mercury: Basic Information," the Environmental Protection Agency online at www.epa.gov/hg/about.htm, accessed August 30, 2013

[313] "What You Need to Know about Mercury in Fish and Shellfish," Environmental Protection Agency, 2004, online at http://water.epa.gov/scitech/swguidance/fishshellfish/outreach/advice_index.cfm , accessed August 30, 2013

[314] "Study finds more mercury in freshwater fish, " by Marie Savard, Jessica Hoffman and Lara Naaman, August 21, 2009, ABC News online at http://abcnews.go.com/GMA/mercury-found-fish-streams-country/story?id=8369324, accessed August 30, 2013

[315] "Mercury in Fish More Dangerous Than Believed," by Dominique Mosbergen December 4, 2012, *Huffington Post* online at www.huffingtonpost.com/2012/12/04/mercury-in-fish-study-more-dangerous-treaty-un-talks_n_2238923.html, acccessed August 30, 2013

[316] "The 'Reagan Doctrine' is announced," History Channel online at www.history.com/this-day-in-history/the-reagan-doctrine-is-announced, accessed September 10, 2013

[317] "Kent State Incident," History Channel online at www.history.com/topics/kent-state, accessed September 3, 2013

[318] "Pentagon Papers," Encyclopedia Britannica online at www.britannica.com/EBchecked/topic/450326/Pentagon-Papers, accessed September 3, 2013.

[319] "Pentagon Papers," United Press International archives online at www.upi.com/Archives/Audio/Events-of-1971/The-Pentagon-Papers/#ixzz2dqQz7Upr, accessed September 3, 2013

[320] Ibid.

[321] "COVER STORY: Pentagon Papers: The Secret War," *TIME Magazine*, June 28, 1971, online at www.cnn.com/ALLPOLITICS/1996/analysis/back.time/9606/28/index.shtml, accessed September 3, 20 13

[322] "The Pentagon Papers," History Channel online at www.history.com/topics/pentagon-papers, accessed September 3, 2013

[323] "Watergate Scandal," History Channel online at www.history.com/topics/watergate, accessed September 3, 2013

[324] "FBI Finds Nixon Aides Sabotaged Democrats," by Carl Bernstein and Bob Woodward, Tuesday, October 10, 1972, the *Washington Post*, online at www.washingtonpost.com/wp-srv/national/longterm/watergate/articles/101072-1.htm, accessed September 3, 2013

[325] "Watergate Scandal," History Channel online at www.history.com/topics/watergate, accessed September 3, 2013

[326] "David Frost … Dies at 74," by Brian Stelter, September 1, 2013, *New York Times*, online at www.nytimes.com/2013/09/02/world/europe/david-frost-known-for-nixon-interview-dead-at-74.html, accessed September 3, 2013

[327] "The 'Reagan Doctrine' is announced," History Channel online at www.history.com/this-day-in-history/the-reagan-doctrine-is-announced, accessed September 10, 2013

[328] "The Iran-Contra Affair," PBS online at www.pbs.org/wgbh/americanexperience/features/general-article/reagan-iran/, accessed September 10, 2013

[329] "Understanding the Iran-Contra Affairs," a project of Brown University, online at www.brown.edu/Research/Understanding_the_Iran_Contra_Affair/timeline-iran.php, accessed September 10, 2012

[330] "Sandinista National Liberation Front," Princeton University online at www.princeton.edu/~achaney/tmve/wiki100k/docs/Sandinista_National_Liberation_Front.html, accessed September 10, 2013

[331] "The Iran-Contra Affair," PBS online at www.pbs.org/wgbh/americanexperience/features/general-article/reagan-iran/, accessed September 10, 2013

[332] "Case concerning the military and paramilitary activities in and against Nicaragua (Nicaragua v. United States of America)," International Court of Justice, online at www.icj-cij.org/docket/index.php?sum=367&code=nus&p1=3&p2=3&case=70&k=66&p3=5, accessed September 10, 2013

[333] "The Iran-Contra Scandal: The Declassified History (The National Security Archive Document Series)," online at www.amazon.com/The-Iran-Contra-Scandal-Declassified-National/dp/1565840240, accessed September 13, 2013

[334] List of Recessions in the United States, online at http://en.wikipedia.org/wiki/List_of_recessions_in_the_United_States, accessed September 11, 2013

[335] "The Nixon Shock," by Roger Lowenstein, August 4, 2011, *Boomberg Businessweek Magazine* online at www.businessweek.com/magazine/the-nixon-shock-08042011.html, accessed September 11, 2013

[336] Text of Richard Nixon's Address to the Nation Outlining a New Economic Policy, University of California at Santa Barbara's American Presidency Project, online at www.presidency.ucsb.edu/ws/?pid=3115, accessed September 11, 2013

[337] "Nixon's Colossal Monetary Error: The Verdict 40 Years Later," by Charles Kadlec, August 15, 2011, for *Forbes Magazine*, online at www.forbes.com/sites/charleskadlec/2011/08/15/nixons-colossal-monetary-error-the-verdict-40-years-later/, accessed September 11, 2013

[338] "History of Genetic Engineering," American RadioWorks online at http://americanradioworks.publicradio.org/features/gmos_india/history.html, accessed September 11, 2013

[339] "Twenty Years Ago Today: Dan Quayle Announces FDA Policy that Denies Americans Right to Know What's in Their Food," published May 26, 2012, on the Food Democracy Now website, www.fooddemocracynow.org/blog/2012/may/26/twenty_years_ago_today_dan_quayle_announces_policy/, accessed September 17, 2013

[340] "20 Years of GMO Policy That Keeps Americans in the Dark About Their Food," by Dave Murphy, May 30, 2012, for the *Huffington Post*, online at www.huffingtonpost.com/dave-murphy/dan-quayle-and-michael-ta_b_1551732.html, accessed September 17, 2013

[341] Report of the Alliance for Bio-Integrity by Executive Director Steven M. Druker, online at www.biointegrity.org/ext-summary.html, accessed September 17, 2013

[342] Genetically Engineered Foods: Statement of James H. Maryanski, Ph.D, before the Subcommittee on Basic Research, House Committee on Science, October 19, 1999, online at www.fda.gov/newsevents/testimony/ucm115032.htm, accessed September 17, 2013

[343] "20 Questions on Genetically Modified (GM) Foods," World Health Organization online at www.who.int/foodsafety/publications/biotech/20questions/en/, accessed September 17, 2013

[344] "Top Five Myths Of Genetically Modified Seeds, Busted," by Dan Charles, October 18, 2012, For National Public Radio (NPR), online at www.npr.org/blogs/thesalt/2012/10/18/163034053/top-five-myths-of-genetically-modified-seeds-busted, accessed September 19, 2013

[345] "Are GMOs Safe? Global Independent Science Organizations Weigh In," by Jon Entine, August 29, 2013, *Forbes Magazine* online at www.forbes.com/sites/jonentine/2013/08/29/are-gmos-safe-global-independent-science-organizations-weigh-in/, accessed September 19, 2013

[346] "Doctors Warn: Avoid Genetically Modified Food," by Jeffrey M. Smith, May 2009, for The Institute for Responsible Technology, online at www.responsibletechnology.org/doctors-warn, accessed September 19, 2013

[347] "Advocacy Group Pushes For Statewide GMO Label Law," by Michelle Roberts, December 12, 2013, WBZ-TV online at http://boston.cbslocal.com/2013/12/12/advocacy-group-pushes-for-statewide-gmo-label-law/, accessed December 17, 2013

[348] "1970: Hijacked jets destroyed by guerrillas," British Broadcasting Corporation online at http://news.bbc.co.uk/onthisday/hi/dates/stories/september/12/newsid_2514000/2514929.stm, accessed September 19, 2013

[349] "Nixon Statement Announcing a Program To Deal With Airplane Hijacking," September 11, 1970, University of California, Santa Barbara American Presidency Project, online at www.presidency.ucsb.edu/ws/?pid=2659#axzz2fMbJRcg7, accessed September 19, 2013

[350] "Iran Hostage Crisis," The History Channel website, www.history.com/topics/iran-hostage-crisis, accessed September 24, 2013

[351] "Target America: Terrorist Attacks on Americans, 1979-1988," Public Broadcasting System online at www.pbs.org/wgbh/pages/frontline/shows/target/etc/cron.html, accessed September 24, 2013

[352] "The Protection of U.S. Forces Abroad," part of Annex 1 in a Secretary of Defense report to the President, released Sept. 16, 1996, online at www.defense.gov/speeches/speech.aspx?speechid=937, accessed October 1, 2013

[353] Ibid.

[354] "U.S. embassies in East Africa bombed," History Channel online at www.history.com/this-day-in-history/us-embassies-in-east-africa-bombed, accessed October 1, 2013

[355] "Bombs Explode at 2 U.S. Embassies in Africa; Scores Dead," by William Claiborne, Saturday, August 8, 1998, *Washington Post*, online at www.washingtonpost.com/wp-srv/inatl/longterm/eafricabombing/stories/main080898.htm, accessed October 1, 2013

[356] "U.S. Raids in Libya and Somalia Strike Terror Targets," by David D. Kirkpatrick, Nicholas Kulish, and Eric Schmitt, October 5, 2013, the *New York Times* online at www.nytimes.com/2013/10/06/world/africa/Al-Qaeda-Suspect-Wanted-in-US-Said-to-Be-Taken-in-Libya.html?_r=0, accessed October 8, 2013

[357] "The Worst School Massacre In American History Was 'Gun-Free'," by Pete Winn, December 19, 2012, online at CNS News (Cybercast News Service), http://cnsnews.com/blog/pete-winn/worst-school-massacre-american-history-was-gun-free#sthash.zVP4pDc5.dpuf, accessed October 2, 2013

[358] "Timeline: Deadly Mass Killings," December 14, 2012, the *Hartford Courant* online at http://articles.courant.com/2012-12-14/news/hc-timeline-mass-killings-20121214_1_mass-killings-luke-woodham-police-officer-shot, accessed October 2, 2013

[359] "Medway man takes readers behind the 'Mad Bomber,'" by Chris Bergeron, *MetroWest Daily News*, June 13, 2011, online at www.metrowestdailynews.com/news/x1166553376/Medway-man-takes-readers-behind-the-Mad-Bomber#ixzz2ga48vlM0, accessed October 2, 2013

[360] "1969, a Year of Bombings," by Bobby Allyn, August 27, 2009, *New York Times*, online at http://cityroom.blogs.nytimes.com/2009/08/27/1969-a-year-of-bombings/?_r=0, accessed October 2, 2013

[361] "T is for Terror," July 9, 2003, *Newsweek Magazine* online at www.nbcnews.com/id/3070093#.UkxE_H9AR7Q, accessed October 2, 2013

[362] "America's First Bioterrorism Attack," by Philip Elmer-DeWitt, Sept. 30, 2001, *Time Magazine* online at http://content.time.com/time/magazine/article/0,9171,176937,00.html#ixzz2gaGZPRzh, accessed October 2, 2013

[363] "Terror Hits Home: The Oklahoma City Bombing," Federal Bureau of Investigation online at www.fbi.gov/about-us/history/famous-cases/oklahoma-city-bombing, accessed October 2, 2013

[364] "Riverdale Press, Bronx Paper Made Famous By Bombing, Sold," *Editor and Publisher* magazine, June 4, 2008, online at www.editorandpublisher.com/PrintArticle/-Riverdale-Press-Bronx-Paper-Made-Famous-By-Bombing-Sold, accessed September 24, 2013

[365] "World Trade Center Bombed," History Channel online at www.history.com/this-day-in-history/world-trade-center-bombed, accessed September 24, 2013

[366] "Sheik Sentenced to Life in Prison in Bombing Plot," by Joseph P. Fried January 18, 1996, *New York Times*, online at www.nytimes.com/1996/01/18/nyregion/sheik-sentenced-to-life-in-prison-in-bombing-plot.html, accessed October 1, 2013

[367] "Hurricanes in History," National Weather Service's National Hurricane Center, online at www.nhc.noaa.gov/outreach/history/#agnes, accessed October 8, 2013

[368] "Tropical Cyclone Naming," World Meteorological Association online at www.wmo.int/pages/prog/www/tcp/Storm-naming.html, accessed October 8, 2013

[369] . "Hurricane Gloria - September 27, 1985," National Weather Service online at www.erh.noaa.gov/mhx/EventReviews/19850927/19850927.php, accessed October 10, 2013

[370] "The Deadliest, Costliest, and Most Intense United States Tropical Cyclones from 1851 to 2010 (and Other Frequently Requested Hurricane Facts)," National

Hurricane Center of the National Weather Service, online at www.nhc.noaa.gov/pdf/nws-nhc-6.pdf, accessed October 10, 2013

[371] "Hurricanes in History: Hurricane Hugo, 1989," National Hurricane Center of the National Weather Service, online at www.nhc.noaa.gov/outreach/history/#hugo, accessed October 10, 2013

[372] "Hurricanes in History: Hurricane Andrew, 1992," National Hurricane Center of the National Weather Service, online at http://www.nhc.noaa.gov/outreach/history/#andrew

[373] "Hurricane Andrew: 20 Facts You May Have Forgotten," August 2012, *Huffington Post* online at www.huffingtonpost.com/2012/08/21/20-facts-hurricane-andrew-anniversary_n_1819405.html, accessed October 10, 2013

[374] "The blizzard of 1993: 20-year anniversary of March Superstorm," by Don Lipman, March 11, 2013, *Washington Post* online at www.washingtonpost.com/blogs/capital-weather-gang/post/the-blizzard-of-1993-20-year-anniversary-of-march-superstorm/2013/03/11/73e205f6-8a67-11e2-98d9-3012c1cd8d1e_blog.html

[375] "Blizzard of '93: Hundreds Killed, Two Dozen States Impacted," by Alex Sosnowski, Expert Senior Meteorologist for AccuWeather.com, March 15, 2013, online at www.accuweather.com/en/weather-news/blizzard-93-20th-anniversary/7393746, accessed October 14, 2013

[376] "Assessment of the Superstorm of March 1993," National Weather Service, National Oceanic and Atmospheric Administration, online at www.nws.noaa.gov/om/assessments/superstorm/superstorm.pdf, accessed October 10, 2013

[377] "Mt. St. Helens Eruption, 1980" San Diego State University online at www.geology.sdsu.edu/how_volcanoes_work/Sthelens.html, accessed October 14, 2013

[378] "Top 10 Greatest Eruptions in Geologic History," Discovery Channel News, December 12, 2012, online at http://news.discovery.com/earth/weather-extreme-events/top-10-volcano-eruptions-in-geological-history.htm, accessed October 14, 2013

[379] "Mount Rainier: Danger at our door," by Eric Sorensen, May 16, 2000, *Seattle Times* online at http://seattletimes.com/special/helens/story3.html, accessed October 14, 2013

[380] "Remembering the 1980 Mount St. Helens Eruption," May 19, 2002, AccuWeather online at www.accuweather.com/en/weather-news/remembering-the-1980-mount-st/65304, accessed October 14, 2013

[381] "Mount St. Helens Eruption: Facts & Information," by Mary Bagley, February 28, 2013, *LiveScience* online magazine at www.livescience.com/27553-mount-st-helens-eruption.html, accessed October 15, 2013

[382] News report at the University of Utah Seismic Station, online at www.quake.utah.edu/RecentNews/nvews.shtml, accessed October 15, 2013

[383] NVEWS: National Volcano Early Warning System," U.S. Geological Survey online at http://volcanoes.usgs.gov/publications/2009/nvews.php, accessed October 15, 2013

[384] "Volcano Hazards Program," U.S. Geological Survey, online at http://volcanoes.usgs.gov/, accessed October 15, 2013

[385] "Mount Rainier - Living Safely With a Volcano in Your Backyard," by Carolyn L. Driedger and William E. Scott, USGS, Republished from USGS fact sheet 2008-3062; online at Geology.com http://geology.com/usgs/rainier/, accessed October 16, 2013

[386] "Mount Rainier: Danger at our door," by Eric Sorensen, May 16, 2000, *Seattle Times* online at http://seattletimes.com/special/helens/story3.html, accessed October 16, 2013

[387] "Number of Earthquakes in the United States for 1990 – 1999," U.S. Geological Survey online at http://earthquake.usgs.gov/earthquakes/eqarchives/year/info_1990s.php, accessed October 14, 2013

[388] "San Francisco–Oakland earthquake of 1989," History Channel online at www.history.com/topics/san-francisco-oakland-earthquake-of-1989, accessed October 16, 2013

[389] "Northridge earthquake of 1994," History Channel online at www.history.com/topics/northridge-earthquake-of-1994, accessed October 16, 2013

[390] "Earthquakes threaten many vulnerable Calif. buildings, little being done about it, CBS News online at www.cbsnews.com/video/watch/?id=50157319n, accessed October 17, 2013

[391] "When space weather attacks!" by Brad Plumer, July 13, 2013, *Washington Post* online at www.washingtonpost.com/blogs/wonkblog/wp/2013/07/13/when-space-weather-attacks/

[392] Ibid.

[393] "Power Failure in Canada During 1989," Australian Government Bureau of Meterology, online at www.ips.gov.au/Educational/1/3/12 , accessed October 16, 2013

[394] From the National Aeronautics and Space Administration website at www.nasa.gov/topics/earth/features/sun_darkness.html, accessed August 12, 2013

[395] "Massive solar flare narrowly misses Earth, EMP disaster barely avoided," by Paul Bedard,| July 31, 2013, *Washington Examiner* online at http://washingtonexaminer.com/massive-solar-flare-narrowly-misses-earth-emp-disaster-barely-avoided/article/2533727, accessed October 16, 2013

[396] *Civil Defense and Homeland Security: A Short History of National Preparedness Efforts*, 2006, p. 14, prepared by the Homeland Security National Preparedness Task Force; online at http://training.fema.gov/EMIWeb/edu/docs/DHS%20Civil%20Defense-HS%20-%20Short%20History.pdf, accessed May 27, 2013

[397] *Civil Defense and Homeland Security: A Short History of National Preparedness Efforts*, 2006, p. 16, prepared by the Homeland Security National Preparedness Task Force; online at http://training.fema.gov/EMIWeb/edu/docs/DHS%20Civil%20Defense-HS%20-%20Short%20History.pdf, accessed May 27, 2013

[398] *Civil Defense and Homeland Security: A Short History of National Preparedness Efforts*, 2006, p. 17, prepared by the Homeland Security National Preparedness Task Force; online at http://training.fema.gov/EMIWeb/edu/docs/DHS%20Civil%20Defense-HS%20-%20Short%20History.pdf, accessed May 27, 2013

[399] *Civil Defense and Homeland Security: A Short History of National Preparedness Efforts*, 2006, p. 19, prepared by the Homeland Security National Preparedness Task Force; online at http://training.fema.gov/EMIWeb/edu/docs/DHS%20Civil%20Defense-HS%20-%20Short%20History.pdf, accessed May 27, 2013

[400] *Civil Defense and Homeland Security: A Short History of National Preparedness Efforts*, 2006, p. 20, prepared by the Homeland Security National Preparedness Task Force; online at http://training.fema.gov/EMIWeb/edu/docs/DHS%20Civil%20Defense-HS%20-%20Short%20History.pdf, accessed May 27, 2013

[401] *Civil Defense and Homeland Security: A Short History of National Preparedness Efforts*, 2006, p. 21, prepared by the Homeland Security National Preparedness Task Force; online at http://training.fema.gov/EMIWeb/edu/docs/DHS%20Civil%20Defense-HS%20-%20Short%20History.pdf, accessed May 27, 2013

[402] *Civil Defense and Homeland Security: A Short History of National Preparedness Efforts*, 2006, p. 23, prepared by the Homeland Security National Preparedness Task Force; online at http://training.fema.gov/EMIWeb/edu/docs/DHS%20Civil%20Defense-HS%20-%20Short%20History.pdf, accessed May 27, 2013

[403] *Civil Defense and Homeland Security: A Short History of National Preparedness Efforts*, 2006, p. 24, prepared by the Homeland Security National Preparedness Task Force; online at http://training.fema.gov/EMIWeb/edu/docs/DHS%20Civil%20Defense-HS%20-%20Short%20History.pdf, accessed May 27, 2013

[404] "Y2K Bug," Encyclopedia Britannica online at www.britannica.com/EBchecked/topic/382740/Y2K-bug , accessed October 25, 2013

[405] "Y2K prep saves St. Cloud paper ... 11 years later," by David Brauer, February 9, 2011, *Minneapolis Post*, online at www.minnpost.com/braublog/2011/02/y2k-prep-saves-st-cloud-paper-11-years-later, accessed October 25, 2013

[406] "Area Counties Are Prepping for Y2K...," by Marc Levy, *Philadelphia Inquirer* online at http://articles.philly.com/1999-11-18/news/25497189_1_emergency-operations-emergency-management-operations-centers, accessed October 25, 2013

Chapter Four

[407] The USS *Cole* Bombing, Federal Bureau of Investigation website at www.fbi.gov/about-us/history/famous-cases/uss-cole, accessed October 30, 2013

[408] "Terrorist Attack on USS Cole: Background and Issues for Congress," by Raphael Perl and Ronald O'Rourke for the Congressional Research Service, online at the Navy Department Library, online at www.history.navy.mil/library/online/usscole_crsreport.htm, accessed October 30, 2013

[409] "Air Traffic Controllers Recall 9/11," ABC News online at http://abcnews.go.com/2020/story?id=123822, accessed November 9, 2013

[410] "Amerithrax or Anthrax Investigation," Federal Bureau of Investigation online at http://www.fbi.gov/about-us/history/famous-cases/anthrax-amerithrax/amerithrax-investigation, accessed October 30, 2013

[411] "F.B.I., Laying Out Evidence, Closes Anthrax Case," by Scott Shane, February 19, 2010, *New York Times* online at www.nytimes.com/2010/02/20/us/20anthrax.html?ref=bruceeivins&_r=0, accessed December 10, 2013

[412] "9/11 Investigation," Federal Bureau of Investigation online at www.fbi.gov/about-us/history/famous-cases/9-11-investigation/9-11-investigation, accessed October 30 ,2013

[413] Book description, *Writing the War on Terrorism*, online at Amazon.com, http://www.amazon.com/Writing-War-Terrorism-Counter-terrorism-Approaches/dp/0719071216/ref=sr_1_4?s=books&ie=UTF8&qid=1383234289&sr=1-4&keywords=richard+jackson+terrorism, accessed October 31, 2013

[414] USA PATRIOT ACT, U.S. Government Printing Office, online at www.gpo.gov/fdsys/pkg/PLAW-107publ56/pdf/PLAW-107publ56.pdf, accessed October 31, 2013

[415] "Threats And Responses: Government Report: U.S. Report Faults the Roundup Of Illegal Immigrants After 9/11," by Eric Lichtblau, June 03, 2003, *New York Times* online at www.nytimes.com/2003/06/03/us/threats-responses-government-report-us-report-faults-roundup-illegal-immigrants.html?pagewanted=all&src=pm, accessed October 30, 2013

[416] "What is the USA PATRIOT Act?" ACLU online at www.aclu.org/national-security/surveillance-under-usa-patriot-act, accessed October 31, 2013

[417] "National Security Letters," January 10, 2011, ACLU online at https://www.aclu.org/national-security-technology-and-liberty/national-security-letters, accessed October 31,2013

[418] "The Terrorist Threat Confronting the United States," testimony of Dale L. Watson February 6, 2002, Federal Bureau of Investigation online at http://web.archive.org/web/20100410013616/http://www.fbi.gov/congress/congress02/watson020602.htm, accessed November 4, 2013

[419] Video of Senator Rand Paul testimony, online at www.youtube.com/watch?v=4klctRWLiPo, accessed November 4, 2013

[420] "Sen. Rand Paul Defends Constitutional Liberties," Nov 29, 2011, press release at www.paul.senate.gov/?p=press_release&id=390, accessed November 5, 2013

[421] "Civil Defense and Homeland Security: A Short History of National Preparedness Efforts," 2006, p.26

[422] "Civil Defense and Homeland Security: A Short History of National Preparedness Efforts," 2006, p.27

[423] Ibid.

[424] Civil Defense and Homeland Security: A Short History of National Preparedness Efforts," 2006, p.28

[425] Department of Homeland Security website at www.gov.com/agency/dhs/, accessed November 12, 2013

[426] "Domestic Terrorism," September 7, 2009, online at the FBI website www.fbi.gov/news/stories/2009/september/domterror_090709, accessed November 12, 2013

[427] Ibid.

[428] Ibid.

[429] "You Might Be A Terrorist If . . .," February 6, 2012, *Network World* magazine online at www.networkworld.com/community/blog/25-more-ridiculous-fbi-lists-you-might-be-terrorist-if, accessed November 12, 2013

[430] University of Virginia Office of Emergency Preparendess, online at http://www.virginia.edu/emergencypreparedness/documents/SituationalAwareness.pdf, accessed November 12, 2013

[431] "NSA stores metadata of millions of web users for up to a year, secret files show," by James Ball, September 30, 2013, *The Guardian* online at www.theguardian.com/world/2013/sep/30/nsa-americans-metadata-year-documents , accessed November 13, 2013

[432] "When Metadata Becomes Megadata: What the Government Can Learn," by Aubra Anthony, June 17, 2013, Center for Democracy and Technology, online at https://www.cdt.org/blogs/1706when-metadata-becomes-megadata-what-government-can-learn-metadata, accessed November 14, 2013

[433] "Top senator: Obama didn't know of U.S. spying on Germany's leader," by Tom Cohen, October 29, 2013, CNN online at www.cnn.com/2013/10/28/politics/white-house-stopped-wiretaps/, accessed November 13, 2013

[434] FEMA preparedness website, www.Ready.gov, accessed November 12, 2013

[435] "Declassification and Transparency," National Security Agency website online at www.nsa.gov/public_info/declass/, accessed December 3, 2013

[436] "Secret Testing in the United States, PBS online at www.pbs.org/wgbh/americanexperience/features/general-article/weapon-secret-testing/, accessed June 19, 2013

[437] "Protocol for the Prohibition of the Use in War of Asphyxiating, Poisonous or Other Gases, and of Bacteriological Methods of Warfare (Geneva Protocal)", online at the U.S. Department of State website, www.state.gov/t/isn/4784.htm, accessed June 19, 2013

[438] From PBS American Experience series, online at www.pbs.org/wgbh/americanexperience/features/introduction/weapon-introduction/, accessed June 19, 2013

[439] "Bioweapons Tested in U.S. in 1960s," by Associated Press reporter Matt Kelley, on the website of the University of California at Los Angeles School of Public Health, Department of Epidemiology, www.ph.ucla.edu/epi/bioter/bioeweaponstestedus.html, accessed June 27, 2013

[440] Oct. 9, 2002 News release by Dept. of Defense on chem/bio testing at http://www.defense.gov/utility/printitem.aspx?print=http://www.defense.gov/releases/release.aspx?releaseid=3504, accessed June 19, 2013

[441] "Project SHAD," From the website of Rep. Mike Thompson, http://mikethompson.house.gov/issues/issue/?IssueID=14752, accessed June 19, 2013

[442] "Statement of The Honorable Michael Thompson," House Committee on Veterans Affairs, online at http://archives.democrats.veterans.house.gov/hearings/Testimony.aspx?TID=41588&Newsid=249&Name=The%20Honorable%20Michael%20%20Thompson, accessed December 3, 2013

[443] "Nixon Ends Biological Weapons Program," Public Broadcasting Station online at www.pbs.org/wgbh/americanexperience/features/general-article/weapon-nixon-ends/, accessed December 3, 2013

[444] "Then & Now: U.S. Biological Weapons Research," Public Broadcasting Station online at www.pbs.org/wgbh/americanexperience/features/then-and-now/weapon-then-now/, accessed December 3, 2013

[445] "Pentagon seeking vaccine for bioterror disease threat," November 15, 2013, *Military Times* online at www.militarytimes.com/article/20131115/NEWS04/311150010/Pentagon-seeking-vaccine-bioterror-disease-threat, accessed December 3, 2013

[446] "Bioterrorism Agents/Diseases," Centers for Disease Control and Prevention, online at www.bt.cdc.gov/agent/agentlist-category.asp, accessed December 3, 2013

[447] "U.S. nearly detonated nuclear bomb over North Carolina in 1961, new book reveals," by the Associated Press, September 21, 2013, New York Daily News online at www.nydailynews.com/news/national/u-s-detonated-nuclear-bomb-north-carolina-1961-book-article-1.1463241, accessed December 10, 2013

[448] "One cheap switch saved US from nuclear catastrophe in 1961," by M. Alex Johnson, NBC News online at http://usnews.nbcnews.com/_news/2013/09/21/20608882-one-cheap-switch-saved-us-from-nuclear-catastrophe-in-1961-declassified-document-reveals?lite, accessed December 10, 2013

[449] From "American Cryptology During the Cold War, 1945 – 1989," Series VI, Volume 5, Book IV, by Thomas R. Johnson, for the Center for Cryptologic History, National Security Agency, published in 1999, released to the public January 14, 2011. Online in National Security Archives at George Washington University,

www.gwu.edu/~nsarchiv/NSAEBB/NSAEBB426/docs/2.American%20Cryptolog
y%20During%20the%20Cold%20War%201945-
1989%20Book%20IV%20Cryptologic%20Rebirth%201981-1989-1999.pdf,
accessed August 12, 2013

[450] "The USSR and US Came Closer to Nuclear War Than We Thought," by
Douglas Birch May 28 2013, The Atlantic Magazine online at
www.theatlantic.com/international/archive/2013/05/the-ussr-and-us-came-closer-
to-nuclear-war-than-we-thought/276290/, accessed August 9, 2013

[451] "A Cold War Conundrum: The 1983 Soviet War Scare," by Benjamin B.
Fischer, 2007, U.S. Central Intelligence Agency, online at
www.cia.gov/library/center-for-the-study-of-intelligence/csi-publications/books-
and-monographs/a-cold-war-conundrum/source.htm#HEADING1-13, accessed
August 12, 2013

[452] "Russia Nuke Attack Drill As China Selects U.S. Targets," editorial, November
1, 2013, *Investor's Business Daily* online at http://news.investors.com/ibd-
editorials/110113-677675-russia-conducts-nuclear-missile-attack-drill.htm,
accessed December 10, 2013
Read More At Investor's Business Daily: http://news.investors.com/ibd-
editorials/110113-677675-russia-conducts-nuclear-missile-attack-
drill.htm#ixzz2n5akRquJ
Follow us: @IBDinvestors on Twitter | InvestorsBusinessDaily on Facebook

[453] "Pentagon's Global Strike Weapon Stuck In Limbo; Congress Fears Accidental
Nuclear War," by David Axe, December 17, 2012, *Breaking Defense* online
magazine at http://breakingdefense.com/2012/12/pentagons-global-strike-weapon-
stuck-in-limbo-congress-fears-a/, accessed December 10, 2013

[454] "It's official: Recession since Dec. '07," by Chris Isidore, December 1, 2008,
CNN online at http://money.cnn.com/2008/12/01/news/economy/recession/,
accessed December 10, 2013

[455] "Recession officially ended in June 2009," by Chris Isidore, September 20,
2010, CNNMoney online at
http://money.cnn.com/2010/09/20/news/economy/recession_over/, accessed
December 18, 2013

[456] "Years after recession, many in U.S. still struggling, polls show," by Susan
Heavey, September 12, 2013, Reuters online at
www.reuters.com/article/2013/09/12/us-usa-poverty-hunger-
idUSBRE98B1BG20130912, accessed December 18, 2013

[457] "Why is the national debt $16 trillion?," by Glenn Kessler, January 4, 2013,
Washington Post online at www.washingtonpost.com/blogs/fact-
checker/post/why-is-the-national-debt-16-trillion/2013/01/03/e2a85386-55fc-
11e2-8b9e-dd8773594efc_blog.html, accessed December 10, 2013

[458] "The 2003 Northeast Blackout, 10 Years Later," Huffington Post online at
www.huffingtonpost.com/2013/08/14/2003-northeast-blackout_n_3751171.html,
accessed December 18, 2013

[459] "Blackouts: A History," by Patrick J. Kiger, National Geographic Channel online at http://channel.nationalgeographic.com/channel/american-blackout/articles/blackouts-a-history/, accessed December 18, 2013

[460] "The Blackout of 2003," by James Barron, August 15, 2003, *The New York Times* online at www.nytimes.com/2003/08/15/nyregion/blackout-2003-overview-power-surge-blacks-northeast-hitting-cities-8-states.html?pagewanted=all&src=pm, accessed December 18, 2013

[461] "The Stuxnet Worm," Norton antivirus information online at http://us.norton.com/stuxnet, accessed December 19, 2013

[462] "Obama Order Sped Up Wave of Cyberattacks Against Iran," by David E. Sanger, June 1, 2012, *The New York Times* online at www.nytimes.com/2012/06/01/world/middleeast/obama-ordered-wave-of-cyberattacks-against-iran.html, accessed December 19, 2013

[463] "Hacking U.S. Secrets, China Pushes for Drones," by Edward Wong, September 20, 2013, *The New York Times* online at www.nytimes.com/2013/09/21/world/asia/hacking-us-secrets-china-pushes-for-drones.html, accessed December 19, 2013

[464] "Obamacare Website Targeted About 16 Times by Cyber Attacks," by Alyssa Newcomb and Matthew Larotonda, November 13, 2013, ABC News online at http://abcnews.go.com/Politics/obamacare-website-targeted-16-times-cyber-attacks-official/story?id=20878814, accessed December 19, 2013

[465] "Exclusive: FBI warns of U.S. government breaches by Anonymous hackers," by Jim Finkle and Joseph Menn, November 15, 2013, Reuters online at www.reuters.com/article/2013/11/15/us-usa-security-anonymous-fbi-idUSBRE9AE17C20131115, accessed December 30, 2013

[466] "Tsunami of 2004 Fast Facts," August 23, 2013, CNN News online at www.cnn.com/2013/08/23/world/tsunami-of-2004-fast-facts/, accessed November 5, 2013

[467] "History's Biggest Tsunamis," March 11, 2011, LiveScience online at www.livescience.com/13176-history-biggest-tsunamis-earthquakes.html, accessed November 5, 2013

[468] "2005 Kashmir Earthquake," History Channel online at www.history.com/topics/kashmir-earthquake, accessed November 14, 2013

[469] "Haiti Dominates Earthquake Fatalities in 2010," U.S. Geological Survey, online at www.usgs.gov/newsroom/article.asp?ID=2679, accessed November 14, 2013

[470] "Aftershock mapping," U.S. Geological Survey, online at http://earthquake.usgs.gov/earthquakes/aftershocks/?event=2010rja6, accessed November 14, 2013

[471] "Years after a deadly earthquake, Haiti remains in need," editorial, *Keene Sentinel* online at http://www.sentinelsource.com/opinion/editorial/years-after-a-deadly-earthquake-haiti-remains-in-need/article_8526902f-d0ba-5123-bbdc-f9fc52e4429d.html, accessed November 14, 2013

[472] "USGS Updates Magnitude of Japan's 2011 Tohoku Earthquake to 9.0," US Geological Survey online at

www.usgs.gov/newsroom/article.asp?ID=2727&from=rss_home, accessed
November 14, 2013

[473] "Japan Earthquake 2011: 8.9 Magnitude Earthquake Hits, 30-Foot Tsunami
Triggered," *The Huffington Post*, online at
http://www.huffingtonpost.com/2011/03/11/japan-earthquake-
tsunami_n_834380.html, accessed November 14, 2013

[474] "Death Toll Estimate in Japan Soars as Relief Efforts Intensify," by Martin
Fackler and MARK Mcdonald, March 13, 2011, *New York Times* online at
www.nytimes.com/2011/03/14/world/asia/14japan.html?pagewanted=all, accessed
November 14, 2013

[475] "Is Fukushima as bad as Chernobyl?" by Thair Shaikh, April 13, 2011, CNN
online at
www.cnn.com/2011/WORLD/asiapcf/04/12/japan.nuclear.disaster.fukushima/,
accessed November 14, 0213

[476] "Japanese nuclear plants' operator scrambles to avert meltdowns." by Chico
Harlan and Steven Mufson, March 13, 2011, Washington Post online at
www.washingtonpost.com/wp-
dyn/content/article/2011/03/12/AR2011031205493.html, accessed November 14,
2013

[477] "Japan readies additional $30 billion for Fukushima clean-up," by Yoshifumi
Takemoto, November 12, 2013, Reuters online at
http://www.reuters.com/article/2013/11/12/us-japan-fukushima-borrowing-
idUSBRE9AB0H520131112, accessed November 14, 2013

[478] "Two years later, Japan seethes at tsunami recovery," CBS News online at
www.cbsnews.com/8301-202_162-57573526/two-years-later-japan-seethes-at-
tsunami-recovery/, accessed November 14, 2013

[479] "Hawaii Scientists Seek To Calm U.S. Fears About Fukushima Radiation," by
Sophie Cocke, September 3, 2013, *Huffington Post* online at
www.huffingtonpost.com/2013/09/03/hawaii-radiation-
fukushima_n_3862187.html, accessed November 14, 2013

[480] "Flood Blamed on Levee Breaches," PBS News Hour online at
www.pbs.org/newshour/bb/weather/july-dec05/levees_8-31.html, accessed
November 6, 2013

[481] "New Orleans Facts Pre-Katrina," New Orleans online at
www.neworleansonline.com/pr/releases/releases/New%20Orleans%20Facts%20Pr
e%20Katrina.pdf, accessed November 12, 2013

[482] "Hurricane Katrina," History Channel online at
www.history.com/topics/hurricane-katrina, accessed November 13, 2013

[483] "And Now We Are in Hell," by Ann Gerhart, September 1, 2005, Washington
Post online at www.washingtonpost.com/wp-
dyn/content/article/2005/08/31/AR2005083102801.html, accessed November 13,
2013

[484] "Looters Take Advantage of New Orleans Mess," Associated Press, August 30
2005, online at www.nbcnews.com/id/9131493/#.UozjpyeTVJs, accessed
November 20, 2013

[485] "Civil Defense and Homeland Security: A Short History of National Preparedness Efforts," 2006, p. 28

[486] Ibid.

[487] "New Orleans Begins Confiscating Firearms as Water Recedes," by Alex Berenson and Timothy Williams, September 8, 2005, *New York Times*, online at www.nytimes.com/2005/09/08/national/nationalspecial/08cnd-storm.html?pagewanted=all, accessed April 21, 2014

[488] "NRA Lawsuit: New Orleans Gun Owners' Rights Violated During Katrina Firearm Seizures," December 26, 2007, Associated Press, via Fox News at www.foxnews.com/story/2007/12/26/nra-lawsuit-new-orleans-gun-owners-rights-violated-during-katrina-firearm/, accessed April 21, 2014

[489] "NRA to settle suit over Katrina gun seizures," October 8, 2008, USA Today online at http://usatoday30.usatoday.com/news/nation/2008-10-08-nra-katrina_N.htm, accessed April 21, 2014

[490] "Hurricane Katrina: Facts, Damage & Aftermath," by Kim Ann Zimmermann, August 20, 2012, LiveScience online at www.livescience.com/22522-hurricane-katrina-facts.html, accessed November 5, 2013

[491] "Hurricane Katrina," History Channel website at www.history.com/topics/hurricane-katrina, accessed November 6, 2013

[492] "Smaller New Orleans After Katrina, Census Shows," by Campbell Robertson, February 3, 2011, *New York Times* online at www.nytimes.com/2011/02/04/us/04census.html?pagewanted=all&_r=0 , accessed November 13, 2013

[493] "Historic October Northeast storm: Epic. Incredible. Downright ridiculous," by Andrew Freedman, October 31, 2011, *Washington Post* online at www.washingtonpost.com/blogs/capital-weather-gang/post/historic-october-northeast-storm-epic-incredible-downright-ridiculous/2011/10/31/gIQApy7LZM_blog.html , accessed November 14, 2013

[494] "Hurricane Sandy Grows To Largest Atlantic Tropical Storm Ever," by Todd Gutner, Meteorologist, October 28, 2012, WBZ-TV online at http://boston.cbslocal.com/2012/10/28/hurricane-sandy-grows-to-largest-atlantic-tropical-storm-ever/, accessed November 15, 2013

[495] "Forecasters warn East Coast about 'Frankenstorm' next week; damage could top $1 billion," October 25, 2012, Associated Press via Fox News, online at www.foxnews.com/us/2012/10/25/trick-no-treat-forecasters-predict-pre-halloween-freak-hurricane-winter-storm/, accessed November 15, 2013

[496] From "A state-by-state look at superstorm Sandy's impact," U.S. News on NBCNEWS.com at http://usnews.nbcnews.com/_news/2012/10/29/14781430-a-state-by-state-look-at-superstorm-sandys-impact, accessed November 15, 2013

[497] From "Service Assessment, Hurricane/Post-Tropical Cyclone Sandy, October 22–29, 2012, U.S. Department Of Commerce and National Oceanic and Atmospheric Administration May 2013, online at www.nws.noaa.gov/os/assessments/pdfs/Sandy13.pdf, accessed November 15, 2013

[498] From "Superstorm Sandy Deaths, Damage And Magnitude: What We Know One Month Later," by the Associated Press via Huffington, Post online at www.huffingtonpost.com/2012/11/29/superstorm-hurricane-sandy-deaths-2012_n_2209217.html, accessed November 15, 2013 :

[499] From "Tropical Cyclone Report: Hurricane Sandy," National Hurricane Center, February 12, 2013, online at www.nhc.noaa.gov/data/tcr/AL182012_Sandy.pdf, accessed November 15, 2013

[500] From "FEMA Sandy Response Engages 'Whole Community'," December 21, 2012, Huffington Post online at www.huffingtonpost.com/2012/12/21/fema-sandy-response_n_2346958.html, accessed November 15, 2013

[501] "Price gouging, looting and rage: Superstorm Sandy brings out the worst in some," November 5, 2012, Fox News online at www.foxnews.com/us/2012/11/05/superstorm-sandy-starting-to-bring-out-worst-in-public-along-east-coast/, accessed November 20, 2013

[502] "Typhoon Haiyan pushed the limit, but bigger storms are coming," by Alan Boyle, Science Editor NBC News, November 11, 2013, online at www.nbcnews.com/science/typhoon-haiyan-pushed-limit-bigger-storms-are-coming-2D11577486, accessed November 15, 2013

[503] "Typhoon Haiyan Feared to Have Killed Ten Thousand Filipinos as Vietnam and China now prepare for the worst," *Daily Mail* online at www.dailymail.co.uk/news/article-2494635/Typhoon-Haiyan-feared-killed-TEN-THOUSAND.html#ixzz2kkFN2Jf6, accessed November 15, 2013

[504] "Typhoon Haiyan: How a Catastrophe Unfolded," by Te-Ping Chen, James T. Areddy, and James Hookway, November 25, 2013, *Wall Street Journal* online at http://online.wsj.com/news/articles/SB10001424052702304465604579217671422015220, accessed November 26, 2013

[505] "Typhoon Haiyan: How a Catastrophe Unfolded," by Te-Ping Chen, James T. Areddy, and James Hookway, November 25, 2013, *Wall Street Journal* online at http://online.wsj.com/news/articles/SB10001424052702304465604579217671422015220, accessed November 26, 2013

[506] "U.S. Tornado Climatology," National Climactic Data Center of the National Oceanic and Atmospheric Administration, online at www.ncdc.noaa.gov/oa/climate/severeweather/tornadoes.html#overview, accessed November 20, 2013

[507] "Fujita Tornado Damage Scale 1971," NOAA Storm Prediction Center online at www.spc.noaa.gov/faq/tornado/f-scale.html, accessed November 20, 2013

[508] "Enhanced F Scale for Tornado Damage," NOAA Storm Prediction Center online at www.spc.noaa.gov/faq/tornado/ef-scale.html, accessed November 20, 2013

[509] "U.S. Tornado Climatology," National Climactic Data Center of the National Oceanic and Atmospheric Administration, online at

www.ncdc.noaa.gov/oa/climate/severeweather/tornadoes.html#overview, accessed November 20, 2013

[510] "State of the Climate: Tornadoes for Annual 2008," NOAA National Climatic Data Center, published online December 2008 at www.ncdc.noaa.gov/sotc/tornadoes/2008/13, accessed November 21, 2013

[511] Ibid.

[512] "State of the Climate: Tornadoes for Annual 2010," NOAA National Climatic Data Center, published December 2010, online at www.ncdc.noaa.gov/sotc/tornadoes/2010/13, accessed November 21, 2013

[513] "State of the Climate: Tornadoes for Annual 2011," NOAA National Climatic Data Center, published online December 2011 at www.ncdc.noaa.gov/sotc/tornadoes/2011/13, accessed November 21, 2013

[514] "NWS Central Region Service Assessment, Joplin, Missouri, Tornado–May 22, 2011," National Weather Service online at www.nws.noaa.gov/os/assessments/pdfs/Joplin_tornado.pdf, accessed November 21, 2013

[515] "A Rush to Protect Patients, Then Bloody Chaos," by A. G. Sulzberger And Brian Stelter, May 23, 2011, *New York Times* online at www.nytimes.com/2011/05/24/us/24tornado.html?pagewanted=all&_r=0, accessed November 21, 2013

[516] "In Joplin, Looters Prowl For What Twister Didn't Take," by NPR Staff and Wires, May 27, 2011, National Public Radio online at www.npr.org/2011/05/27/136712859/in-joplin-looters-prowl-for-what-twister-didnt-take, accessed November 21, 2013

[517] "Preparation of All Kinds Blesses Saints in Joplin, Missouri," by Melissa Merrill, September 2011, The Church of Jesus Christ of Latter-Day Saints, online at www.lds.org/ensign/2011/09/preparation-of-all-kinds-blesses-saints-in-joplin-missouri?lang=eng, accessed November 21, 2012

[518] "The Tornado Outbreak of May 20, 2013," National Weather Service online at www.srh.noaa.gov/oun/?n=events-20130520, accessed November 21, 2013

[519] "Oklahoma Tornado," by Ramit Plushnick-Masti And Sean Murphy, May. 23, 2013, Associated Press online at www.bigstory.ap.org/article/okla-residents-come-home-pick-pieces, accessed November 21, 2013

[520] "Out-of-state looters descend on tornado-ravaged Moore, Oklahoma," by Timothy Whitt, June 12, 2013, Digital Journal online at http://digitaljournal.com/article/352064#ixzz2lJ17ZnmC, accessed November 21, 2013

[521] "History of Powerful Tornadoes in Illinois," November 18, 2013, CBS Chicago online at http://chicago.cbslocal.com/2013/11/18/history-of-powerful-tornadoes-in-illinois/, accessed November 21, 2013

[522] "November 17, 2013 Tornado Outbreak," National Weather Service online at www.crh.noaa.gov/ilx/?n=17nov13, accessed November 21, 2013

[523] "Washington Mayor: 1,000 Homes Damaged Or Destroyed By Tornado," November 19, 2013, CBS Chicago online at

http://chicago.cbslocal.com/2013/11/19/six-more-counties-declared-disaster-areas-as-tornado-cleanup-continues/, accessed November 21, 2013

[524] Transition Town network online at www.transitionnetwork.org/, accessed December 11, 2013

[525] "What is a Transition Town?", by Samuel Alexander, July 21, 2012, Permaculture Research Institute online at http://permaculturenews.org/2012/07/21/what-is-a-transition-town/, accessed December 11, 2013

[526] "What is sustainability?," U.S. Environmental Protection Agency, online at www.epa.gov/sustainability/basicinfo.htm, accessed December 18, 2013

Chapter Five

[527] Interview with James Wesley Rawles, October 28, 2013

[528] Kellene Bishop interview November 6, 2013

[529] Interview with Ron Douglas, September 4, 2013

[530] Judge Andrew Napolitano 2010 interview with Jack Spirko on Fox News' Freedom Watch, archived on YouTube at www.youtube.com/watch?v=8813kVYzYxU, accessed January 9, 2014

[531] From The Survival Podcast, episode #1267, online at http://www.thesurvivalpodcast.com/calls-12-16-13, accessed December 17, 2013

[532] "What I saw at the doomsday prepper convention," by David Z. Morris, November 11, 2013, CNNMoney online at http://tech.fortune.cnn.com/2013/11/11/life-changes-be-ready/, accessed January 3, 2014

[533] U.S. Population Clock, United States Census Bureau online at www.census.gov/popclock/, accessed January 7, 2014

[534] Judge Andrew Napolitano 2010 interview with Jack Spirko on Fox News' Freedom Watch, archived on YouTube at www.youtube.com/watch?v=8813kVYzYxU, accessed January 9, 2014

[535] About Self-Reliance Expo, online at www.selfrelianceexpo.com/about-us/, accessed January 7, 2014

[536] "Grief and Depression," WebMD online at www.webmd.com/depression/guide/depression-grief, accessed January 7, 2014

[537] "About Us: Ten Principles of Preparedness," Preparedness Pro online at www.preparednesspro.com/about-us, accessed January 14, 2014

[538] The Survival Podcast: Modern Survival Philosophy, online at www.thesurvivalpodcast.com/articles-by-jack/modern-survival-philosophy-2, accessed January 14, 2014

[539] "Getting Started in Prepping," American Preppers Network online at http://americanpreppersnetwork.com/getting-started-in-prepping, accessed January 14, 2014

[540] "About Us" at PreparednessPro.com, online at www.preparednesspro.com/about-us, accessed January 4, 2014

[541] "Why I Hate Preppers," by Allen C., The Survival Blog online at www.survivalblog.com/2012/09/why-i-hate-preppers-by-allen-c.html, accessed January 26, 2014

[542] Online Survival Radio Show at www.thesurvivalpodcast.com/about-tspc/landingpage-1, accessed January 4, 2014

[543] The American Preppers Network at http://americanpreppersnetwork.com/, accessed January 14, 2014

[544] Survival Blog Subject Areas, online at www.survivalblog.com/about.html, accessed January 6, 2014

[545] "Health Officials: 'No Concern' Over 500% Increase In Radiation Levels On Cali. Beach," by Mikael Thalen, January 6, 2014, Infowars.com, online at http://www.infowars.com/health-officials-no-concern-over-500-increase-in-radation-levels-on-cali-beach/, accessed January 6, 2014

[546] "The Economic Collapse," online at http://theeconomiccollapseblog.com/, accessed January 6, 2014

[547] The Mark Levin Show online at www.marklevinshow.com/common/page.php?pt=podcasts&id=191&is_corp=0, accessed January 6, 2014

[548] "Supervolcano Under Yellowstone Could Alter Global Climates, Lead to Mass Extinction of Other Species," by Myles Collier, January 6, 2014, Christian Post online at www.christianpost.com/news/supervolcano-under-yellowstone-could-alter-global-climates-lead-to-mass-extinction-of-other-species-112092/, accessed January 6, 2014

[549] Survival Summit Schedule, online at http://thesurvivalsummit.com/schedule-3/, accessed January 27, 2014

[550] Permaculture Design Principles online at http://permacultureprinciples.com/principles/, accessed December 11, 2013

[551] Jack Spirko profile on the Worldwide Permaculture Network, online at http://permacultureglobal.com/users/4607-jack-spirko, accessed January 16, 2014

[552] Permaculture Voices Conference 2013, Jack Spirko bio, online at www.permaculturevoices.com/tag/jack-spirko/ , accessed January 16, 2014

[553] Geoff Lawton resume, Permaculture Research Institute online at http://permaculturenews.org/2005/10/16/geoff-lawtons-resume/, accessed January 27, 2014

[554] Geoff Lawton bio, Transition Towns New Zealand, online at www.transitiontowns.org.nz/node/3434, accessed January 27, 2014

[555] "Grow Wild: Paul Wheaton's at the forefront of a permaculture revolution," by Erika Fredrickson, July 26, 2012, Missoula Independent, online at http://missoulanews.bigskypress.com/missoula/grow-wild/Content?oid=1669018, accessed January 28, 2014

[556] "Podcast 227 - Spreading Permaculture with Geoff Lawton Part 1," Permies online at www.permies.com/t/18925/podcast/Podcast-Spreading-Permaculture-Geoff-Lawton, accessed January 28, 2014

[557] Master Food Preserver Program, University of Maine online at http://umaine.edu/food-health/food-preservation/master-food-preservers/, accessed January 16, 2014
[558] Master Food Preservers Program, Utah State University, online at http://extension.usu.edu/utah/htm/masterfoodpreservers, accessed January 16, 2014
[559] National Center for Home Food Preservation, Preserving Food at Home: A Self-Study, online at https://spock.fcs.uga.edu/ext/food/nchfp_elc/, accessed January 16, 2014
[560] "The Congressman Who Went off the Grid," by Jason Koebler, January 2014, for *Politico Magazine* online at www.politico.com//magazine/story/2014/01/roscoe-bartlett-congressman-off-the-grid-101720.html#.UuqXSfvWBEm, accessed January 30, 2014
[561] "Former GOP congressman builds survivalist compound in remote West Virginia woods," January 5, 2014, Daily Mail online at www.dailymail.co.uk/news/article-2533946/Former-GOP-Congressman-Roscoe-Bartlett-builds-survivalist-compound-remote-West-Virginia-woods-prepare-doomsday-living-grid.html#ixzz2swV8KZdd, accessed February 10, 2014

Chapter Six

[562] "Assault on California Power Station Raises Alarm on Potential for Terrorism," by Rebecca Smith, February 4, 2014, *Wall Street Journal* online at http://online.wsj.com/news/articles/SB10001424052702304851104579359141941621778, accessed February 7, 2014
[563] GlobalSecurity.org history, online at www.globalsecurity.org/org/overview/history.htm , accessed December 19, 2013
[564] "Attack Ravages Power Grid. (Just a Test.)," by Matthew L. Wald, November 14, 2013, The New York Times online at www.nytimes.com/2013/11/15/us/coast-to-coast-simulating-onslaught-against-power-grid.html, accessed December 19, 2013
[565] Biographies of EMP commissioners, online at www.empcommission.org/bios, accessed December 28, 2013
[566] "Report of the Commission to Assess the Threat to the United States from Electromagnetic Pulse (EMP) Attack, Critical National Infrastructures," April 2008, page ix
[567] "Report of the Commission to Assess the Threat to the United States from Electromagnetic Pulse (EMP) Attack, Volume 1: Executive Report, 2004," page 5
[568] "Report of the Commission to Assess the Threat to the United States from Electromagnetic Pulse (EMP) Attack, Volume 1: Executive Report, 2004," page 15

[569] "How North Korea Could Cripple the U.S.," by R. James Woolsey and Peter Vincent Pry, May 21, 2013, *Wall Street Journal* online at http://online.wsj.com/news/articles/SB10001424127887324482504578455451910 706908, accessed December 30, 2013

[570] "Report of the Commission to Assess the Threat to the United States from Electromagnetic Pulse (EMP) Attack, Volume 1: Executive Report, 2004," page 13

[571] "Report of the Commission to Assess the Threat to the United States from Electromagnetic Pulse (EMP) Attack, Volume 1: Executive Report, 2004," page 13

[572] Captain William D. Sanders, U.S. Navy, in the Afterword of *One Second After*, published by Tom Doherty Associates, LLC, 2009

[573] *One Second After*, MacMillan Publishers online at http://us.macmillan.com/onesecondafter/WilliamForstchen, accessed December 28, 2013

[574] Foreword, *One Second After*, page 12, published by Tom Doherty Associates, LLC, 2009

[575] "Homeland Security" What EMP Action Plan?" by F. Michael Maloof, September 19, 2013, WorldNet Weekly online at www.wnd.com/2012/09/homeland-security-what-emp-action-plan/, accessed December 12, 2013

[576] "North Korea developing 'electromagnetic pulse weapons'," AFP News via Yahoo, online at http://ph.news.yahoo.com/n-korea-developing-electromagnetic-pulse-weapons-135357782.html, accessed December 30, 2013

[577] "North Korea developing 'electromagnetic pulse weapons'," AFP News via Yahoo, online at http://ph.news.yahoo.com/n-korea-developing-electromagnetic-pulse-weapons-135357782.html, accessed December 30, 2013

[578] "Electric Grid Still Vulnerable to Electromagnetic Weaponry," by Janet Raloff, for Science News, posted July 27, 2009 at *U.S. News and World Report* online at www.usnews.com/science/articles/2009/07/27/electric-grid-still-vulnerable-to-electromagnetic-weaponry?page=2, accessed February 5, 2014

[579] "Doomsday Fear: Could an EMP Throw World into Chaos?" by Douglas Main, August 13, 2013, LiveScience online at www.livescience.com/38848-emp-solar-storm-danger.html, accessed December 28, 2013

[580] "What If the Biggest Solar Storm on Record Happened Today?," by Richard A. Lovett, March 2, 2011, for National Geographic News, online at http://news.nationalgeographic.com/news/2011/03/110302-solar-flares-sun-storms-earth-danger-carrington-event-science/, accessed February 10, 2014

[581] National Space Weather Program, online at http://www.nswp.gov/, accessed December 30, 2013

[582] "Officials Meet in Washington to Discuss Solar Storms, Great and Small," National Aeronautics and Space Administration online at www.nasa.gov/mission_pages/sunearth/news/swef-2013.html, accessed December 30, 2013

[583] "Officials Meet in Washington to Discuss Solar Storms, Great and Small," National Aeronautics and Space Administration online at www.nasa.gov/mission_pages/sunearth/news/swef-2013.html, accessed December 30, 2013

[584] "Officials Meet in Washington to Discuss Solar Storms, Great and Small," National Aeronautics and Space Administration online at www.nasa.gov/mission_pages/sunearth/news/swef-2013.html, accessed December 30, 2013

[585] Maine State Legislature Resolve 45, online at www.mainelegislature.org/legis/bills/bills_126th/chapters/RESOLVE45.asp, accessed April 16, 2014

[586] "Billionaire Tells Americans to Prepare For 'Financial Ruin'," Money News online at www.moneynews.com/Outbrain/Trump-Aftershock-American-Economy/2012/11/06/id/462985?PROMO_CODE=10999-1, accessed December 10, 2013

[587] "Billionaire Tells Americans to Prepare For 'Financial Ruin'," Money News online at www.moneynews.com/Outbrain/Trump-Aftershock-American-Economy/2012/11/06/id/462985?PROMO_CODE=10999-1, accessed December 10, 2013

[588] "We're Unable to See the Coming Economic Collapse," by Terry Burnham, PBS News Hour online at www.pbs.org/newshour/rundown/2013/07/ben-bernanke-as-easter-bunny-why-the-fed-cant-prevent-the-coming-crash.html, accessed December 10, 2013

[589] "Economic Pearl Harbor Will Strike; America Not Prepared," by Christian Hill, March 13, 2013, *Money News* online at www.moneynews.com/MKTNews/economic-pearl-harbor-america/2013/03/13/id/494512, accessed April 15, 2013

[590] *Boomerang*, by Michael Lewis, p. 191

[591] *Boomerang*, by Michael Lewis, pp. 193-194

[592] *Boomerang*, by Michael Lewis, p. 196

[593] "Struggling, San Jose Tests a Way to Cut Benefits," by Rick Lyman and Mary Williams Walsh, September 23, 2013, *New York Times* online at www.nytimes.com/2013/09/24/us/struggling-san-jose-tests-a-way-to-cut-benefits.html

[594] "A Multi-Billion Dollar Pension Crisis Threatens Chicago's Future," by Sarah Burnett, Dec. 10, 2013, Associated Press via *Business Insider*, online at http://www.businessinsider.com/a-multi-billion-dollar-pension-crisis-threatens-chicagos-future-2013-12, accessed December 11, 2013
Read more: http://www.businessinsider.com/a-multi-billion-dollar-pension-crisis-threatens-chicagos-future-2013-12#ixzz2nCSwrXR2

[595] "Detroit isn't alone. The U.S. cities that have gone bankrupt, in one map," by Brad Plumer, July 18, 2013, *Washington Post* online at www.washingtonpost.com/blogs/wonkblog/wp/2013/07/18/detroit-isnt-alone-the-u-s-cities-that-have-gone-bankrupt-in-one-map/, accessed December 11, 2013

[596] "California Shuts Major Water Supply as Drought Worsens," by Kate Pickert, January 31, 2014, TIME Magazine online at http://nation.time.com/2014/01/31/california-shuts-major-water-supply-as-drought-worsens/, accessed February 11, 2014

[597] "Western residents face threat of water rationing as feds reduce water flow, by Kelly David Burke, January 28, 2014, Fox News online at www.foxnews.com/politics/2014/01/28/western-residents-face-threat-water-rationing-as-feds-reduce-water-flow/, accessed February 12, 2014

[598] "Chemical levels in West Virginia water drop, but still no end in sight to ban," by Greg Botelho and Tom Watkins, January 11, 2014, CNN Online at www.cnn.com/2014/01/09/us/west-virginia-contaminated-water/, accessed February 11, 2014

[599] "From 'Freedom Industries' to 'Patriot Coal'," by Steve Benen, February 11, 2014, MSNBC News online at www.msnbc.com/rachel-maddow-show/freedom-industries-patriot-coal, accessed February 12, 2014

[600] "California Drought Impact Seen Spreading From Fires to Food Cost," by Jennifer Oldham and Michael B. Marois, February 7, 2014, *Bloomberg News* online at www.bloomberg.com/news/2014-02-07/california-drought-impact-seen-spreading-from-fires-to-food-cost.html, accessed February 12, 2014

[601] California Agricultural Production Statistics, California Department of Food and Agriculture, online at www.cdfa.ca.gov/statistics/, accessed February 12, 2014

[602] "Shopping chaos ensues in Louisiana Walmart stores after EBT cards stop showing credit limits," by Deborah Hastings, October 14, 2013, *New York Daily News* online at www.nydailynews.com/news/national/chaos-la-walmart-stores-ebt-cards-dump-spending-limits-article-1.1484953#ixzz2t8MAXkcQ, accessed February 12, 2014

[603] "Lie of the Year: 'If you like your health care plan, you can keep it'," by Angie Drobnic Holan, December 12th, 2013, online at www.politifact.com/truth-o-meter/article/2013/dec/12/lie-year-if-you-like-your-health-care-plan-keep-it/, accessed February 12, 2014

[604] "Obamacare is a 'massive, massive income redistribution'," by James Capretta, December 1, 2013, "Fox News Sunday," as reported by PolitiFact online at www.politifact.com/punditfact/statements/2013/dec/05/james-capretta/capretta-says-obamacare-massive-income-redistribut/ , accessed February 12, 2014

[605] "Rep. Paul Ryan: Obama Presidency 'Increasingly Lawless'," by Benjamin Bell, February 2, 2014, ABC News online at http://abcnews.go.com/blogs/politics/2014/02/rep-paul-ryan-obama-presidency-increasingly-lawless/, accessed February 12, 2014

[606] "Hot spots of Terrorism and Other Crimes in the United States, 1970 to 2008," National Consortium for the Study of Terrorism and Responses to Terrorism, online at www.start.umd.edu/sites/default/files/files/publications/research_briefs/LaFree_Bersani_HotSpotsOfUSTerrorism.pdf, page 1, accessed February 12, 2014

[607] Ammunition solicitation, February 7, 2014, Federal Business Opportunities portal online at

www.fbo.gov/index?s=opportunity&mode=form&id=94034530e947269f2603ada738cbbdb1&tab=core&_cview=0, accessed February 12, 2014
[608] "Ohio National Guard Training Envisions Right-Wing Terrorism," by Jesse Hathaway, February 10, 2014, Media Trackers online at http://mediatrackers.org/ohio/2014/02/10/ohio-national-guard-training-envisions-right-wing-terrorism, accessed February 12, 2014

Chapter Seven

[609] "Preparing for Disaster," by Gary F. Arnet, *Emergency Preparedness and Survival Guide* (1989–2003), p.21, published by Backwoods Home Magazine, Inc.
[610] "The Five Principles of Preparedness," American Preppers Network online at http://americanpreppersnetwork.com/what-is-a-prepper/the-five-principles-of-preparedness, accessed February 14, 2014
[611] "Minimum Equipment For Standard Bug-Out-Bag," by Talon, SurvivalBlog online at www.survivalblog.com/2013/05/minimum-equipment-for-standard-bug-out-bag-by-talon.html, accessed February 14, 2014
[612] "Kit Storage Locations," FEMA readiness website online at www.ready.gov/kit-storage-locations, accessed February 18, 2014
[613] Interview with Judge Andrew Napolitano, on Foxnews.com/freedomwatch, 2010, on YouTube at www.youtube.com/watch?v=8813kVYzYxU, accessed February 18, 2014
[614] "Food Storage," The Church of Jesus Christ of Latter-Day Saints, online at www.lds.org/topics/food-storage, accessed February 17, 2014

Chapter Eight

[615] Costco American Preparedness 2-Person / 7-Day Emergency Preparedness Kit, online at www.costco.com/American-Preparedness-2-Person--7-Day-Emergency-Preparedness-Kit.product.11249169.html , accessed March 3, 2014
[616] BJ's Ready America Grab 'n Go 3-Day Deluxe 4-Person Emergency Survival Kit, online at www.bjs.com/ready-america-grab-n-go-3-day-deluxe-4-person-emergency-survival-kit.product.222908, acccessed March 3, 2014
[617] LifeStraw Personal Water Filter, online at www.buylifestraw.com/products/lifestraw-personal, accessed March 3, 2014
[618] LifeStraw 1.0, online at www.buylifestraw.com/products/family, accessed March 3, 2014
[619] Katadyn Products online at www.katadyn.com/en/katadyn-products/products/katadynshopconnect/katadyn-wasserfilter-endurance-series-produkte/katadyn-pocket/, accessed March 3, 2014

[620] Berkey Water Filters online at /www.berkeyfilters.com/berkey-water-filters/systems/?gclid=COrY2tPc9rwCFdTm7AodjnQAXQ, accessed March 3, 2014

[621] Sam's Club online store at www.samsclub.com, accessed March 4, 2014

[622] Costco online store at www.costco.com, accessed March 4, 2014

[623] BJ's Wholesale Club online at www.bjs.com, accessed March 4, 2014

[624] Food Storage Calculator online at http://lds.about.com/library/bl/faq/blcalculator.htm, accessed February 26, 2014

[625] Starter Kit, LDS Store online at http://store.lds.org/webapp/wcs/stores/servlet/Product3_715839595_10557_30744 57345616706370_-1__195787, accessed February 26, 2014

[626] Food Storage Analyzer online at http://beprepared.com/company/food-storage-analyzer, accessed February 27, 2014

[627] Emergency Essentials Year Supplies and Combos, online at http://beprepared.com/premium-2000-one-year-supply.html, accessed February 27, 2014

[628] Emergency Essentials online at http://beprepared.com/company/about-us, accessed March 1, 2014

[629] The Ready Store online at www.thereadystore.com/food-storage/supply-size/1-year-supplies?dir=asc&order=price, accessed March 1, 2014

[630] Wise Food Storage online calculator at http://wisefoodstorage.com/food-storage-calculator.html, accessed March 5, 2014

[631] Survival Retreat Consulting online at http://survivalretreatconsulting.com/survival-retreat-consulting/our-consulting-services.html, accessed March 5, 2014

[632] Ultimate Bunker online at www.ultimatebunker.com, accessed March 5, 2014

[633] Luxury Survival Condo, press release online at www.survivalcondo.com/?page_id=107, accessed March 5, 2014

[634] Luxury Survival Condo online at www.survivalcondo.com/?page_id=107, accessed March 5, 2014

Chapter Nine

[635] "National Strategy Recommendations: Future Disaster Preparedness," Executive Summary, Department of Homeland Security Fiscal Year 2013 Report to Congress, published September 6, 2013

[636] "Hurricane Sandy Was Second-Costliest In U.S. History, Report Shows," by David Porter, February 12, 2013, Huffington Post online at www.huffingtonpost.com/2013/02/12/hurricane-sandy-second-costliest_n_2669686.html, accessed March 12, 2014

[637] "National Strategy Recommendations: Future Disaster Preparedness," Executive Summary, Department of Homeland Security Fiscal Year 2013 Report to Congress, published September 6, 2013, pp 2 and 3

[638] Presidential Policy Directive / PPD-8: National Preparedness, online at www.dhs.gov/presidential-policy-directive-8-national-preparedness, accessed March 12, 2014

[639] "National Mitigation Framework," online at www.fema.gov/media-library/assets/documents/32209?id=7363, accessed March 12, 2014

[640] National Mitigation Framework, p. 8

Index

Appendix

Prepper Jargon

If you know any preppers, or if you visit prepper websites, you may encounter some unusual words or phrases. Following is a sampling, to help you understand the lingo.

Term	What it means
Black Swan	An intense, unexpected event that could cause TEOTWAWKI
BOB	Bug-out bag; an emergency kit to help you survive at least 72 hours if you have to evacuate your home
BOL	Bug-out location; survival retreat; where you go when you have to bug out
BOV	Bug-out vehicle; what you use when you bug out; sometimes set up to be a mobile survival retreat
Bug in	Shelter in place to deal with TEOTWAWKI
Bug out	Evacuate your home
Camo	Short for camouflage; could be useful attire in an outdoor survival situation or if you're bugging out to your survival retreat
Carrington Event	A massive solar storm that took place in 1859 and disrupted telegraph communications all over the world
CME	Coronal mass ejection from the sun; the thing that caused the Carrington Event

CYA	Cover your assets
DHS	Department of Homeland Security
DIY	Do it yourself
Doomer	Someone who believes that Peak Oil will bring about TEOTWAWKI
EDC	Every-day carry; the things a prepper has with him at all times in case of emergency
EMP	Electromagnetic pulse; a side effect of a nuclear bomb detonated high in the atmosphere; shuts down any electronic equipment in its path
False Flag	A covert military or paramilitary operation designed to give the appearance that it is being carried out by people, groups, organizations, or nations other than those who were actually responsible. False flag operations have been known to be used by governments to give the appearance that they are the target, while conducting attacks against their own people.
FEMA	Federal Emergency Management Agency; also known to some preppers as "Foolishly Expecting Meaningful Aid"
Get-home bag	Similar to a bug-out bag, only it's carried with you at all times and is stocked with whatever emergency supplies you might need to get back home if the SHTF while you're on the road
Go bag	Another term for a bug-out bag
GOOD	"Get Out of Dodge" — what you do when you bug out
Hubbert's Peak	The highest point on a bell curve developed by geologist M. King Hubbert, depicting the peak and

	ensuing decline in the worldwide production of oil
INCH	"I'm Never Coming Home"; code for the family if you can't make it home when the SHTF and you don't want them to stay there waiting for you if they need to bug out
KISS	The classic "Keep It Simple, Stupid!"
MRE	Meals Ready to Eat; servings of food that can be eaten right out of the package; often stocked in BOBs
LTFS	Long-term food storage; a supply of foods that can be relied upon for survival over a long period of time
OPSEC	Operations Security; a concern for preppers, which includes providing for security about your personal information, your location, and your plans, as well as understanding and countering risks to your vulnerabilities.
Para	Paracord; a useful item to have in a BOB
Peak oil	A term coined by geologist M. King Hubbert back in the 1950s, which refers to an eventual peak and subsequent decline in worldwide oil supplies. According to Hubbert, "When the energy cost of recovering a barrel of oil becomes greater than the energy content of the oil, production will cease no matter what the monetary price may be."
Prep	To prepare (verb); the things you accumulate to help you become prepared (noun)
Prepper	One who prepares for the unexpected
SHTF	Sh*t hits the fan; a scenario that brings about TEOTWAWKI

Survival retreat	A dwelling in a remote location set up for self-sufficiency and survival if the SHTF; could be a primary dwelling or a BOL
TEOTWAWKI	"The End of the World as We Know It"; not the end of the world necessarily, but a change to the way of life people have known
WROL	Without Rule of Law; a lawless situation; a time when police and the military no longer have control of civilization
Zombie	The hordes of desperate people who are unprepared for TEOTWAWKI, and after the SHTF will try to take what you have

Prepper Websites

Name	Web Address	Description
American Preppers Network	www.americanpreppersnetwork.com	General information on all things preparedness, from bug-out bags to gardening
Backdoor Survival	http://www.backdoorsurvival.com/	Offers "tools for creating a self-reliant lifestyle through thoughtful prepping and optimism"
Backwoods Home Magazine	http://www.backwoodshome.com/	Information and blogs on self-reliance
Bug-out Survival	http://www.bugoutsurvival.com/	Preparedness blog; online resource for emergency planning
Bushcraft Survival	http://bushcraftusa.com	Forum for discussion about preparedness and survival
Camping Survival Blog	http://campingsurvivalblog.com/	Information on camping and outdoor survival
Catastrophe Network	http://www.catastrophenetwork.org/	Encourages people to "be prepared, informed, and networked for the numerous natural and man-made threats that we face in this world today"
EDC and Prepping Blog	http://edc-prepping.blogspot.com/	Blog about Every Day Carry items and general prepper information and ideas
Emergency Home Preparation	www.emergencyhomepreparation.org	Articles and information on emergency preparedness and self-reliance
Emergency Preparedness and Response (Latter-Day Saints)	www.lds.org/topics/emergency-preparedness	Basics of emergency preparedness
Getting Prepped	http://gettingprepped.com	Emergency preparedness education and supplies

Granny Miller	www.granny-miller.com	A journal of agrarian life and skills
Graywolf Survival	http://graywolfsurvival.com	Preparedness information, from car emergency kits to bunkers
Growing Freedom Podcast	http://www.growingfreedom.yolasite.com/growing-freedom-podcast.php	"Growing freedom and liberty by going beyond permaculture and building resilient systems"
Homestead Survival	http://thehomesteadsurvival.com	Homesteading, emergency preparedness, frugal living, food storage, self-sufficiency
Learn to Prepare	http://learntoprepare.com/	"Beginning and improving preparedness planning"
Living Off the Grid	www.off-grid.net	"Reports on the people, technologies, events and influences throughout the global off-grid community"
Mike Marlow's Survival Blog	http://mikemarlow.com/	One man's take on self-reliant living and preparedness with contributions from online community
Modern Survival Online	http://modernsurvivalonline.com/	Survival, self-reliance, preparedness, firearms, and "thoughts on the world today"
Modern Survival Blog	http://modernsurvivalblog.com/	Preparedness information; commentary on national and world events as they relate to preparedness
Natural News	http://www.naturalnews.com/	Alternative news; articles on natural medicine
No Tech Magazine	http://www.notechmagazine.com/	Articles on DIY projects, alternative power, living with minimal technology
Off Grid Survival	http://offgridsurvival.com	Preparedness information and gear; commentary on national and world events as they relate to preparedness
Outdoor Life Survival	http://survival.outdoorlife.com/	"How to" information on preparedness and wilderness survival and gear

Outdoors Native	http://outdoorsnative.com/	Alternative news; survival information and gear
Permaculture Institute	http://www.permaculture.org/	permaculture concepts and techniques
Practical Preppers	https://practicalpreppers.com/	Survival consultation
Prepared Christian	http://preparedchristian.net	Christian views on preparedness; general preparedness information
Prepared for Survival	http://preparedforsurvival.blogspot.com/	Food storage and preparedness information
Preparedness Advice Blog	http://preparednessadvice.com/	General information on preparedness, alternative energy, safety, survival
Preparing Your Family	http://preparingyourfamily.com/	Blog with tips and advice on how to create an emergency plan, general preparedness, and commentary on preparedness as it relates to world events
Prepper Groups	http://www.preppergroups.com	Form for preppers to connect with like-minded people
Prepper Journal	http://www.theprepperjournal.com/	Prepping and survival basics, videos, gear reviews, commentary on national and world events
Plan-Prepare-Mitigate	www.fema.gov/plan-prepare-mitigate	Information on what to prepare for and how
Preparedness Pro	www.preparednesspro.com	Principles of preparedness, food storage, recipes, self-reliance
Prepper Central	http://preppercentral.com	Blog about preparing for emergencies, from TEOTWAWKI to financial disaster
Prepper Resources	www.prepper-resources.com	Forums, product reviews, commentary on preparedness topics

Prepper Website	www.prepperwebsite.com	Articles on preparedness topics
Preppers Meetup Groups	http://preppers.meetup.com	Forum for preppers to connect with like-minded people
Ready Nutrition	http://readynutrition.com/	Homesteading, food storage, preparedness
Rule of 3 Survival	http://www.ruleof3survival.com/	Forum where people can discuss preparedness
SHTF Plan	http://www.shtfplan.com/	Alternative news, commentary on preparedness as it relates to national and world events
Suburban Prepper	http://www.suburbanprepper.com	Preparedness information and advice for those who live in moderately populated areas
Suburban Survival Blog	http://suburbansurvivalblog.com/	Education in preparedness and survival targeted to those living in suburban settings
Survival Blog	www.survivalblog.com	Virtual community of people concerned about preparedness; contributions from members on myriad preparedness topics and commentary on national and world events as they bear on preparedness
Survival Medicine	www.doomandbloom.net	"Dr. Bones" and "Nurse Amy" offer strategies to stay healthy during disaster situations
Survival News Online	www.survivalnewsonline.com	Articles on gear, preparedness strategies, economics, national events as they related to freedom and preparedness
The Survival Doctor	http://www.thesurvivaldoctor.com/about/	Medical information to use if professional help isn't available

The Survival Podcast	www.thesurvivalpodcast.com	"Helping you live a better life if times get tough, or even if they don't"; podcast on topics related to preparedness and self-reliance; member forum
Zombie Squad	http://www.zombiehunters.org	Tongue-in-cheek goal is zombie removal; real goal is educating the community about the importance of disaster preparedness; network has 47 chapters across the country

Prepper EXPOS and Conferences

There are expositions and conferences held across the country every year, offering information on self-reliance and assorted subjects related to preparedness. Here are a few:

Conference Name	Location, Dates	Website/Contact
Arizona Survivalist / Prepper Expos	Prescott Valley, AZ; late May-early June	arizonasurvivalistshows@gmail.com
Back to Basics Sustainable Living and Survival Expo	Dallas, TX; November	918-366-3191 www.backtobasicsshow.com
Berryville Gun and Prepper Expo	Berryville, VA; November	High Caliber Events 110 West Main St. Berryville, VA 22611 www.highcaliberevents.com
Crossroads of the West Gun Shows	Arizona, California, Nevada; April-May	801-544-9125 www.crossroadsgunshows.com
East Tennessee VOAD Emergency Preparedness Fair	Knoxville, TN; September	http://prepfair.org
Great Lakes Emergency Preparedness Expo	Birch Run, MI; April	800-880-2485 info@greatlakespreppers.com
International Disaster Conference & Expo	New Orleans, LA; February	504-582-3072 info@idcexpo.net
Kansas Prepper Expo	Holton, KS; May	kansasprepperexpo@yahoo.com
Life Changes, Be Ready Preparedness and Gun Expo	Seminole County, FL; October	Fortress Management Group www.lifechangesbeready.com

Conference Name	Location, Dates	Website/Contact
Mid-Atlantic Emergency Preparedness and Survival Expo	Boonsboro, MD; August	301-573-5142 midatlanticsurvivalexpo.com
Mountain Prepper Home, Gun & Outdoor Expo	Sevierville, TN; May	828-349-4354 www.mountainprepperexpos.com
National Preppers & Survivalists Expo	Tulsa, OK; April	504-281-4430 www.npsexpo.com
The NW Preparedness Expo	Prosser, WA; May	509-786-3177 info@nwpreparednessexpo.com
Outdoor Enthusiasts Festival	Hedgesville, WV ; April	540-338-2437 www.appalachianreadiness.com
P4P Preparedness 4 Preppers Self Reliance Expo	Pomona, CA; June	909-346-0277 p4pexcpo@gmail.com
Prepared and Spared – Off the Grid Expo	Dayton, OH; late May-early June	937-361-9196 info@preparedandspared.com
Preppers Festival	Newcastle, VA; April	540-309-6650 www.preppershpwsusa.com
Self-Reliance Expo	Mesquite, TX; April	877-618-0065 www.selfrelianceexpo.com
SunCoast Gun Shows	Florida, various locations; January - June	330-963-6964 erica@suncoastgunshows.com
Survival Gardening & Disaster Prep Expo	Twin Falls, ID; April	530-622-2333 www.facebook.com/events/138953090139010/?ref=22
Survival Preppers Expo	Bloomington, MN; April	info.survivalpreppers@gmail.com www.survivalpreppersexpo.com
Sustainable Preparedness Expo	Oregon, May; Tennessee, June; Washington, September	https://sustainablepreparedness.com

Made in the USA
Las Vegas, NV
29 September 2021